PENGUIN BOOKS

SMALL MAN IN A BOOK

Rob Brydon is the award-winning star of many critically acclaimed comedy series, from the darkly funny *Human Remains*, *Marion and Geoff* and immensely popular *Gavin and Stacey* to his recent outing alongside Steve Coogan in Michael Winterbottom's *The Trip*, as well as host of *Would I Lie to You?* and *The Rob Brydon Show*. Rob has five children and lives in London.

Small Man in a Book

ROB BRYDON

PENGUIN BOOKS

PENGUIN BOOKS

Published by the Penguin Group
Penguin Books Ltd, 80 Strand, London WC2R 0RL, England
Penguin Group (USA) Inc., 375 Hudson Street, New York, New York 10014, USA
Penguin Group (Canada), 90 Eglinton Avenue East, Suite 700, Toronto, Ontario, Canada M4P 2Y3
(a division of Pearson Penguin Canada Inc.)
Penguin Ireland, 25 St Stephen's Green, Dublin 2, Ireland (a division of Penguin Books Ltd)
Penguin Group (Australia), 250 Camberwell Road,
Camberwell, Victoria 3124, Australia (a division of Pearson Australia Group Pty Ltd)
Penguin Books India Pvt Ltd, 11 Community Centre,
Panchsheel Park, New Delhi – 110 017, India
Penguin Group (NZ), 67 Apollo Drive, Rosedale, Auckland 0632, New Zealand
(a division of Pearson New Zealand Ltd)
Penguin Books (South Africa) (Pty) Ltd, Block D, Rosebank Office Park,
181 Jan Smuts Avenue, Parktown North, Gauteng 2193, South Africa

Penguin Books Ltd, Registered Offices: 80 Strand, London WC2R 0RL, England

www.penguin.com

First published by Michael Joseph 2011
Published in Penguin Books 2012

003

Copyright © Rob Brydon, 2011
All rights reserved

The moral right of the author has been asserted

Welsh Landscape and *For Instance* by R. S. Thomas © Phoenix, an imprint of The Orion Publishing Group.
Extracts from *Marion and Geoff* and *Human Remains* scripts © BBC.

All images courtesy of the author except: Rob Brydon meeting Bruce Springsteen © Chris Lopez/Photoshoot;
Rob Brydon with Tom Jones and Ruth Jones © Trevor Leighton; press cuttings of 'Rob Lands a job with Sky',
'An Oscar for *Sweet Charity*?' and 'Join the Carousel' © *Glamorgan Gazette*.

Set in 12.74/15 pt Garamond MT Std
Typeset by Jouve (UK), Milton Keynes
Printed in England by Clays Ltd, St Ives plc

Except in the United States of America, this book is sold subject
to the condition that it shall not, by way of trade or otherwise, be lent,
re-sold, hired out, or otherwise circulated without the publisher's
prior consent in any form of binding or cover other than that in
which it is published and without a similar condition including this
condition being imposed on the subsequent purchaser

ISBN: 978-0-241-95482-9

www.greenpenguin.co.uk

MIX
Paper from
responsible sources
FSC® C018179
www.fsc.org

Penguin Books is committed to a sustainable
future for our business, our readers and our planet.
This book is made from Forest Stewardship
Council™ certified paper.

For
Katie, Harry, Amy, Tom and George

Foreword

Here is the story of some of my life. I start on the day I was born and stop thirty-five years later at the end of the year 2000, the point at which I finally had the first sniff of the 'success' I had been so doggedly searching for. Within this timescale I occasionally jump forward into the new millennium when I feel the stories will add to the reader's enjoyment, and also because I've always been fascinated by our inability to know what lies ahead.

By the time this success arrived, I had married and had three beautiful children. As I sit here at my desk and write these words in the summer of 2011, I find I am the proud father of five children, and married – to my second wife, Claire.

This book makes no mention of my divorce and its accompanying sadness. My children are of an age where reading about the intimate details of their parents' lives holds little appeal and great potential for social embarrassment. Coupled with this, their mother – my first wife, Martina – shares none of my desire for attention, nor my willingness to parade around for the amusement of strangers. It is for this reason, and this reason alone, that she features less in these pages than her major role in my life surely warrants.

In not meeting me until 2002 Claire has ensured that she features even less, making a grand total of zero

appearances in the autobiography of her husband –
something that feels very wrong but, having structured
the book in the way that I have, is, I'm afraid, inevitable.
We have been together now for nearly ten years and, were
it not for her, I doubt very much that I would have reached
a position where I was asked to write an autobiography.

If that is indeed the case, then should you find the
book is not to your taste, it's really her fault, not mine.

PART ONE

'Born in the USA'
(The Uplands of Swansea, actually . . .)

I

I was born on Monday the 3rd of May 1965 at a maternity home in Swansea, South Wales, which was called, rather prophetically, The Bryn. I have often wondered how differently my life might have turned out if my parents had instead chosen the nearby James Bond Home For Expectant Mothers. Bryn, as you may know, means 'hill' in Welsh, and the home sat on top of one such hill in Killay, the Uplands area of Swansea. Mum and Dad – Joy and Howard – were just twenty and twenty-one years old at the time and had arrived there the previous evening after the contractions began while they were at home watching the television. These were the dark days before Sky+ and so on Mum's insistence, and despite the lengthening and by now rather painful contractions, they waited until *The Fugitive* had finished before making a move.

Just like Dr Richard Kimble, I was keen to escape and by the time the programme was over I could wait no longer. Mum waddled out of the house, and squeezed into the car, which Dad then steered over to Swansea. On arrival at The Bryn, Mum's waters had still not broken; they did so as the midwife was examining her. My mother was the midwife's first delivery after a lengthy period of maternity leave, and the time away from the job had softened the poor woman sufficiently that when the moment arrived and the levee finally broke, on witnessing the deluge, she promptly passed out. That's right, a midwife passing out at the sight of someone's waters breaking. Not wishing to appear rude my father followed suit. Bang, down he went, leaving my mother staring at the two of them in a heap on the floor. The delivery doctor – an older and, in my mother's recollection, quite stern gentleman – had to administer to both the fainters before he could turn his attention to the job at hand. He guided Dad out to another room, where he might regain his composure, and then two hours later, shortly after twenty past five in the morning, returned with the words, 'It's a boy, and it works . . .' This last part of his news a reference to the fact that I had urinated on him in a most enthusiastic fashion as soon as I was out and into the world. On leaving the room he turned back to my dad and, in a glorious example of the politically incorrect 1960s, gave the following advice with regard to my mother, 'Keep them pregnant and barefoot; they won't go very far.'

After coming in to meet his son and check on the wellbeing of his wife, Dad returned home to Baglan to spread the news, full of pride at having passed out only once. Mum stayed at the home for a whole week, in her own little room, surrounded by flowers and cards, her only disturbance being the sound of one baby in particular who could be heard screaming at the top of its lungs night and day from the nursery where all the newborns were herded together to give their novice parents a break. From the comfort of her bed she couldn't help feeling sorry for the mother of this noisy little child who was surely in for a rough ride once she got home. On her departure Mum received the splendid news that the child in question was

4

my good self, her little cherub, her firstborn. It was decided that I was suffering from colic, and as mother and child left the home we did so with the advice that I would benefit, even at this young age, from mashed-up Farley's Rusks to settle my poor little stomach.

The pattern was set, and Mum swears I didn't sleep for the next five years. She and my poor sleep-deprived father would take it in turns to walk me around the bedroom on their shoulder while they sang in what Dylan Thomas described as the slow, black, crowblack darkness of the Welsh night, waiting for my body to go limp and my breathing to slide into the telltale rhythm of sleep. Mum's repertoire consisted of 'Lili Marlene', 'You Are My Sunshine' and the now-forgotten song that sounded like the set-up to a Jackie Mason gag, 'The Three Jews' ('Once upon a time there were three Jews / Once upon a time there were three Jews / Juh-ewuh, Jew, Jew, Jew / Juh-ewuh, Jew, Jew, Jew / Once upon a time there were three Jews . . .'), all the while patting my back in rhythm with the song. Dad opened his set with the first verse of 'We Plough the Fields and Scatter' repeated ad infinitum before moving on to 'There is a Green Hill Far Away'. There he was, circling the room in the gloom, a lone desperate voice in the wilderness.

> There is a green hill far away,
> Without a city wall,
> Where the dear Lord was crucified,
> Who died to save us all.

Crucifixion, while an extreme and (one would hope) last resort, must surely have crossed his mind.

*

We lived at Woodside, a large manor house in Baglan, just next to Port Talbot in South Wales. It belonged to my maternal grandparents – Bob and Margaret – who had bought the place, kept the best bit for themselves and converted the rest into flats to provide an income. Nan and Grandpa had one side of the ground floor; Mum, Dad and I occupied the other, while the upper floors were taken by a variety of tenants. Most of my memories are of being in my grandparents' part of the house or in the large sloping garden, which wrapped round one side of it. It was a magnificent, imposing house with a long winding driveway and grand steps sweeping up to a veranda and large central door. Mature rhododendron bushes in which I would climb and play at Robin Hood and Tarzan bordered the driveway; there was also a haystack along the way in which I would leap from one bale to another and slide down the gaps in between. Behind and around the house were fields, with a small farm just off to the side, and the whole thing sat high up on a mountain from which it was possible to see the coast at Aberavon, while beyond and off to the right lay the shimmering excitement of Swansea.

If it seems as though I am painting a picture of a bucolic idyll, it is because that is how it now appears in my mind. The rhododendron bushes, perfect for small arms and legs to climb through, seemed identical to the surroundings that Hawkeye found himself in each week on the BBC's *Last of the Mohicans* (which I would watch wide-eyed and then re-enact the following day). Even now, all these years later, if I see a rhododendron bush at close quarters, perhaps while walking through a park,

I will have to suppress a strong urge to climb in and dangle from a branch.

My memories of those early years at Woodside (we lived here on and off for some time) are all late sixties film stock colour-soaked loveliness. Cosy winter evenings with hot buttered toast and Ivor the Engine parping away on the television as he puffed around his imaginary North Wales. Long summer days with the French windows open and the net curtains blowing in the breeze as Mum and Nan sat glued for interminable hours to the BBC's coverage of Wimbledon and I'd wander in and out of the room wondering what all the fuss was about and when it would end.

The television was contained within its own lacquered wooden cabinet, the doors rolling back to reveal the screen, and it was here that I would sit and worship at the altar of entertainment. *Pinky and Perky*, *Bill and Ben* and *The Herbs* as a small child, before my tastes matured and I was able to appreciate the more complex plots of *Marine Boy*, *Champion the Wonder Horse*, *Robinson Crusoe* and *Skippy*. We were able, thanks to the house being high on a hill, to pick up the English local ITV provider Westward. The station had a fluffy puppet of a rabbit that would sit with the presenter as he read out the birthdays at teatime. When the age of the child was revealed, Gus Honeybun, for it was he, would perform the requisite number of bunny hops in celebration. Perhaps my earliest memory is of my second birthday party and the television being surrounded by aunts and mothers of friends, who all erupted in celebration as my name was read out and Gus began to bust some moves. A chorus of Welsh ladies' voices rang out, a shrill clarion call of, *'It's Robert!'* They rose to their feet in collective triumph: *'It's doing it, it's doing it! The rabbit is hopping for Robert!'* In the process, blocking my view of the screen and rather scaring me.

I wasn't having much luck with birthdays. Twelve months earlier, on my very first one, I'm told I had been applauding myself for having blown out my solitary candle when the cat stepped up and quite deliberately scratched my face, as if to tell me off for attracting attention to myself.

If he was hoping to quell any ambitions in that area, he didn't succeed.

Great swathes of my childhood come back to me in vivid colour, with a decidedly American flavour or tone. The Americanization of my memories may be attributed to several factors, in no particular order. My maternal grandfather was Canadian. Robert Arthur Brydon (I was named after him, Robert Brydon Jones) spoke with a Canadian accent, which to my young ears sounded American and therefore rather exotic and exciting. He came to Britain during the war and met my grandmother, Margaret Thomas, in London in 1942. They were at the United Services Library and were both writing letters home. Years later, once I was around and old enough to notice, I'd hear him call up the stairs to his wife, *'Maaarg!'* I wonder if having this unusual accent in such close proximity contributed to my being able to mimic different voices. Probably not – I suspect it's a lucky trick, more to do with the make-up of your ear and how it relates to your mouth. It must also tie in with an inbuilt desire to perform, something I certainly had from a young age and was never shy to express.

Grandpa was a builder. He built houses. He built the one that frames my strongest memories of him, Hawthorn Cottage on the edge of Baglan as it becomes Briton Ferry. This was the house that we moved into in 1981 when Dad's business became a victim of the recession, a year or so after Grandpa had passed away. He died not long after going into hospital with a complaint that the doctors failed to cure. I only have one fleeting memory of him in his final days, sitting at home on his reclining chair. This was perhaps the only time I saw him unshaven.

The bulk of my memories are of a strong man, eating sausage and mash on a Saturday lunchtime with just one hand. I should make it clear that he held a fork in the one hand. He wasn't an animal – nor, for that matter, an amputee – but he liked to cut up his meal first and then allow the knife to rest while he slowly and methodically picked out morsels of food one by one, like hostages being selected for death. These lunches would follow a Saturday morning when he'd take me, his first grandchild, to Swansea Bay Golf Club where he was twice champion. If you pop in while you're passing on your way to Swansea, you'll see his name, *R. Brydon*, still there on the champions' board. Every Saturday we would drive over and stroll to a practice tee where we'd hit a bag of balls with a 7-iron. Let's be clear about this: we would take the balls out of the bag first and hit them each individually. I wasn't standing there hitting a cloth bag full of balls in a peculiarly Welsh and golf-centric premonition of *The Karate Kid*.

Although we would go to the course once a week, I didn't really develop a love of the game until many years later when I hit my forties and it seemed rude not to.

Memories of Grandpa also include trips to the timber merchant in Briton Ferry where selected the materials needed for his current projects, which at one point included a pair of semi-detached houses on Old Road in Baglan into which Mum, Dad and I were to move. Our house had a small spare room in which I one day became trapped when the door handle came off on the inside and I shouted and shouted until I lost my voice. It was also where we lived during my Basil Brush phase, a curious time of my life when I was equally drawn to and terrified of the cheeky little waistcoat-wearing fox. I clearly remember my father reassuring me that in the unlikely event of a visit from Basil, he would throw him over the garden wall. Given that we lived on the edge of a fairly high drop, this would surely act as a deterrent.

Many years later, while working as a radio presenter for the BBC in Cardiff, I would finally come face to face – or, at least, voice to voice – with Basil, now long past his heyday, in a phone interview. I was surprisingly nervous, but delighted, when he ended our exchange with one of his poems.

> The girl stood on the burning bridge,
> Her leg was all a-quiver.
> She gave a cough,
> Her leg fell off,
> And floated down the river . . .
> *Boom, boom!*

While this house was being built I would spend time with Grandpa 'helping' him. I was three years old at the time and I dare say my help was indispensable. After a suitable period of hard toil, we would break and Grandpa would take out a glass bottle of Corona lemonade, or 'pop' as we called it. I don't recall how much he would drink but I would have mine served from the cap – he would fill the cap of the bottle with lemonade, and I would drink the contents.

Mum and Dad met in 1961. Mum had finished her O levels and was at the Corner House Café, opposite the Plaza cinema in Port Talbot with a friend. Dad worked at the Blue Star Garage, next to the café, fitting tyres and batteries. The owner of the café was a friend and would loan Dad his brand-new Ford Zephyr, with leopardskin seat covers, in which he would then try to impress the girls. Mum walked over to Dad on this fateful evening and asked if he'd take her friend out for a spin in his car. Dad declined the invitation but said that he'd gladly take Mum; he's still driving her around today.

As a young boy, I would go with my family to church on a Sunday, to St Catharine's in Baglan. It was where Mum and Dad were married and I had been christened. Our vicar was Islwyn Lewis, a lovely man who would encourage me to get up on the steps of the pulpit and perform to the congregation. My signature act was to hide deep inside Vicar Lewis's flowing robes and then spring out with a song or a funny face. I dare say that nowadays encouraging young boys to hide in your ecclesiastical robes is frowned upon, but these were more innocent times and services at St Catharine's were considered to have been something of a disappointment if I hadn't popped in and out at least once. I took centre stage too when Vicar Lewis officiated at the wedding of Mum's sister, my Aunty Ann. I was a pageboy and kept trying to pull focus by bowing at every opportunity during the service.

On Sunday afternoons we would go for a run in the car, perhaps east to the seaside at Ogmore or west to Oxwich. When it came to holidays we travelled to spots in Britain and beyond into Europe, where on a trip to Italy I caught mumps and the hotel owner encouraged us to leave earlier than planned. Closer to home we stayed at Mullion Cove in Cornwall with Uncle Colin, Aunty Dilys and my cousin Kim, all travelling down in Grandpa's metallic-blue Mark IX Jaguar. Once at the hotel Dad became known to the other guests, most of whom were English, as Jones the Jag. Fittingly enough, for a child who would go on to find a career in comedy, we once stayed at the Gleneagles Hotel in Torquay, famously the inspiration for *Fawlty Towers*. My parents remember being in the bar one night at around ten o'clock, enjoying a drink with the other guests, when the owner suddenly pulled down the grille, switched out all the lights and went to bed, leaving his guests in the dark. Perhaps someone had mentioned the war.

Nan and Grandpa would often take me to stay with Aunty Ann and Uncle Peter, who lived now in England. My first ever memory of London is of being driven by Uncle Peter along the Embankment and having Cleopatra's Needle pointed out to me. I wasn't especially impressed.

I was a happy little boy, sociable, stoical and keen to entertain, whether it was at home, popping out from behind the long wine-coloured curtains in the living room, or at the little preschool nursery I attended at the age of three, run by Mrs Salvage. I had a group of friends here; we would dress up in a variety of outfits and I would entertain them with songs and jokes. Dressing up was a big part of my life in those early days. Each Christmas I would receive a new outfit and wear it that afternoon when we visited my Aunty Margaret, Uncle Tom and my cousin Jayne who lived further up the hill in Baglan. I would knock on the door, then hide out of sight until Uncle Tom came and expressed shock at the vacant doorstep. This was my cue to leap into view and blast him with my ray gun or pistol (depending on whether I was a spaceman or cowboy), at which point he would feign injury – or sometimes, if I'd been a particularly good shot, death.

Mum and Dad made those early Christmases truly magical. The excitement at the prospect of a visit from Father Christmas was almost as difficult to bear then as it is to comprehend now. The house would fill with satsumas, nuts and tinsel; lights of red, green, gold and blue would be hung on the tree. Like the shopkeeper in *Mr Benn*, my presents would always appear, as if by magic, at the foot of my bed. I can still remember waking in the early hours and glimpsing their shadowy outline in the darkness, pillowcases stuffed full of surprises and delights. One year I received a Dansette record player in red with a cream-coloured lid and sat cross-legged on my bedroom floor at five o'clock in the morning, playing a Rupert Bear record again and again, marvelling at the sound coming out of the little mono speaker hidden away in the housing of the machine.

Throughout my childhood I always had all the toys of the moment: Spirograph, Flight Deck, Ker-Plunk, Cluedo, Mastermind, Mouse Trap, Operation, The K-Tel Record Selector. They all came into the house in pristine condition and then left piece by piece, slowly and mysteriously, over the coming years, like British soldiers slipping quietly out of Colditz – oddly enough, the one game I didn't own.

2

By 1970, just after my fifth birthday, it was time to start school proper. I went to a private school in the nearby coastal town of Porthcawl. St John's, an idyllic-looking prep school for boys, was set at the end of a tree-lined driveway and had as its motto *Virtus, Sapientia, Humilitas* (Virtue, Wisdom, Humility). As luck would have it, very much my own watchwords at the time.

My first day at St John's was a rather traumatic one. I cried bitterly as my mother tried to extricate herself from my soggy clutches. As she struggled to leave, another boy came over and, straight from the pages of a novel, said, 'Don't worry, ma'am, I'll look after your little boy.' Such kindness. The school, though in Newton, Porthcawl (on the South Wales coast), is forever frozen in my memory as a minor English public school; it seemed very precise and just so. Dad remembers hearing a teacher once shouting at a pupil from some distance, '*Wackerbath! Get orf the grass!*'

They were very strict about uniform, not just with the pupils but also with the parents. I don't mean that fathers had to drop off their sons wearing shorts and a cap, but that the school was especially particular with regard to where the uniform had been purchased. We duly set off for the prescribed outfitter, Evan Roberts on Queen Street in Cardiff, a rather imposing store, from which every item on the long list of garments had to be bought – even the grey V-neck jumpers, which would surely have looked no different if they'd been picked up for a fraction of the price at the Port Talbot Peacock's. I was kitted out with all the necessary uniform and equipment. Unfeasibly long shorts and socks, along with a still stiff new shirt for rugby (a game that terrified me), all contained in a soft brown cloth drawstring bag. We wore shorts in the summer as part of our uniform along with a blazer and cap. Everything was new, not a hand-me-down in sight, one of the advantages of being the first child. I had a brand-new leather satchel for my first day, a wonderful, robust and shiny vessel that smelled of leather in a way that nothing has smelled of leather before or since. This glorious smell has stayed with me all these years and now, on receiving a gift of a leather diary or perhaps a wallet, I'll immediately plunge my nose in and stay there for a minute or so. I'm back at St John's and everything is new and unknown; it's all to play for.

It was very much an old-fashioned school inasmuch as competitive sports were encouraged and the food was appalling. Beetroot appeared on the menu with frightening regularity, as did rice pudding, both dishes way too exotic for my limited palate. The competitive sports took place mainly on a large field to the left of the drive-way as you approached the school, or on the dreaded rugby pitch over on the other side. I have a collection of Polaroid photographs taken on a bright summer's Sports Day; in one of them I'm competing in the sack race and still hopping along in my hessian prison while the rest of the course is clear, the other boys all having finished the race, completed the random drugs test and set about preparing themselves mentally for the next event. People often ask if my work is autobiographical, and I'll typically say no, cleverly throwing them off the scent. In fact, this photo appears in the first episode of *Human Remains* as an example of my character Peter's ineptitude at sport.

It could just as easily be me.

I remember very little of the actual lessons at St John's – in fact, try as I might, I can only conjure up two classroom-based memories from my whole time there. The school taught maths in a very peculiar way involving small coloured pieces of wood, each colour corresponding to a particular length of wood and representing a number. There is a name for this method but it escapes me, as did the ability to gain even the most basic understanding of its workings. I remember the colours, though, and the feel of the little wooden sticks, which I would use to build tiny houses while the teacher had turned to face the blackboard. It is in this classroom that my other, far more specific memory is found. It is a sunny day (I have no memories of St John's where the sky is not clear blue and the sun is not shining), the teacher is talking, it's maths again and my mind is wandering out through the window and up into the trees from where I can survey the fields and the roofs of the buildings. I have a compass in my hand, the sort used for drawing circles rather than for finding true north. I'm attempting, unsuccessfully, to harpoon the top of the pencil with the point of the compass. Try as I might, it won't go in. And so I give it one last big push, and in it goes – into my thumb. I look down and see the instrument buried deep in the fleshy pad of my fattest digit and want to say something, '*Ouch!*' ideally, but know that this would attract attention. So, instead, I calmly remove the compass, wrap my thumb in my handkerchief and carry on as if nothing had happened.

And that's about it as far as memories of St John's go.

After a couple of years at St John's I switched schools. Following a bout of measles when I was three I had by now paid a couple of visits to hospital for operations on my ears, and my hearing was far from perfect. Mum was concerned that this was holding me back in class; I was struggling in maths, especially. She remembers the school not being entirely sympathetic or willing to hold my poor hearing solely responsible for my academic shortcomings. They may have had a point. This, and the fact that the promised introduction of a minibus service from Port Talbot to Porthcawl never materialized, was enough to prompt a change. I headed west to Swansea and Dumbarton House School, another private establishment, though this time co-ed.

It was 1972, I was seven and I remember going with my mother to visit the school for the first time. It was in the Uplands area of Swansea, not a million miles away from The Bryn, where I had made my entrance seven years earlier. We approached the school from the rear, driving down a spectacularly steep hill and stopping at the back entrance, a tiny wooden door lost in the centre of a huge red-brick wall. The bottom of the door didn't quite reach the ground; visitors had to step up and over perhaps ten inches of red bricks, and for some reason this struck me as very exciting indeed. It gave the place a Narnian, other-worldly quality that remained on entering the school grounds.

The buildings were spread out over perhaps three levels, the main, rather grand Victorian house being the lowest, then up a little for more classrooms and the gymnasium/hall, before going a little higher again for the library and the canteen-cum-art room. The main house possessed a grand central staircase and a smaller side staircase, which had originally been solely for servants. There was also, at one end of a narrow playground on the lowest level, a most remarkable construction that I can only describe as a multi-storey graveyard for desks. Under a corrugated roof, but open on two sides, were piled desk upon desk, stretching upwards far higher than the average child could reach. Again, like the little door in the red-brick wall, this gave the school an air of mystery. What lay inside this labyrinth of old wooden work stations, beyond the empty crisp packets and the variety of balls (tennis and foot) that remained tantalizingly out of reach? Had any pupils ever dared to crawl through the twisting tunnels that lay inside? I was an avid reader of Alfred Hitchcock's series of books *The Three Investigators*, and the desk cemetery seemed reminiscent of the headquarters described in the books – a large trailer hidden in a junkyard behind and beneath piles of scrap iron and waste from where Jupiter, Pete and Bob would solve many a mystery.

The school was full of higgledy-piggledy bits of architecture, from the home-made table-tennis tables where the bigger boys would congregate at lunch and break times, making the balls spin and hover in the air, to the appallingly Heath Robinson toilet facilities. These were a curious indoor/outdoor affair consisting of an intermittent corrugated-iron sloping roof, a few rickety cubicles and a trough at which we boys would stand while trying not to breathe; the poorly plumbed system and the partly alfresco nature of the arrangement creating a heady aroma of cold damp Swansea air married with stale and fresh urine. While our own sanitary arrangements at home were second to none, I spent enough time at the school to think that this was how all toilets smelled, and over time actually became quite fond of the stench – to the extent that if I now find myself in close contact with shoddy drainage (on, say, a farm or using the external facilities at a very old pub), I'll be transported back to my schooldays and lost for a while in my happy memories. There must be men and women of my age all over Britain who secretly yearn for an occasional whiff of this acrid perfume. I can't help wondering if Jo Malone and the boffins at Molton Brown are missing a trick.

The school had been started in 1923 by the head master Elmer Thomas and his brother. When I arrived in the seventies, Mr Thomas's son and daughter, Aled and Judith, were also teachers there. Both Mr Thomas and his son (known as Mr Aled) were kind men and wonderful teachers, though you wouldn't have wanted to get on the wrong side of Mr Thomas. In my memory he is strolling around the school, his black gown flapping in the breeze like the Dark Knight, his head a neat blanket of snow-white hair, dropping in on lessons unannounced, or filling in when teachers were taken ill. He would be used as a stick to wave at an unruly class, especially by Mrs Mosford, our Welsh teacher, who in the face of pupil disruption would tilt her ear towards the door in an almost pantomime fashion, her eyes widening as she screamed in a stage whisper, '*He's coming! Mr Thomas is coming! Mr Thomas is coming!*' He had a way of opening a textbook which, I now realize from my lofty position as a mature and especially wise adult, conveyed a love of and a respect for knowledge. He would open the pages with relish, as though setting off on an adventure, using his thumb to drive a crease down the inside of the spine and ensure that the book remained open and able to do its job.

Each morning we would have an assembly, headed by Mr Thomas, when hymns would be sung to the accompaniment of an upright piano, played with delightful flamboyance by Mr Croote, our history teacher. His favourite appeared to be 'It Fell Upon a Summer Day', which he would begin with a positively Liberacean zeal and perform in a rhythm and style reminiscent of the theme tune to the popular seventies BBC sitcom *It Ain't Half Hot Mum*: 'Meet the gang 'cause the boys are here / The boys to entertain you!' That was what I and, I'm sure, many of the other children had in mind as we sang:

> It fell upon a summer day,
> When Jesus walked in Galilee,
> The mothers from a village brought
> Their children to His knee.

Mr Croote's history lessons were held on the top floor of the main building. There was a large double window in the classroom, which looked out on to a mature tree in which could be found a family of wood pigeons who would provide a cooing accompaniment to our studies. I would gaze out at them and imagine myself living in the tree with the birds, or flying off to Swansea Bay, and all the while Mr Croote's sonorous and soothing voice would be humming and bubbling away in the background.

'In 1536 Henry the Eighth ordered the dissolution of the monasteries . . .'

His lessons seemed to feature a lot of dictation; we would sit there in rows, hanging on and writing down his every word.

'New paragraph . . . However, Thomas Cromwell began to . . .'

This was one of Mr Croote's signature moves. He seemed unable to begin a new paragraph with any word other than 'however'; he had a screenwriter's instinct for conflict. He would stand at the front of the class, beside a ream of paper, and gently rub his fingers over the top sheet in a circular fashion, causing the pages to fan out symmetrically in such a magical fashion that he wouldn't have been out of place at Hogwarts. With his colourful rings, slightly powdery face and frequent use of cologne, Mr Croote's home life was the subject of some conjecture among the pupils and, looking back now, I suspect he was ahead of his time in many ways. He was popular with the children and once referred to me as a 'little sirocco'; I didn't know what it meant at the time but now I suspect he was spot on.

March 1st is an important day in Wales; it is St David's Day, the festival of our patron saint, and tradition dictates that schools across the land put on an eisteddfod, a little festival of music, poetry and performance. Each year we would leave the school en masse and walk two abreast in a slowly snaking crocodile of children, travelling the short distance to the nearby Henrietta Street Chapel. Our joint national symbols, the daffodil and the leek, would be worn on the lapels of our blazers – sometimes little cloth representations, but often the real thing – with some of the rowdier boys competing to see who could attach the largest flower or vegetable to their chest. Once at the chapel we would file into the pews and wait for the proceedings to commence, the air heavy with the scent of leeks and daffodils. It was the one day of the year that we all felt like greengrocers.

When it came time to perform we would gather in small groups for songs, and for our attempts at choral speaking. This was the reciting of a poem as a group, and the poem always seemed to be T. Llew Jones's 'Y Wiwer', Welsh for 'The Squirrel'. As the morning wore on, some of the rowdier boys – those with less regard for authority than me – would crane their necks to one side and begin to chew at their leeks. A few tentative nibbles would soon be followed by full-on unbridled chomping, which would then be complemented by a chorus of belching. Once the eisteddfod was completed, with the air of the small chapel now heavy with the aroma of vegetables and the gaseous emissions of young children, we would return to the school, from where we would disperse for a much-anticipated afternoon off.

These were happy, carefree days at Dumbarton and it was here that I made the first significant relationship of my life, my first best friend. David Williams was three months younger than me; his birthday was in August, a month he would spend much of in Majorca where his family had an apartment in the seaside resort of C'an Pastilla and from where he would return each year with a stomach tanned to mahogany. His father Gwynfa owned a chemist's shop in Port Talbot, several in other parts of Wales and one in Hounslow, just outside London. He had a debenture in the North Upper Stand at Cardiff Arms Park and I would often go as David's guest to see Wales play, although my interest in rugby was not especially keen. We would drive up in the family Jaguar with the personalized number plate and park on Cathedral Road where David's Uncle Em(lyn) had a house, then we would walk down to the ground, stopping at the Beverley for a pre-match drink where David would have a pint and I would have a lemonade. I had no interest in drinking as a child, a youth or indeed as a young man. I had tried beer and found it a most unpleasant taste, so would spend the hour or so in the pub like a Nonconformist minister sent to the Valleys to save the men from themselves.

On leaving the pub we would join a growing throng of men, women and children as it moved slowly down Cathedral Road, over the Castle Street Bridge and onto the ground. The security in those days was not what it is now and it was quite common at this stage of the journey to see opportunistic enthusiasts trying to gain entrance to the ground via the banks of the River Taff, clambering up the slopes, legs wet to the knee, pint precariously balanced in one hand, flag in the other.

There was, and still is, a hell of an atmosphere in Cardiff on match day. We would buy a programme – a modest, far simpler publication than today's glossy sporting pornography that costs a fortune – then squeeze our way past the scarf and flag sellers, the hot dog and rosette (whatever happened to *them*?) stands before entering what seemed to me to be the largest man-made structure in the world, Cardiff Arms Park. These were the glory days of Welsh rugby, with Gareth Edwards, Phil Bennett and J. P. R. Williams on the field and Max Boyce at the top of the charts, but it was all rather lost on me then. Having said that, my lack of interest didn't stop me from following David for a triumphant trot onto the pitch after Wales's Grand Slam triumph against France in 1978.

David was a huge sports fan, and his dad also had access to tickets for football matches at Wembley. We went on more than one occasion to see the FA Cup Final, staying at the flat above the chemist shop in Hounslow and getting the tube into central London on the Saturday morning. On one such visit we made a detour into Soho so that David's brother John, eight years older and about to get married to Sian, could visit the tailor responsible for his morning suit. David and I shuffled along behind the grown-ups, sneakily glancing into the doorways and shopfronts of ill repute. It wasn't like Swansea.

With his chain of chemist's shops, David's father was a very successful and canny businessman, but he took great delight in playing the innocent; perhaps it wrong-footed business adversaries. He came to our house once, shortly after we'd taken delivery of one of the first video recorders in the area, and pretended to be utterly baffled at how the machine could send out pictures when it wasn't pointing at the screen, like a projector.

This faux naivety masked a sterner side, glimpsed one stormy night in Majorca when David and I returned later than promised to the apartment after an evening spent playing pool in a bar. We tiptoed in an hour later than expected, hoping to find Mr and Mrs Williams tucked up in bed, only to be greeted by the furious silhouette of David's dad as he stood in front of the double glass doors that led to the balcony. He exploded at David, '*Where the hell have you been?*' As he laid down the law in a most forceful manner, he was beautifully backlit by the lightning as it flashed angrily outside in the stormy night, swiftly followed by deafening claps of thunder. He directed not one word of his dressing-down at me, but nonetheless I was terrified. In a few minutes the ordeal was over and we shuffled off to the bedroom with our tails between our legs. I had never witnessed anything like this from my dad and was in shock as I sat down on my bed. I turned to David to ask if he was all right; he must surely be shocked and upset too, but he just laughed. He'd seen it all before. At breakfast the next day it was as though it had never happened.

I went out to the apartment a few times with David and his parents, and once (when we were in our late teens) just with David, to decorate the flat and have a little holiday at the same time. We had strict instructions as to the colour of paint and trekked off to the local paint shop, returning fully equipped and ready for action. In accordance with my desire to always be at the cutting edge of alternative culture, we worked to the soundtrack of Wham's album *Make It Big*, their much-anticipated follow-up to *Fantastic*, on vinyl of course, and had the whole place done in a week. We had arrived on the island as boys but now returned home as men; not just any men, but painting and decorating men. It wasn't until David's mother went out for a short stay a few months later that it was discovered her cut-price painters and decorators had done the whole place in gloss.

I began at Dumbarton a couple of weeks before David, and on the day of his arrival he was told to sit next to me as my regular deskmate was away. It was Miss Leahy's class and she was reading to us from *The Lion, the Witch and the Wardrobe*, appropriately enough, given my initial reaction to entering the school via the tiny door at the back. Talking to David I discovered that he lived just a few streets away from me in Baglan and would therefore be travelling to school with me every morning on the bus. This was as long and tortuous a route as it is possible to plot from Baglan to Swansea. Every morning I would board the bus outside a row of shops a few streets away from home and we'd trundle along through Baglan, picking up David en route, then through Briton Ferry, past the Metal Box factory in Neath, along to Birchgrove, through Llansamlet and then finally, an hour after I'd got on, we'd arrive at school.

David says that it was on these interminable journeys that he first saw me perform, entertaining a captive audience desperate for any form of diversion from the monotony of the transit. Apparently my repertoire included Hartley Hare (a puppet from the children's programme *Pipkins* whose voice I found I was able to replicate), characters from the Welsh comedian Ryan Davies's television programme, Kermit the Frog and a creature of my own making, the Wild Mandango, who specialized in smelling people. I had forgotten all about these bus journeys to and from school but, talking again to David, my little flights of fancy stood out in his memory as being an important stage in my early development as a performer.

I can certainly remember being the one at school who would want to make people laugh, whether it was simply impersonating the teachers or by pulling more elaborate stunts such as the time I hid in the box during PE. In a chilling premonition of the Small Man in a Box I decided that it would be fun to hide in the box – the piece of apparatus made up of sections, all leading to a leather top, over which we would vault – and stay there for the whole of the class. The gym teacher, Mr Jones, was unaware of my presence, but the other boys knew I was there. David remembers seeing a pair of eyes peeping out from the hand-hold holes at the side while Gareth Morris, never the most coordinated of boys (he once put his school trousers on over his wet swimming trunks and then smashed a window with his hand while attempting to kill a wasp), delighted in running head first into the box in an effort to unnerve me and give the game away. I hadn't factored in getting back out of my little box and when I finally did, the other boys had gone, and with them my clothes.

I took an almost Dadaist pleasure in walking into the next class in my underwear and enquiring in a calm and perfectly reasonable voice, 'Excuse me, sir, I wonder has anyone seen my trousers?'

The kids all laughed but the teacher, Mr Cope, took a very dim view.

'You think you're very funny, don't you? Well, you're not and you're not going to amount to anything until you stop playing the fool.'

He wasn't happy.

Autobiographies are typically full of tales where the protagonist is suffering verbal or physical abuse at the hands of an unkind or insensitive teacher, but I have only this minor altercation with Mr Cope to offer up. This and the time he called me 'short-arse' in front of the class. Not the crime of the century but, at the risk of sounding like a teacher myself, I have to say it was his own time he was wasting.

3

While these early efforts at entertainment were small-scale, spur-of-the-moment affairs, I was soon to expand and widen my horizons with the mounting of my first play – an ambitious and, as far as I'm aware, entirely unprecedented stage adaptation of *Star Wars*. It was 1979 and we were all in the grip of the film, which had created quite a stir in Swansea. Oddly, I don't remember anything of seeing the film for the first time myself but have vivid memories of the trailer, especially the part where Luke and Leia swing across an abyss on an unfeasibly thin rope. It looked impossibly exciting. David and I wrote the script; naturally I cast myself as Luke Skywalker, Helen Williams was Princess Leia and Gareth Morris, the wasp killer himself, made an imposing Darth Vader. David, not bitten by the performing bug, was happy to essay the lesser role of Chief Stormtrooper, dressed in cricket whites, skateboard helmet and plastic stormtrooper mask, bought at Swansea market. We had battery-operated toy light sabres and, in lieu of an R2-D2 (who was deemed too challenging a build), constructed instead an impressive K9 from *Dr Who*. He was built out of a large cardboard box, with a smaller box for his head, and pulled along the stage by a length of string.

We performed to the school and before the play began I went out in front of the curtain and gave what I suppose was my first ever stand-up comedy routine. It consisted of a few words of welcome and some jokes memorized from my beloved *Two Ronnies' Joke Book*. I especially recall seeing a teacher's face change from smiling appreciation of my efforts to a portrait of narrow-eyed disapproval when I told the one about the naked Swedish woman who had been pulled from the North Sea by Scottish trawlermen and covered with an old mackintosh. Mr Angus Mackintosh of Fife, who was delighted. See, it still works.

Our play began with the Stormtroopers, led by David, crashing through the tinfoil door we had constructed upstage right and arriving on the Death Star. The idea was that the fall from my old partner in crime the gym box, placed behind the foil door, would be softened by the presence of a crash mat on the other side. But in his excitement at his first and entirely unwanted stage appearance, David forgot to place the mat. This left him arriving on the stage rather inelegantly, crashing down on his shoulder from a great height and crying out in pain. Audiences often think this sort of occurrence is intentional, and I seem to remember that being the case in this instance: 'Fair play, that can't be easy . . .'

We carried on despite this and a catalogue of other setbacks, including K9's head falling off mid-scene and the light sabres snapping open during the fight between Darth Vader and Obi-Wan Kenobi. It's hard to communicate the poignancy of, 'If you strike me down I shall become more powerful than you can possibly imagine,' while two Eveready size 'C' batteries land with a resounding clunk on the hollow wooden floor and begin slowly rolling towards the edge of the stage, before dropping off and into the audience. Despite our technical shortcomings the production was considered a success and I was well and truly bitten by the acting bug.

I suppose the only other thing of note when it comes to our stage version of *Star Wars* is that, unless she was off ill that day, a very young Catherine Zeta Jones would have been in the audience. The future Queen of Wales was a pupil at the school although, she being some few years younger than me, we weren't friends. There was one occasion when I bumped into Catherine's mother while on my way into school. She had just dropped off her daughter and then realized she'd forgotten to give her the lunch money for that day. Instead, she handed it to me and asked if I would pass it on. I of course said I would, and then went on my way, completely forgetting about the money until I found it nestling in my pocket at lunchtime while at the shops with friends. I spent it on some sweets. I've told this story innumerable times on a variety of talk shows, so shan't repeat it here. Hmm, I think I already have – apologies if you've heard it before.

I would eventually meet Catherine, very briefly, twenty-four years later at a party after that year's BAFTA ceremony, at which she had won an award for her role in the film musical *Chicago*. Someone at the do knew that we'd been to the same school and thought it would be a good idea to introduce us. I'd had a few glasses of champagne at this point, otherwise I think I'd have said a polite 'no thank you'. There's nothing worse than being introduced to a big star who has no idea who you are. The embarrassment of standing there while a well-meaning third party trots out a potted history of your relatively modest achievements to the bewilderment of the increasingly impatient celestial being is not worth the brief moment of pleasure when you get to say how much you like their work. However, I'd had a drink and so walked over to where she and her husband, the great Michael Douglas, were receiving a line of well-wishers who had formed an orderly queue just off to their right. Being a little tipsy, I happily joined this queue and waited my turn.

It was like meeting minor European royalty and, as I got closer to the front, I began to pick up more and more of the brief exchange that each congratulant enjoyed after having at last reached the top of the queue. Catherine was in that awkward position of really being unable to say anything beyond 'thank you' – faced, as she was, with an unending barrage of compliments. Her voice had that familiar mid-Atlantic to often full-on American twang, '*Thaaank you!*' Understandable, given the amount of time she spends there and her being married to Captain America. This was what I heard repeated as I edged and shuffled towards the front of the queue and my moment: '*Thaaank you, thaaank you . . .*' My plan was to congratulate her, accept my American '*thaaank you*' with a good grace, then tell her that we'd been at the same school, a very small school, in Swansea, at the same time as each other. I thought she'd welcome something a bit different, and happily passed the remainder of my waiting time imagining her and Michael inviting me back to the Dorchester, where we'd hook up with Danny DeVito and talk about old times. I was woken from my reverie by suddenly finding myself in front of my prey, and so launched into my well-rehearsed congratulations.

'Hello, Catherine, I just wanted to say congratulations, really well done!'

'*Thaaank you, thaaank you –*'

'And I wanted to tell you that I went to Dumbarton too –'

At this point her voice shot out of LA, across the Atlantic at the speed of light, and settled back into its natural sing-song Swansea loveliness.

'Really?! I saw Mr Aled yesterday!'

And with that she turned and was gone, closely followed by a man who looked like Gordon Gekko.

I slunk back to my table with my tail between my legs, my dining companions anxious for a debriefing.

'How did it go? How was she? Did she remember you?'

'Um, yes, err . . . could you pass the wine, please?'

I suppose I had been performing long before my first, witnessed by future Hollywood royalty, moment on a stage. After school and at weekends I would usually be found with David, riding our bikes around Baglan, two abreast, pretending to be Starsky and Hutch in the red Ford Gran Torino with the white stripe down the side and hearing the crackle of the radio as it alerted us to crimes newly perpetrated: *All units, we have an APB on a suspect, corner of Sunset and Main . . .* We would swing into action: *Zebra Three, Zebra Three, we're on our way!* We'd be off, pedalling furiously down Lodge Drive and towards the park, always right next to each other so as to maintain the illusion of being in the Torino.

At that time the thought of being able to drive was exciting beyond belief. I struggled to understand how anyone ever left their car once they'd got a licence. When I was old enough to try, I passed the test on my first attempt despite getting a few of the questions wrong and telling the examiner that in the event of a blowout on the motorway I would pull over and wait for help on the cold shoulder.

David and I would cycle all around Baglan and beyond, often over the bridge to The Ferry Boat Inn for a lemonade and sometimes even as far as Swansea, singing Beatles songs as we went. David's brother John had the red and the blue Greatest Hits albums; we would sneak them out of his bedroom and listen to them, trying not to allow any scratches onto the vinyl. John was away at boarding school in Llandovery and so David and I would make frequent raids on his bedroom. On one occasion we came back across the landing to David's room with the glossy programme for Rod Stewart's 'Blondes Have More Fun' tour, which John had rather excitingly been all the way to London to see, at the impossible cathedral of glamour that was Earl's Court.

David's house, on the corner of Lodge Drive, was bigger than ours and kept in immaculate condition by his mother, Pam, who waited on David hand and foot. He really did live like a maharajah, returning from school and entering the smelling-of-furniture-polish house, whereupon he would sit down in front of the television and wait for his mother to bring him his tea on a tray, which would then be consumed while watching *Magpie* or some such show. The house had an open wooden slatted seventies-style staircase which was kept polished to such an extent that it became quite dangerous. Every time I visited I would take off my shoes in the kitchen and David and I would pad around the house in our socks. He would tear up and down the stairs at breakneck speed, by now familiar with the amount of slippage, whereas I would cautiously make my way up and down while gripping the banister like a man slowly regaining mobility around his home after a serious accident at work.

Once we'd negotiated our way down the ice wall of a staircase, we'd run outside to the field behind the house to play football. I'd be happy to be in goal so long as he'd tell me where he was going to place the ball and I could execute a dramatic dive. That was part of being an actor; I was always aware of how things looked and wouldn't mind engineering a situation where I would be the butt of the joke, providing it got a laugh, providing it was interesting. After an evening playing outdoors with David I'd arrive home out of breath and head straight to the kitchen, where I'd pour myself a few glasses of water, passing Mum and Dad in the living room sitting in the oh-so-1970s brown fabric swivel pod chairs, bought at the furniture warehouse set up in an old aircraft hangar at Llandow.

In my mind *Robin's Nest* is on the television, the windows are steamed up because Mum's been boiling fish and my little brother is on the floor. Pete was born in 1973, eight years after me, a gap large enough to mean that I always felt as much a paternal influence on him as a fraternal one. We never fought or were competitive with each other. There was no sibling rivalry whatsoever, to the extent that when I had my own children many years later, with just a few years between them, I was amazed at how siblings can fight. I'd never known anything like it. Having said that, in researching this book I came across a picture of a young me and a very young Pete, in which I'm glowering at him as though he was the most unwelcome guest to ever arrive anywhere!

I think back on the eight years before Pete was born as years in which I was an only child, but this is not the case. In April of 1971 Mum gave birth to my brother Jeremy. I was about to turn six in May. I'm afraid I have no memories at all of Jeremy, the only image I can conjure up when I think of him is of my mother sitting on the settee at Woodside, crying. Jeremy died, without warning or explanation, in August of that year, a victim of sudden infant death syndrome. I can't imagine how this affected my parents; it is unbearable to try.

As a young child I can remember a comforting glow of certainty in my surroundings; while Dad was often away at work, Mum was always with me, ferrying me around here, there and everywhere, to Swansea, Neath, Briton Ferry . . . you name it, we went there. In my hazy childhood memory we're in a Vauxhall Viva, the one with the rectangular speedometer. We're waiting, Nan and I, in the car outside C&A while Mum pops in for something. It's raining hard and the wipers are flapping across the windscreen.

I have a very strong memory of being snug between Mum and Dad in bed and feeling that all was well with the world. 'Snug as a bug in a rug,' as Dad would say.

Dad was always as much a friend as a father. He was also quite flashy; he had a way with words that betrayed his profession, that of a salesman. He sold cars. When I was little, he sold them from a large showroom in Margam that is now buried deep under the M4 motorway as it prepares for its flight of avoidance over Port Talbot; after Margam Abbey Motors he struck out on his own and set up a second-hand car dealership. I would join him on trips to the car auctions at Southampton. It was always raining and the trips always smelled of cigarettes – this, for me, was the smell of the seventies. Mum and Dad both smoked; they were quite keen, and it is them I have to thank for my never having been tempted. Without knowing it they carried out an early form of aversion therapy and I grew up with an almost pathological dislike for cigarettes, matches, ashtrays. In fact, any of the paraphernalia connected with smoking. I even disliked holding an unopened packet.

When I would hear The Beatles singing 'She's Leaving Home', I'd always love the line about the man who worked in the motor trade. That was my dad, he was a man from the motor trade. As part of his devotion to this trade he had a Jet garage for a while. I remember the orange glow of the lights as they indicated a pump being used, and the *Man from U.N.C.L.E.* exoticism of the little safe that was built into the floor under the cashier's chair. I would gaze down at it from the swivel chair and imagine a masked criminal forcing me to unlock it and empty the contents into a bag.

At home I would hear Dad talk on the telephone to clients and he would be full of energy and charm, his voice shifting from its natural soft Port Talbot lilt and edging towards a mild mid-Atlantic twang. It was the seventies, so the phone in question was a Trimphone or Slimphone; I forget the name now. It was one of those narrow phones and it was probably a shade of green. Whatever the colour, it was undoubtedly the phone of the day, the very latest in telecommunications style.

We were in many ways early adopters in the area of consumer durable technology. A Sony cassette deck was purchased one Saturday afternoon on a trip to Swansea, soon to be augmented by tapes of Barry White, the Carpenters, the *Doctor Zhivago* soundtrack and Herb Alpert. I imagine it was quite swish in its day, with its FM tuner, slider volume controls and dark-wood casing and speakers. I used to play a double cassette on it that I'd received for Christmas, a compilation of hits of the day that included 'Sad Sweet Dreamer' by Sweet Sensation and 'Devil Gate Drive' by Suzi Quatro. I also enjoyed sliding the volume controls and making the transporter-room noise from *Star Trek*, pretending that I was beaming down to another planet. The room also had a rug with two circles on it, which to me represented the platforms in the transporter room from which Captain Kirk would teleport. Although state of the art, it wasn't long before the Sony cassette deck became faulty and started chewing up the tapes, which would then have to be painstakingly removed before a pencil was inserted into the spool and careful rewinding began. On future plays, whenever the mangled bit of tape was reached the sound would acquire an odd 'underwater' quality that would last for as long as the damage stretched, before the music would come into the clear again, as though waking from a fitful sweaty sleep or emerging unscathed from a dense forest of thorns.

My pretend beaming would take place in the lounge, the 'best' room. It wasn't a 'best' room in the traditional Welsh sense – that is to say, we *did* use it all year round – but it was also the room that grandparents would sit in on a Sunday. I can see my father's mother with a cup of tea; Nanny Margam, she was known as (given that she was my nan and she came from Margam). She still lived, as a widow now, in the house that my dad had grown up in, number 51 Wern Road, just up the street from Anthony Hopkins and his parents. Hopkins's father was a baker, and it was from his bakery that Dad and my Aunty Margaret and uncles Colin and Leighton bought their bread. My only memory of my grandfather Emlyn is of standing at the foot of his bed while paying a visit to the house; he died when I was very young.

Nanny Margam would come to our house on Sundays, always bearing a freshly made egg custard tart (still the best I have tasted), and we would discuss that week's show by our shared favourite, Benny Hill. I would recount one of his sketches and she would tut under her breath, 'Well well, there's comical . . .' before we'd listen together to 'Ernie (The Fastest Milkman in the West)'.

For the rest of the week this best room was somewhat underused, and I remember it now for just two reasons. It had a glass fireplace, which I once put my head through after twirling round and round in an effort to make myself dizzy. When I think of the room, I always remember that incident. The other memory was

Mum and Dad in 1964, event unknown.

As a baby, shortly after stumbling across my dad's merkin.

With Nan and Grandpa at Woodside.

A young Brando.
(Marlon Brando.)
(. . . the actor.)

'I declare this meeting of
the Junior Book Club open.'

Riot!

Dad, Grandpa, Nan, Just William, Mum, Cousin David,
Aunty Ann, Uncle Peter.

My fourth birthday and Nanny Margam is
disappointed by the quality of the catering.

A little put out by the arrival of my brother Pete.

Plotting his demise . . .

In Spain with Dad and Pete. Mum is on the other side of the camera.

Before the inferno. Pete and I on *The Prophet* in 1977. In an unrelated incident, Elvis would soon be dead.

Me and David in Lawrenny. Insert your own crab joke:

I place my mind elsewhere as Santa reaches his own conclusion.

I'd be happier if I could see his other hand.

Please do what he says or he will kill me.

Finally, a Santa I can trust.

My first year at Porthcawl Comprehensive.

I like Elvis.

'One day in class, she wrote her name on my arm, and I nearly fainted.'

of Saturday mornings spent sitting on the floor cross-legged with a bowl of Sugar Puffs and copies of *Roy of the Rovers* and *Tiger* laid out on the carpet in front of me. They would be delivered on a Saturday morning and I would rush downstairs full of excitement, while Mum and Dad slept on above me.

I've always felt that, as a child, I had an above-average interest in several things; comedy was one of them, but magazines were also high up on the list. I had an ability then – and still do, to a lesser extent – to fixate on something and to elevate it to a loftier position than it deserves. Every week along with *Roy of the Rovers* and *Tiger*, I would also get *Look-in*. This was a TV-oriented magazine with features on shows such as *Supersonic, The Six Million Dollar Man* and other hits of the day. One week it was giving away a dragon pendant, cashing in on the success of the *Kung Fu* TV series. When my copy arrived the pendant had already gone and there ensued a quest, which lasted for some weeks, as I tried to track down another. I can't remember whether or not I turned up anything, but the smell of magazines will take me right back to opening the comic and the horrible feeling in the pit of my stomach as I realized that the prized free gift was missing.

I must have spent a lot of time in newsagents as a child; the smell of newsprint, especially on a cold frosty morning, is one of the most evocative for me as an adult, right up there with the leather of my satchel at St John's. Mulling it over, perhaps the comics weren't delivered; perhaps I went down to Flares, the newsagent just down the hill on the corner, and bought my comics myself, hurriedly bringing them back in time for *Swap*

Shop – a fine BBC programme, and one to which I was devoted.

It's fair to say that I was a BBC child, faithful to *Blue Peter* and *Swap Shop*, with only occasional forays into the racier fields of *Magpie* and *Tiswas*, which seemed, as Alan Bennett's mother would say, 'common'. This is not to say that we never dipped our toes in the murky waters of ITV – far from it. We loved *Rising Damp*, *Only When I Laugh* and *The Kenny Everett Video Show* but were really more naturally at home with the BBC where, like millions of others, we were regular viewers of *The Two Ronnies*, *Top of the Pops*, *Mike Yarwood* and *The Generation Game*.

A lot of my childhood seems to have been spent in front of the television, and yet I was just as content outdoors, roaming around Baglan with my friend Robert George. Robert was known as Georgie and loved the outdoors even more than I did. Together we climbed trees looking for birds' eggs, a pursuit rightly frowned upon now but at the time it was all the rage and not seen as being at all cruel. We would cross over the main road and on to the marshy fields with their tiny waterways, where we built makeshift rafts with bits of wood and discarded plastic barrels. Once constructed, these fine vessels would carry us off to uncharted territories. While on the marshy ground we would collect frogspawn and bring it home in buckets, to be transferred into a water-filled bin just outside the back door, where it would sit until the frogs arrived. We were forever building dens, and this meant that I was always gathering sticks, boughs and branches, dragging them back to the house and trying to make some kind of shelter or hideaway with them.

From 1971 we lived on what might be called the nursery slope of a larger hill in Baglan and had a steep narrow lawn at the front of the house, perfect for sending Action Man hurtling down on a suicide mission in his jeep. I was very fond of Action Man and loved nothing more than suspending him on a length of string and dangling him from the top of the stairs, out through the banisters and down the wall at the side. I'd do this for hours, perfectly happy to watch him swing back and forth like a pendulum. In my mind he was scaling a cliff face or the walls of the castle to reach the lair of an evil mastermind. He would often have been stripped of his uniform long ago and, in a form of exhibitionism frowned on by the military, be attempting his mission naked. This was quite common in Action Men. I had several of them, almost a platoon, and within minutes of emerging from their boxes they'd be naked, huddled together in a heap like a drunken support group. With their toned muscular bodies, crew cuts and gripping hands, one wonders with hindsight exactly what sort of action these men were looking for.

Mine would soon be out of their uniforms and in their bespoke outfits that I'd made from old socks. A hole would be cut at the toe for their head to pop through, followed by two smaller holes at the side for the arms, with an elastic band serving as a belt. It was a sort of Roman slave tunic inspired, I suspect, by Kirk Douglas in *Spartacus*, the first film I ever cried at, sitting on the sofa between Mum and Dad, watery eyes glued to the telly. I made quite a few little outfits for my Action Men; this, combined with a love of not only Donny Osmond but also the Bay City Rollers, might prompt the reader to a few conclusions with regards to my young self and matters of orientation. Rest assured that I always knew where to draw the line when it came to my slightly fey leanings.

I offer as proof the time that my grandmother bought me a purple T-shirt on which was printed the face of Donny Osmond. Much as I loved what he and his crazy brothers were doing in challenging the perceived norms of contemporary music, I knew deep inside that it would simply be wrong for a young boy of my age to wear such a T-shirt. And so I broke Nan's heart with my refusal, 'Good God, woman, no! What the hell were you thinking?!' That's what a more forceful, not to say rude, child might have said. I politely declined, offering up all manner of excuses.

Despite waving the flag for sensitive, artistic children everywhere I was also involved in more boyish pursuits, and my love of trees and dens continued to grow unabated. One particularly ambitious Sunday morning I decided to build an extensive new lair in the garden, and soon realized that I needed far more in the way of raw materials if I was to do justice to my architectural vision. So I set off just down the hill from our house to a point where a few trees stood on a grass verge at the side of the road. I climbed up, knife in hand, for twelve feet or so to where the tree divided off into a network of branches and then, sitting on one, began to saw at a limb. I tugged away at the branch with one hand while hacking at it with the other, all the while blind to the laws of physics, which confidently predicted my imminent downfall. Not unlike the splendid Wyle E. Coyote in the Road Runner cartoons – when he speeds off a clifftop and only falls when he looks down and realizes what he's done – at the point that the branch parted company with the tree I suddenly recognized the folly of my ways and plummeted downwards, landing in a dead weight on the grass and knocking myself out cold in the process. Luckily for me a local man, George Williams, happened to be passing, walking his dog, and he witnessed my fall. Were it not for him, I might still be there now.

He hurried over to find my lifeless body lying limp and abandoned amongst the long grass and, no doubt aware of the weight of responsibility dictating that he should do the right thing, immediately flagged down the next person he saw. As luck would have it, that next person was my father, returning from the pub, where he'd been enjoying his traditional pre-Sunday-lunch drink.

'Come and look, Howard! Whose boy is this?'

Dad wandered over to help, full of public-spiritedness, only to receive the awful shock of seeing his own son lying in the long grass. Rather like George Cole's Arthur Daley in *Minder*, when realizing that one of his plans had gone asunder Dad uttered a quick, 'Oh my good God!' and then concentrated on not passing out himself. I was ushered into the car and taken, still unconscious, to the nearby Neath hospital and wheeled along a corridor to be examined by a doctor; all the while Dad was leaning over me in a concerned manner. Bear in mind that he'd come upon me directly from the pub and so each time he gazed down at my pale unflinching face he breathed out a constant stream of, frankly, alcoholic fumes. (Probably worth pointing out here that it was the fumes that were alcoholic, not Dad.) On examining me, the doctor couldn't help but notice the sweet stench of beer and enquired, not unreasonably, 'Has your son been drinking?'

Mum would not have been pleased at such a suggestion; I would only have been seven or eight years old, and I've no doubt she would have put the doctor straight in a direct and unambiguous manner. Anyway, I came around eventually and all was well, although I must have liked the hospital as I was to return a few weeks later, this time conscious but in some pain, after attempting to build a slide in the back garden. (Mum says I was accident-prone as a child, and these stories do tend to back up her argument.) I thought it would be a good idea, again on a Sunday morning – a particularly dangerous time for me, it would appear – to build a slide in the garden, a rollercoaster almost. To do this I took a ladder and placed one end up on the top of a low wall. This positioned the ladder at roughly forty-five degrees. Perfect. I then placed a plastic sledge, specifically a sand sledge – we used to go regularly to the sand dunes at Merthyr Mawr near Bridgend (as seen in *Lawrence of Arabia* – no, really . . .) and career around on these little sledges – at the top of the dunes. My plan was to slide down the ladder, and I was curious as to how far I would continue to travel once I hit the ground.

Holding the sledge in place with one hand, at the summit of my slide, I carefully climbed on to my chariot and surveyed the scene. Everything looked good. The sky was clear, there was little wind and, in my opinion, forty-five degrees was steep enough to get a bit of speed up but not so steep that I might come to any harm. I launched myself off and hurtled down, reaching the ground with a bump and stopping just inches from the foot of the ladder. The only thing out of the ordinary to have happened on my fantastic journey was the unmistakable ripping sound I heard as I reached the bottom, a kind of tearing noise. Strange. I stood up and noticed that a length of fabric from the left leg of my trousers, Sunday best trousers at that, was hanging down at my side, torn. That would explain the noise, then. I glanced at the sledge and saw that it too had suffered some damage, a huge tear down the left side, a gaping hole in the hull of the vessel.

This was when I realized that I'd made the mistake of placing the top of the ladder at the bottom of my slide. The top of the ladder was where the metal hooks, the sharp metal hooks through which you could slide another ladder, were located. I felt a curious sensation in my leg and looked down. There, in full view thanks to the torn trouser, was my thigh, hanging open and exhibiting what, even to my untrained eye were evidently several layers of me. Lovely. That was when it began to hurt, only once I'd *seen* it. Very strange. I went in the house to find Mum and first apologized for ripping my best trousers before showing her the collateral damage. Off we went to the hospital again, not returning until my poor little thigh had been stitched up. The scar is still there, just below my bum.

If you're ever in the area, do have a look.

4

Through my early childhood we had often hooked a caravan up to the car and headed off to a couple of spots around Wales – Brecon, and New Hedges near Tenby – and across the Severn Bridge into Dorset. Then, in the spring of 1977, Mum and Dad bought a large static caravan on a site in Lawrenny, West Wales, in those days a few hours' drive from Baglan through lovely countryside, though now a considerably shorter journey thanks to the expanding motorway. Well done, the M4. A few friends already had places there, and the idea was that we would spend weekends and school holidays at the caravan with Mum, being joined by Dad when he could get away from work. Lawrenny is a tiny village, not a million miles away from Tenby, and the small caravan site was adjacent to Lawrenny Yacht Club where many of the caravan dwellers had boats in which they would sail, motor or paddle on the Cleddau Estuary. The estuary goes out past Pembroke Dock and Milford Haven to the Irish Sea and inland as far as Haverfordwest. We bought a little red speedboat, a Picton Speedmaster, and would take it out on the water most weekends.

I loved Lawrenny. It's surrounded by trees, and that's where you would find me when I wasn't on the water. I was in den-building heaven, scampering out to the woods from the moment I woke up in the little bedroom at the back of the caravan, where Pete and I had bunk beds with me in the Ronnie Barker spot on the top bunk and Pete taking the Richard Beckinsale role on the bottom. I'd head out and into the woods, ideally before Pete could claim to have heard me calling out girls' names in my sleep, and joyfully take to the trees. There was a spot a few minutes' walk into the woods, near the banks of the estuary, at the remains of some old brick cottage, where a few friends and I had built a tree house of sorts with a ropeway connecting two trees on which I'd walk back and forth, imagining I was Tarzan.

Further inland, away from the water, past the ditch we'd covered with thin sticks and leaves, creating a primitive yet successful mantrap where we once disabled a fully grown man and his dog, was a slope with a large tree from which we'd hung a swing. There were two options with the swing: the straightforward back and forth approach that, depending on the speed of trajectory, could take you out over the nearby barbed-wire fence, high into the air; or the more ambitious sweeping sideways motion that would take you round the tree and dangerously closer to the barbed wire. Far more kudos was at stake with this method, especially if your dirty Adidas or Puma trainers could be seen to have only just cleared the barbed wire.

I was happiest, though, back at the tree house and would often spend time there on my own, once climbing to the very top of the tree on an especially windy day. From here I could see the peaks of the neighbouring trees, and also the estuary as it headed off in both directions. When the wind picked up, I was at first scared, but then began to relish holding onto the tree as it swayed, gently at first, with each new gust. The wind became stronger and the tree began to move a few feet each way. I closed my eyes and hung on tightly, breathing the fresh salty air through my nose and hearing the angry rush of the wind as it chased itself through the leaves and branches all around me. This most singular experience has stayed with me and is one of the most evocative of my childhood. It is responsible for my continued love of the sound trees make as they're buffeted by the wind.

It was on the water that we spent most of our time at Lawrenny; we had the little speedboat in which we would buzz around here, there and everywhere. Then after a while, Dad wanted something bigger and was tempted to buy a little cruiser. *The Prophet* was a 24-foot-long Cleopatra 700 with a 140-horsepower inboard engine; she was canary yellow with a bench seat at the back, two raised seats at the cockpit and a spacious cabin inside. We've often wondered since if the name was incomplete. Had the words *of Doom* been washed away by the corrosive salty water as it slammed the hull on previous misadventures? Dad's friends, who knew more than a thing or two about boats and boating, had advised – warned, even – against buying it, but Dad didn't listen and coughed up regardless. He was keen to see his family take to the high seas in a larger, more impressive vessel than the faithful little Picton that never let us down.

For our first outing, we filled her up to her full 55-gallon capacity and set off inland to Cresswell Quay and a lovely little pub, the Cresselly Arms, run in those days by a Mrs Davies. Indeed, you wouldn't say you were going to the Cresselly Arms, you'd say you were going to Mrs Davies's. It was, and still is, one of the few pubs in Wales where the beer is served from jugs. It was only possible to reach Cresswell Quay by water when the tide allowed. Once there, departure was again dictated by the tide; leave it too long and you'd be stuck, waiting for the tide with only the pub for company. Maybe that was the appeal. On arrival, boats would tie up to the quay wall (and here also it was wise to exercise caution, as the wall contained a sewage outlet under which many unlucky novice sailors had left their vessels only to return an hour or so later to a nasty shock). On arrival, Mum and Dad would head inside with their friends, while Pete and I would stay outside with our friends and provisions in the form of Coke and crisps.

We made many trips here over the years, but the one that stands out for me is the time we were standing on the grass by the wall and I was challenged to a race by former Wales and British Lions scrum-half Rex Willis. I suspect he had been put up to it by Dad, and my suspicions were confirmed when I won. I say my suspicions were confirmed, but it's only now, looking back, that I realize he let me win. At the time I was convinced that I'd somehow, through sheer bloody-mindedness, got the better of this world-class athlete.

To return, though, to our first visit to Mrs Davies's in *The Prophet* . . .

We had filled her up, and then pootled along the river in a small flotilla until reaching our destination, tying up well away from any falling unpleasantness, and enjoying the delights of the pub. Then, and still in good time, we returned with the tide to Lawrenny. It was at this point, the completion of our maiden voyage, that Dad noticed that *The Prophet* was a little thirsty when it came to fuel; almost half the tank had been consumed. After some investigation it was discovered that *The Prophet* – or should that have been *The Loss*? – had a corroded and leaking fuel tank. Lovely. Given the number of cigarettes Mum and Dad smoked in those days, it's a wonder we didn't explode.

At no small expense, a new tank was built and fitted. We returned to the water, confident that a new era in luxury water-based fun was just beginning. By his own admission Dad was no expert on matters nautical; this, coupled with a fear of the water and his lack of ability when it came to swimming, made him far from the most inspiring captain.

One of our first trips in the newly refurbished *Prophet* was to Dale, a lovely beach beyond Milford Haven where the estuary meets the sea. The anchor was dropped, and a picnic enjoyed. After a couple of hours it was time to return, and so Dad attempted to lower the propeller. He pressed the appropriate button but it wouldn't budge, and so he did what all fearless captains would do in such circumstances – he put on a life jacket, attached a rope round his waist and ventured out over the back of the boat, where he stood on the shaft of the propeller and attempted to force it down. It still wouldn't budge. Mum held onto Dad with one hand (she knew how nervous he was of falling into the deep water), and he continued to perform little jerky jumps on the shaft, trying to get it to go down. Again, nothing shifted.

We were beginning to wonder if we'd have to call for help when Mum noticed a man, about ten feet from the boat, enjoying a paddle with his trousers rolled up, Blackpool fashion, around his knees. The tide had gone out during our picnic and the propeller was refusing to budge for the simple reason that it couldn't – it was resting on the sea bed. To regain his authority, Dad had to execute an Inspector Clouseau-like, 'Ah, yes, of course! The sea bed, yes . . .' as he reached for an oar to push us off.

There was worse to come. On another trip, the boat full of family and friends, we were heading once again to Dale and had got as far as the suspension bridge near Pembroke Dock when I came out of the cabin, where I had been playing cards with Pete and a few friends, to tell Dad that I thought there was smoke appearing. Not unlike Basil Fawlty when he sent Manuel back into the burning kitchen in *Fawlty Towers*, Dad assured me that I was imagining things and ushered me back into the cabin. A few minutes later I came out again, this time coughing a little.

'Dad! Dad! I really [*cough*] think there's smoke in there [*cough*]!'

Just as he had when discovering my lifeless body under the trees in Baglan, Dad let out a plaintive, 'Oh my good God!'

The smoke was pouring out of the cabin. Dad switched off the engine, and a huddle of watery-eyed children was ushered out and into the open air. Friends who had been travelling with us drew up in their boat and everyone hopped and clambered over into the safety of the reassuringly non-burning craft, which was sitting lower in the water with each new refugee that joined it. With the survivors being ferried back to civilization, another friend came and towed *The Prophet* back to its mooring, where it stayed for a while before leaving the water and heading in disgrace to dry dock at Pembroke to be fixed. I never saw it again.

In the meantime, on returning to dry land, Mum and Dad discovered a few friends from back home had arrived unannounced and were keen to get out on the water. With Dad having repaired to the pub for a calming pint or three, it was left to Mum to take the friends out in the Picton. She got as far as the bridge – the scene, just hours earlier, of the evacuation – when she ran out of petrol. The two male friends (who shall remain nameless, as they don't come out of this story very well) stayed in the boat, not wanting to spoil their suits, while Mum hopped over the side and swam to shore with the petrol can, filling up just enough to get home.

On many levels, you could argue that we weren't cut out for boats.

We had wonderful times at Lawrenny. The pub, the Lawrenny Arms, had a pool table, a dartboard and a jukebox. It's hard for children now to imagine the excitement of a jukebox, harder still for them to imagine paying to hear a song in a pub. But that's what we did – again, and again. The jukebox at the Lawrenny Arms was very much of its time, a mid- to late-seventies squat little oblong metal and glass affair that pumped out the hits of the day: Blondie's 'Heart of Glass', Abba's 'The Name of the Game' and Elvis Costello's 'Oliver's Army'.

In the process it provided the soundtrack to our years in this lovely countryside idyll. In my memories the juke-box is always playing Justin Hayward singing 'Forever Autumn' – quite fitting, perhaps, as those youthful days in Lawrenny shift further and further away in my mind. 'The summer sun is fading as the year grows old, And darker days are drawing near.'

5

In 1979 we left Baglan and moved ten miles or so east, to the seaside town of Porthcawl. I had spent some time there already through my couple of years at St John's, and we had friends there; a few families from Port Talbot had already made the move. With my brother's asthma being a growing concern, it was felt that the sea air at Porthcawl might be a help, away from the steelworks of Port Talbot and, closer to home, the huge BP chemical plant at Baglan Bay. Mum had been very involved in an action group campaigning against the plant, their objections based largely on grounds of health. We moved into a very nice house in Nottage, a brisk walk over fields and golf links to the sea, and I was assured of a pleasant cycle ride from the school.

Isn't it odd which peculiar moments stand out when looking back into the past? I have very strong memories of lemonade and other fizzy drinks being delivered by the milkman on a Thursday, and of steak being a regular mealtime treat that evening. When it came to food, we were – in keeping with the times – far from adventurous: meat, fish, stew, sausages, potatoes, that kind of thing. Only recently, when talking about our diet in those days, Mum remarked, 'I remember in the seventies when spag bol and lasagne came in, thinking, Well, this is madness!'

For the first few months in Porthcawl I continued to commute to school in Swansea, but after a while it was decided that I would change. The daily commute was a long one and so, in the Easter term of 1980, I began at Porthcawl Comprehensive. The thought of moving from the fantastically small, polite *niceness* of the fee-paying, well-to-do Dumbarton to the savage inner-city urban decay of life at a comprehensive school was rather unsettling to a well-mannered young chap like me. My only glimpse of a comprehensive education had come via the BBC children's television programme *Grange Hill*, which I loved but at the same time found to be a bit harsh with its themes of bullying and general pupil-based misery.

I was to start in the Easter term of the fourth form and went along prior to this with Mum to meet the headmaster in his office. We sat opposite him, and Mum told him all about me and my interests. Coming so soon after the triumph of the world's first stage production of *Star Wars* (attended by the future wife of the son of Kirk Douglas), these interests consisted of one thing: acting.

'Ah well,' began Mr Ebsworth, 'we have a wonderful drama department here. We put on a musical every year – this year it's going to be *West Side Story*. You could go along and audition for that . . .'

This was exciting; maybe I'd get to be in a show. I didn't know that going along and auditioning would have such a massive influence on the rest of my life and the path I would follow. We left the meeting, encouraged by the thought of being able to get involved with the school show. This, to some extent, allayed my fears surrounding the move.

The day arrived and I set off for school. I remember standing near the language labs when the bell went for lunch and staring wide-eyed at what appeared to be thousands upon thousands of children pouring out of the surrounding buildings and onto the playground. Like a computer-enhanced battle scene from *The Lord of the Rings* they spilled ever forward as I stood rooted to the spot, just trying to take in the enormity of it. It was so different from what I was used to; I really was overwhelmed by the size and scale of it all.

For the first week or so I kept myself to myself, rather like Sylvester Stallone beginning a jail term for a crime he didn't commit. I wasn't looking for trouble. I faced the right direction in class, and when lunchtime came made my escape to the nearby town centre where I would walk up John Street, buy a *Daily Mirror* at the newsagent and then sit in Sidoli's Café and have lunch. This consisted of sausage and chips followed by a glass of milk and a Kit Kat, my confectionery safety blanket. I would arrive home at the end of the school day and look forward to night-time and the warm secure feeling of lying in my bed, watching the numbers on the *Groundhog Day*-style digital alarm clock flap over to ten o'clock and the sound of John Peel lulling me off to sleep by the time his third record had begun.

After this first week spent not knowing a soul, and struggling to take in the scale of my new environment, I trudged home one day to find Mum in the garden.

She asked me how it was going.

I replied, a tad overdramatically it now seems, 'I'm the loneliest boy in the world . . .' I might even have allowed my lower lip to tremble.

This must have been heartbreaking for Mum, but she didn't let it show, instead promising that if I felt the same way at the end of the term I could return to Swansea.

The lessons at Porthcawl were more difficult than they'd been at Dumbarton, where the classes were smaller and the teachers were able – in theory, at least (and often in practice) – to give more attention to individuals. It was annoying that the O level curriculum in several of my subjects was different to what I'd been studying at Dumbarton. This meant being handed piles of work to catch up with, and so it was decided that I would be given the work of Marie Claire Pearman, a model pupil. She kindly handed over her files and I took them home, the idea being that I would copy them and soon be up to speed with the rest of the school. It didn't quite work like that, although the fact that I had been given the books of a girl with as dreamily romantic a name as Marie Claire was a great source of amusement to Mum, Dad and Pete, who delighted in imagining the romantic possibilities in such an arrangement.

I can't pretend that Porthcawl Comprehensive was in any way a *rough* school, although compared to the vaguely gentleman's club atmosphere of Dumbarton it was certainly a little edgier. The pupils seemed more worldly-wise and, in the absence of fees, inevitably came from a greater variety of backgrounds. The banter in the playground had a harsher edge to it. There was a very kind boy named Michael Jenkins. (This is not of course his real name; I'm sure the last thing he needs is someone accosting him in the street and telling him how much they enjoyed hearing about his childhood afflictions.) Michael was one of the first to befriend me, but unfortunately he suffered from eczema, giving his face, hands and I dare say other more delicate areas of his body a rather florid appearance and forcing him to rub himself frequently for relief. This would be met with cries of, '*Itch! Itch! Itch!*' from his friends and classmates, which I thought was pretty unfair and couldn't imagine happening back in Swansea. They of course didn't limit this cry to the times poor Michael was mid-scratch. He would often be met by a cheerily sadistic chorus on entering a room, or simply as he passed by in the playground.

There were many playgrounds or open areas where the children congregated at break times, far more than at Swansea. They would always be buzzing with activity and, from my slightly nervous perspective, potential danger. I had arrived at the school in the middle of a new and very popular craze, which involved boys approaching each other and asking, 'Can you cope?' This related to a television documentary, unseen by myself, involving a boy with some kind of mental disorder who apparently at a given point in the programme had indicated that he could/couldn't cope. It had caught the imaginations of my new classmates and they took great pleasure in roaming the school, uttering this peculiarly cruel enquiry with broad smiles on their faces. Like friendly Nazis.

I was never picked on, although some time later –

once I had settled into the school and found my own friends – I had the pleasure of being headbutted, from behind, by a lovely chap called Fat Ed. I was walking through an underpass one day, minding my own business when he popped up from behind and, quite without provocation, headbutted me. It was a shock, and it hurt a bit. But, more than that, I was perplexed as to why he would do it. I suppose it can't have been easy, being known as Fat Ed. (Although, if truth be told, his name was Ed and he was a little portly.) Perhaps he was just lashing out at an unjust world. Then again, perhaps he just liked hitting people. I've never been a big fan of violence, especially when it's directed at me; unless there's a *reason*, something to explain it, I just don't understand it at all.

It was at Porthcawl Comprehensive that I made my first tentative steps towards girls. For a moment there I considered using the word 'lunges' rather than steps, for comic effect, you understand, in the hope that it might raise a wry smile. I'm afraid it would be entirely inaccurate to use so forceful a word. I never once came close to a lunge, more's the pity. With hindsight I was far too cautious and wary of rejection and subsequent humiliation to ever threaten a lunge. Instead, I contented myself with gazing adoringly from afar. I could list you an impressive roll-call of beauties who all managed to remain tantalizingly out of reach during and, on reflection, beyond my time at the school. It would read like this: Katie Davies Williams, Rhian Grice, Meryl Metcalfe, Liza Milza and Helen Phillips. All these enchanting creatures were at one time or another subject to, at the very least, a wistful gaze from the young me, and all of them, as mentioned earlier, went on to successfully complete their schooling without any input from these quarters.

Katie was the first one I noticed. She was a beautiful, captivating girl – although, as I write these words, I'm sad to discover that I can't bring up a faithful reproduction of her features in my mind's eye. I remember the impression she created, though, and the effect she had on me. She was sunny, cheerful and cheeky with just the right amount of hippy to her; that is to say, she displayed a free spirit but her personal hygiene was never in question. She had long hair. Did she use to crimp it into that smoky-bacon Frazzles look? She brought to mind a young Kate Bush and, as Miss Bush herself had done only recently, Katie stirred hitherto unknown sensations deep within. She possessed a wonderfully mysterious gypsy-like quality, giving the impression that when out of my sight she floated wispily from here to there, carried on the breeze like a dandelion seed. She was a delicious mutant hybrid of the health-threateningly exciting Kate Bush and *Rumours*-era Fleetwood Mac (female members). At that year's eisteddfod she performed a fantastic, inappropriately erotic piece of interpretive dance to Kate Bush's 'Breathing', with Keith Davies (who was playing Tony in *West Side Story*). I sat sulking in the audience as the two of them wrapped their young, leotard-clad bodies around each other, creating a shape-shifting ball of togetherness. Or exclusion, depending on your viewpoint. And I knew where I stood on the matter.

Katie and I got on very well, probably too well. One day, in class, she wrote her name on my arm and I nearly fainted. She was entirely comfortable as the first occupant of my still-pristine pedestal, long before it would become scuffed by the heels of the girls who followed. She worked on a Saturday in Porthcawl's only health-food shop, where I would spend an inordinate amount of time apparently concerned for my health, browsing the various nuts and berries while secretly pining for the girl at the till. To this day I can't sniff a dried banana without filling up. I never once told her how I felt, although I often dreamed of doing so, time and again lying in bed at night telling myself that *tomorrow* was the day. Of course when the moment came I would invariably retreat, afraid that I might spoil the lovely friendship we had. The fear of rejection is a powerful emotion in a young mind and it held a tight grip on me throughout my teenage years.

Katie eventually went off to America for a while, perhaps around the end of the sixth form. I knew the time of her flight; it was a warm Sunday afternoon and I was washing the dishes after Sunday lunch, staring out of the window and thinking about her flying away from me. On the radio Jimmy Savile played Frankie Valli's 'My Eyes Adored You'. I cried.

This time of my life comes with its own soundtrack album, not available in the shops. In the midst of my mooning over Katie I heard Gordon Lightfoot on the radio singing 'Daylight Katy'. I was sure it had been written about her. 'But she doesn't have to get up in the morning, With her hair so soft and long . . .'

I'd ride around Porthcawl on my bike, often in the rain, listening with a heavy heart to my Walkman and Joe Jackson singing 'Is She Really Going Out With Him?'.

Pretty women out walking with gorillas down my street . . .

And, in conclusive proof that there was no credibility apartheid on my little cassette player, I would also take comfort from the, at that time, still-undecorated Cliff Richard and 'Dreamin'. 'If you could only see through my eyes, Then you'd know just what I'm going through . . .'

Poor me! If only I'd had the nerve to make a move . . . I'm afraid I was far too polite.

It was around this time that I discovered James Dean after watching *Rebel Without a Cause* on the television one night. The next day I began a considerably lengthy phase of wearing a white T-shirt and not washing my hair for a few days at a time so that it would stand up like his. Nowadays I'd have scoured the Internet for information on him, but back then I made do with hopping on my bike and cycling down to the library, where they had a couple of books on his brief life and career. Looking back, I suspect this was the extent of my teenage rebellion – a refusal to wash my hair for up to three days at a time, a brief interruption of my polite ways, after which normal service was resumed.

Some of the girls on my list made less impact than others. Meryl Metcalfe, for example, cannot be said to have cast her spell for an extended period but earns her place nonetheless for the sheer delight she has given my children whenever I recount to them the time my teenage self lay on the grass above Rest Bay one summer's day and gazed at her from afar. She was sitting with her friends, perhaps eating ice cream. Certainly, when they make the film of my life she'll be eating ice cream. Depending on the certificate, it might even be an ice lolly that she's getting to grips with. She was sitting on the grass, just being, and I was maybe thirty yards away, also sitting down and, had I only known it then, *chillin'*. Somewhere in the vast chasm between us a bicycle lay discarded; the wheel framed my view of her, the spokes giving an out-of-focus, softly pornographic haze to her already enticing features. That was it – I just gazed and thought, hoping that telepathy would do the rest and she might glide towards me and make the first move.

I realize now, that was what I was always waiting and hoping for, that the girl might make the first move. It was a mistake. To any young readers I would thoroughly recommend making the first move yourself. If you're lucky, the girl will have the second move up her sleeve ready to go. If you're very lucky, she might show you the third and fourth moves. If you're not lucky, who cares? You'll have some stories to tell your kids.

Helen Phillips was in my English class; her mum was a teacher at the school and involved in the drama productions. We got on famously. I always got on well with the parents of the girls I fancied, especially the mums (always a big hit with the mums). Not in a Mrs Robinson kind of way, although the thought did cross my mind, but just in an, 'Aw, Rob's great, isn't he?' kind of way. If anything, this made the lack of romantic interest from their daughters even harder to take. I have to stress *romantic* interest as opposed to interest generally. I got on hugely well with all these girls – not so much with Meryl, who was more your distant, bicycle-framed goddess type – but all the others thought I was an absolute hoot. I would make them laugh like drains with my pithy observations and wry comments scribbled in the margins of their ring binders. That's not a euphemism.

This was the case with Helen and with Liza, who sat near me in English classes during my third year in the sixth form. (This extended tour of duty was brought about by an appalling performance at O level – only two passes at the first attempt. This meant that, rather than going back a year, I just hung around and waited for the year behind to eventually arrive, like shoddy guests at a dinner party.) Liza Milza, like Meryl, had a pleasingly exotic name that just added to her already substantial appeal. Again, we got on terribly well and I was sure I detected the green shoots of a relationship sprouting underfoot. Alas, it wasn't to be. Liza showered my little green shoots not with kisses but with weedkiller in the form of politely declined advances.

But of all these distant glittering prizes it was Rhian who held my heart hostage for the longest during my teenage years. We met at drama class and again got on wonderfully. She was a lovely girl with an exceptionally pretty face, and I was smitten from the start. Just like in *Jerry Maguire*, she had me at hello. By now it won't surprise even the most casual reader to learn that any romantic leanings were painfully one-sided. Rhian had a tall, good-looking surfing boyfriend named Mike. My God, I've just remembered, it was Mike Metcalfe, Meryl's brother. That bloody family! What did they have against me?

Mike surfed, as did many of the cool boys at the school (Porthcawl sitting neatly on the South Wales coast, almost midway between Cardiff and Swansea). I toyed for a while with the idea of surfing. Dad had a friend who owned Pyle Marine, a boat shop next to a garden centre in Pyle, and he had some surfboards in stock. But, explained Dad, they didn't have fins so I would have to buy a fin myself. The fin, as any surfers will know from their own surfing escapades, is the rudder-like device that juts down from the back of the board and helps with the steering. I went to a surf shop in Porthcawl and bought an exciting-looking fin, made out of glittery red translucent plastic, as well as some wax for the expected board. For whatever reason, I never got the board. There I was, in an effort to impress Rhian, left standing boardless with just a shiny red fin in my hand, bereft and (what was worse) entirely ignorant of the horrific metaphorical implication of my situation. I kept that fin for years, on the off chance that I might one day answer the ocean's call. I never did.

I was already very taken with Rhian when we were cast opposite each other in *Guys and Dolls* as Sky and Sarah. We had been rehearsing for some weeks when we finally arrived at the point in the play where the two characters kiss. It comes at the end of a song; all through that song, all I could think was that in a moment I would have to kiss her. Now, bear in mind that at this point I hadn't kissed a girl. My God, I was nervous as I sang the last note, looking into her eyes. I think she might have been nervous too; her face looked a little flushed as we leaned in and kissed – a chaste, closed-mouth kiss – and I nearly caught fire. Her mouth appeared to be aflame; anyone watching closely would have witnessed my closed eyes opening and my eyebrows arching in shock. Spontaneous combustion was a real concern. I'd never known a feeling like this – was this what kissing was like? I'd better carry a bucket of sand around with me. I think I looked anywhere but at her as we disjoined, my head reeling as I tried to retain a nonchalant gait and conceal the furnace inside.

I suppose I spent the rest of my time at school trying to get back to that intimacy with Rhian; it had felt so real, but of course it was entirely contrived. We kissed a few more times in rehearsals and also during each of the three performances (who's counting?) but it never felt like it did that first incredible time. How could it? And so it went. We were great friends in that classic 'I want to be more than friends' *ménage à un* scenario that breaks so many hearts, and I moped about pining and feeling sorry for myself.

Things reached their platonic peak in the run-up to my eighteenth birthday. We had arranged to go out to dinner and I was *so* excited at the prospect I could hardly wait. The night before, she called to say that she couldn't come as she had to revise. Looking back, I suppose she realized that this dinner was a very different proposition for me than it was for her, and felt it best to call it off.

I certainly didn't understand at the time; it was the eve of my eighteenth birthday, and I was heartbroken. Still, my birthday arrived and I went to Swansea with David Williams to see Dustin Hoffman in *Tootsie*. We had a good time.

We had a very good time.

I can honestly say that in all these years neither David nor Dustin has ever let me down.

6

It was in the drama studio that I began to feel at home in my new school. I auditioned for *West Side Story* and ended up playing Snowboy, one of the Jets. I think his one line was a loud, sarcastic, 'It hurts! It hurts!' which I hoped to imbue with enough passion to mark me out for a bigger role in next year's show. To do that I had to impress the show's director, head of the drama department Roger Burnell. Roger was in his late twenties when I arrived at the school. He had trained as an actor at the Cardiff College of Music and Drama and stayed on another year to qualify as a teacher. On leaving the college he worked for a year as an actor before deciding he'd rather teach; and what a teacher he was.

It's no exaggeration to say that the hours spent under his guidance helped shape the direction my life would take, and we remain friends to this day. He had a way of talking and relating to his pupils that simply inspired confidence; for me it was a hugely liberating experience to work with him and to feel that here was an area of school life in which I might excel. He has said that schools often don't cater for children who are bright and sharp but do not possess an academic attitude. That just about sums me up at school. In most subjects I felt average at best – often, far worse – but in the drama studio, creating, rehearsing and building a performance, I felt smart, I felt clever, as though I had something to offer the world. This did a great deal for my self-confidence and was a huge factor in finding my feet in the new school, and it was all down to him. Thank you, Roger.

Most of the time, when I wasn't required to be somewhere else, you would find me in the drama studio, and each year when the big musical production came round I would go for bigger parts. *Sweet Charity* followed *West Side Story*; I played Oscar in a thinly veiled Woody Allen impression. After this was *Guys and Dolls* with the knee-trembling kiss, then finally *Carousel* in which I played Billy Bigelow. Billy is a barker for a carnival, working on the carousel of the title. He's thought of as a rough, tough, muscular kind of fellow and in most people's minds he surely peaks at more than my rather disappointing five feet and seven inches. To correct this injustice I borrowed a pair of soft leather zip-up boots from my Uncle Tom. The boots had a generous heel and it was felt this would help lend the required boost to my stature. To a degree it did, shooting me up to a terrifying five foot eight and a half, but the boots brought with them their own problem.

Stages are often sloped, running from the back of the stage (upstage) down to the front where the stage meets the audience (downstage); this arrangement is called the 'rake' of the stage, and the angle can vary depending on the venue. At the Grand Pavilion in Porthcawl the rake is quite steep and this, combined with my towering new heels, meant that when standing facing the audience I was in great danger of falling over. I felt as though I was standing at forty-five degrees, like Michael Jackson in his

'Smooth Criminal' video. It was only through sheer will-power, self-discipline and exquisite calf muscles that I managed to avoid joining the orchestra.

Billy is a splendid part and contains the wonderful Rogers and Hammerstein 'Soliloquy', often known as 'My Boy Bill', which ends with a long-held-out note that would leave me light-headed. I would exit the stage after completing the song and stand swaying in the wings, feeling dizzy, and with the sound of applause rushing around my head. That may have been the moment that I glimpsed what lay ahead for me in my life. Low blood pressure and tinnitus.

It was through the drama department that I met some-one who would become a lifelong friend and who, many years later, would be responsible for handing me one of the best roles of my career. And I'll tell you for why . . .

Ruth Jones was two years younger than me but shared my love of acting. We became friends through rehears-als, although our respective casting meant that we never really acted together. In *Guys and Dolls* she stole the show as Miss Adelaide, and in *Carousel* she was an excellent Carrie Pipperidge; I can still remember her singing 'When I Marry Mr Snow'. Ruth was never on my pining list; we were good friends, more like brother and sister, although this didn't stop my own brother insinuating that something was going on between us. Pete used to love raising his eyebrows at the mere mention of her name. Ruth and I stayed in touch once we'd left school, through the lean years when the acting work was less than forthcoming, and I take some pride now in having once sat with her in a Cardiff café and talked her out of packing it all in and getting a proper job.

We've both benefited from that decision.

While all the acting and sudden interest in unattainable girls was going on I was also introduced to two things that would have a huge influence on me and stay with me for the rest of my life. Bruce Springsteen and acne.

Bruce came first; I hadn't thought much about him since hearing 'Born To Run' while making my precocious local radio debut as a junior DJ on Swansea Sound (of which more later), but I was now noticing his new record 'Hungry Heart' being played on the radio. I liked it enough to set off for Woolworths at the top of John Street in Porthcawl and to invest my hard-saved pocket money in his double album *The River*, essentially my first grown-up record purchase. I had bought ELO's *New World Record* previously, but that doesn't count. I'd also had Sparks' album *Propaganda* on cassette at nine, a record I still love today. But it was when buying *The River* that I felt as though I had come of age. I can still remember the excitement at hurrying the discs home and up to my bedroom. I hid away for a few hours listening to them and studying the glossy printed lyric insert, the first of its kind that I had ever encountered. I read along to 'Stolen Car'; I'd never heard a song like that before, and found it entirely transporting and captivating. It was the weekend and Nan was staying with us, so I took the sheet of lyrics to show her: 'Look! It's like poetry.' My love affair with Bruce had begun.

My more tempestuous relationship with acne was also in its first flush; just a few perfectly anticipated and acceptable teenage spots at first, then a slow and gradual remapping of my face until it could be said that the condition had moved in and declared squatter's rights. The problem with acne is that friends and family, keen not to upset the sufferer, will often declare that 'it's not that bad, really' when in fact it's appalling.

It was some years before I finally went to see a dermatologist, who reacted with horror and informed me that my face was home to chronic acne. He put me on a heavy course of vitamin A, which dried out my skin and more or less put an end to the condition, although by now much of the damage had been done and the scars that I still bear today were well and truly in place. Hurrah!

As well as the acting that I was doing in rehearsals for the annual show, I was made aware of the National Youth Theatre of Wales and their month-long course in the summer, which culminated in a series of performances at Cardiff's Sherman Theatre. Some of my fellow cast members had been on the course in previous years and spoke of it in glowing terms. There were a limited number of places available, and students would have to audition and prove themselves worthy of inclusion. So it was that a few of us hopefuls were driven up to a school in Pontypridd on a wet spring day in 1982 and sat nervously in a corridor waiting to go into the room set aside for auditions. Applicants had to perform two pieces of text: a passage from Shakespeare's *Measure for Measure* and, if memory serves me well, a bit of Archie Rice from *The*

Entertainer. The third piece could be anything at all and I had chosen, rather than a piece from a play, to perform a poem. It came from *Twelve Modern Anglo-Welsh Poets*, an anthology belonging to my mother. The poem was 'For Instance' by R. S. Thomas, a particularly bleak and uncompromising poet, best known perhaps for his 'Welsh Landscape' in which he describes my perfectly innocent, minding-their-own-business fellow countrymen as:

> . . . an impotent people,
> Sick with inbreeding,
> Worrying the carcase of an old song.

'For Instance' is a lament from a man who has been left a widower. I pulled a few plastic chairs into a row and lay across them as though I was lying on a bed. Then, staring up at the ceiling, my sixteen-year-old self began:

> She gave me good food;
> I accepted;
>
> Sewed my clothes, buttons;
> I was smart.
>
> She warmed my bed;
> Out of it my son stepped.
>
> She was adjudged
> Beautiful. I had grown
>
> Used to it. She is dead
> Now. Is it true
>
> I loved her? That is how
> I saw things. But not she.

I think I might have managed to force out a tear on the last line. It was all a bit heavy for a young teenager; with hindsight, perhaps a little prophetic of *Marion and Geoff*, the series of monologues I would go on to find success with many years later (a connection I make only now). As is always the case with auditions, the poor actor leaves the ordeal none the wiser and then tries to forget about it. But I didn't forget about it; I thought of little else until a few weeks later I discovered, much to my delight, that I had been accepted.

And so, that August on a warm summer's day, Mum and Dad drove me up to Cardiff and dropped me and a select collection of my belongings off at Senghennydd House, a student hall of residence, just on the edge of the city centre and down the road from the Sherman Theatre. This whole experience was a dress rehearsal for heading off to college, four weeks spent away from home, fending for yourself and meeting new people. There was a lively mix of young personalities and types, all jostling and bumping along, trying to find their place and standing within the larger group. The only thing that linked us was a love of theatre, of acting, of performance – and the fact that, within our respective schools, we were the ones who were good at drama, the standouts, the little stars.

Here it was different; our position at the top of the league table was no longer assured. It soon became obvious to me that I was slipping down towards the relegation zone and had no need to worry myself with the responsibility of anything approaching a lead role. There were older actors there who seemed light years ahead of me in terms of confidence and accomplishment and, perhaps more notably, worldliness. They possessed a swagger which suggested that they had been around a few more blocks than I had, and might even have lingered a while on the corner of some of them.

On the first day of the course we all sat in the front few rows of the auditorium at the Sherman Theatre, knowing that in a few weeks we would be up on the stage playing to a full house. The Sherman was a modern theatre, built in the seventies, and a world apart from the pre-war design of the Grand Pavilion in Porthcawl, where we put on our yearly musical. As I sat mulling over this step up into the big time, all the students were asked to take to the stage, one at a time, and sing a song for the rest of the group. I recall Patrick Brennan, a veteran it seemed of the NYTW, ambling forward confidently to the stage and beginning a relaxed, I'm-in-my-natural-environment rendition of Fats Waller's 'Ain't Misbehavin'', all twinkly-eyed charm. Fats Waller? Why wasn't he doing a pop song of the day? He must be quite sophisticated. He appeared to be decades older than me; he even had a beard. It wouldn't have surprised me to learn that *The South Bank Show* was planning a retrospective of his life and work. Song complete, he sauntered back to his seat to general applause and awe.

When my turn came, I chose to stand in front of my recently appointed peers and sing Michael Jackson's moving ballad 'The Lady in My Life' from his album *Thriller*. What a sensitive soul I must have seemed. And probably was.

So many of them seemed older and smarter than me,

and none more so than the mighty Peter Wingfield. Peter went on to become well known for his many roles, including the *Highlander* television series in America. I met him in between being crowned Welsh National Trampoline Champion and going on to study medicine at Oxford (him, not me); you could say he was a high achiever. His popularity and ease with girls was matched by his spectacular – and I use that word advisedly – ability to put his athletic gifts to everyday use. There was a tall black metal gate that led from the halls of residence out onto Salisbury Road; it must have been over six feet high. Peter would sprint up and vault over this obstacle in effortlessly superhuman fashion, during which feat he would reach a midpoint that would find him upside down, perfectly straight, with his hands gripping the top of the gate and his feet pointing skywards. He would then spring off and sail through the air to the ground, where he would land like Superman, checking the surroundings for wrongdoers.

I would watch, wide-eyed in admiration at this and other stunts, such as the time he suggested some of us visit Cardiff's now vanished Empire Pool with its Olympic-height diving boards. A few of us ordinary boys splashed around and maybe jumped feet first off the lowest board, desperately trying not to belly flop and do ourselves an injury. In the midst of our adolescent malarkey one of the group pointed to the sky, 'Look!' We craned our necks upward whilst treading water. Is it a bird? Is it a plane? No, it's Peter. He's leaping off the highest board, spinning, twisting and turning as he plummets downwards and makes a perfect entry into the pool. My hero.

I would look at someone like Peter and his levels of skill, which can only have come about through hours and hours of practice, and it would be hard not to wonder: *What have I been doing with my time?*

Athletics were not the only arena in which Peter excelled. He had the room next to mine at Senghennydd House and my nights were greatly enlivened by the sound of his many and varied conquests as noises seeped through the thin wall that divided our cell-like rooms. I would lie in my bed with my Sony Walkman on, probably listening to Bruce or, if I was feeling adventurous, Hall and Oates, perhaps even Dire Straits, and then slide off my headphones, enjoy a minute or so of the Welsh Warren Beatty next door, before returning to my more innocent pursuits.

As well as befriending the superhuman Peter, I also found boys closer in experience and outlook to myself. Ian Hughes came from Merthyr Tydfil, the once great industrial town in the Rhondda Valley, and had brought his guitar with him. We spent hours singing Paul Simon and Springsteen songs together in his room. Ian would thrash wildly at his guitar and belt out early Chris de Burgh tunes; his virtuosity with his instrument again caused me to wonder what I'd been doing all these years. He went on to great success in the theatre, joining the Royal Shakespeare Company and playing the Fool to Robert Stephens's King Lear.

The great friendship formed at the National Youth Theatre of Wales that still remains intact was with Steve Roberts, now known as Steve Speirs. Steve also came from Merthyr and though we had never met prior to this course, I'd already heard his name spoken of in hushed tones. He was a legendary figure at my school for his many exploits, witnessed by boys who had met him on previous drama courses and who had come back to regale me with their hard-to-believe tales.

Darren Gadd, Nathan to my Sky in *Guys and Dolls*, was himself no slouch when it came to benign antisocial behaviour; witness his setting off the fire hose one lunchtime in the youth wing, resulting in an impressive archipelago of puddles as far as the eye could see. The deputy head, when confronted with the small-scale flood for himself, remarked, 'Right! Who has been spitting?'

Darren felt Steve was a man to admire and was sure we'd get on, as indeed we did. He was big, six foot one, prematurely balding (although he would now protest it was a receding hairline), a little overweight and very, very funny. Steve could find humour in anything; he had a deadpan, Tommy Cooper quality that made just looking at him funny. Unfortunately, all jokes require a victim and I unwittingly became the victim of one of Steve's after moaning about my poor skin and bad acne which, it has to be said, was continuing its advance on my face with a determination that should have won it a Queen's Award for Industry. Steve listened sympathetically to my woes before kindly sharing with me the secret of a special 'Valleys' cure that was guaranteed to work and leave me with a clear complexion. It involved sugar and water, as simple as that. It sounded like it made sense. No one spoke of 'organic' anything in those days – although, if they had, this scam would surely have qualified. It involved mixing some sugar with some warm water and then rubbing it, with some gusto, all over the affected areas of the face.

The morning after Steve had been compassionate enough to enlighten me, I made my way into the communal washroom and checked that the coast was clear before beginning the treatment as prescribed by Dr Roberts. It hurt. It stung. *That probably means it's doing me good*, I thought, as I persevered with what was surely an early form of the now popular 'self-harming'. After I felt I'd given my cheeks a thorough going-over, I patted them dry and made my way off to rehearsals. My ravaged, bloodied face and I arrived to howls of laughter from Steve and enquiries from everyone else as to whether I'd got the details of the other driver.

I swore revenge. I'm still swearing.

The whole course was geared towards the final few days of public performance. Each actor would appear in two plays, one on the main stage and one in the smaller studio space. The first year we did *Under Milk Wood* and a new play about its author, Dylan Thomas, *This Side of the Truth*, the title being borrowed from one of his poems. I can't remember what I played in *Under Milk Wood*; it certainly wasn't a big part or, as I think I've proved quite unequivocally, especially memorable. Perhaps I was one of the drowned sailors that haunt the dreams of Captain Cat. It's just come to me, I was Nogood Boyo – not many lines and, in my portrayal of him, entirely innocent and naive with regards to what he was doing that was no good.

The play was directed by Hugh Thomas, an actor/director known to us primarily for his recent appearance in *Not the Nine O'Clock News* in which he played a mad politician in a *Question Time* sketch, memorably shouting 'We're all going to die!' The fact that Hugh had worked on such a zeitgeist show added hugely to his kudos, yet his popularity had a downside with his frequent departures from rehearsals, as he once again dashed off to the stage door to take a phone call from his agent.

The other play was what would now be termed a 'biopic'. I brought a smattering of infinitesimal roles vividly to life, although I faltered at what I now recognize was my first stunt. While some action was going on downstage, I stood upstage dressed in a nightgown and holding a lit candle. At a given moment in the proceedings I had to snuff out the flame with my thumb and forefinger, very dramatic. As a child I had an acute aversion to flames, matches, candles and to fire in general. This tiny bit of stage business used to cause me heaps of anxiety as I stood there doing bugger all at the back of the stage while the other actors got to emote their hearts out, considerably closer to the audience. Any member of that audience not transfixed by the principal players may have felt their gaze wander to the little chap at the back with the candle. *Goodness me, I think his hand is trembling. Must be cold in his nightgown.* The play had a song, written for the occasion by Dorian Thomas, which we all sang in harmony. I think it was called 'I Remember Dylan'. It has since become the soundtrack to which many of these happy memories are set.

> I remember him, I knew him well.
> Met him once, he was drunk, yes
> He was a boor. He was a gentleman,

He was just a child, yes
I remember him, I knew him well.
Doesn't anyone else remember Dylan?
Dylan,
I remember Dylan.

Singing was part of the course and we would attempt it every morning with the singing coach, David Blackwell. This would take place on the main stage, which at that time appeared to me to be a vast open space, larger than any stage I'd known. I've since gone on to play on stages that are huge by comparison, and now look on the Sherman as a little friendly space, perfect for trying stuff out on. It's like Bruce Springsteen says in his song 'Straight Time':

. . . you get used to anything,
Sooner or later it just becomes your life.

Any performer or artist who experiences any kind of significant success also experiences major changes to their life, if only in the size of venue in which they perform. After a while, the shock and wonder at the bigger spaces subsides and you just get on with it. Sometimes it's good to stop and look back down the road you've just trundled along; it can surprise you. David would tell us to imagine the sound of our voices coming over our heads like a hood: 'Pull the hood over your head!' I think he subscribed to the idea of singing slightly above the note, a good discipline for someone like me who still has a tendency to sing flat. I'm not saying I do that too often – at least, I hope not – but given the choice between flat and sharp I'll tend to take the flat option.

Before or after the singing session we'd have a period of movement/dance under the instruction of a very lithe Scot called Ian Stuart Ferguson. He would slink around the stage to the sound of George Benson's version of 'On Broadway' and we would do our warm-up. It was good; for a brief moment it was as though we were part of *A Chorus Line*.

I almost felt like a dancer. For that feat alone he deserves a medal.

With the course taking place in August, the evenings were warm and long and would often be spent outdoors on the grass in front of the halls of residence. Guitars were played, someone plucking the introduction to 'Romeo and Juliet' by Dire Straits. Food was eaten, drink was drunk, and above us in the night sky Peter Wingfield would soar past, cape flapping in the breeze, en route to Planet Sex. Not really. Although the reality isn't far off. He would sit on the ledge of his third-floor window, legs dangling over the edge while playing the flute, before enticing a girl back to his room and encouraging her to attempt something similar.

Steve and I would often walk into the town centre and visit one of the cinemas on Queen Street – the ABC or the Odeon. The two of us went one night to see *Star Trek II: The Wrath of Khan* and both cried when Spock 'died'. Another time a small group of us went to see *Rocky III* and I was delighted when one of the girls said she felt I looked a little like Sylvester Stallone (very much my hero at the time).

I think the perceptive girl in question was called Sarah,

and I remember having quite a crush on her. In accordance with my crushes at school, this involved me getting on very well with her, teasing her a little, making her laugh and then waiting. And waiting. And waiting while another boy, slightly older and in this instance called Phil, stepped in and claimed the prize with his barbaric, Neanderthal directness. It was the sort of situation where I thought I was making progress, Phil merely popping up occasionally in my peripheral vision, until suddenly it dawned on me: *Damn, he's with her, and it looks like he's been there for some time.*

Much as I wanted to hate Phil, I just couldn't. He'd only recently loaned me *Pièce de Résistance*, a legendary bootleg cassette featuring Bruce's concert at New Jersey's Capitol Theatre on the 19th of September 1978, part of his renowned 'Darkness on the Edge of Town' tour. Many regard this as Bruce's finest ever live performance and while I'd heard rumours of the existence of this tape I'd never seen one, let alone heard one. Well, here it was. It was mine, for a while; I was allowed to borrow it! My eyes lit up as I scampered back to my little room clutching my treasure. Clever, clever Phil; he'd cunningly used the two little C-90 cassettes like a burglar throwing a poisoned lump of steak to a particularly dim-witted guard dog.

Woof, woof.

I returned to the National Youth Theatre of Wales the following year, this time to renew old friendships and play slightly, ever so slightly, bigger parts. We did Brecht's *The Caucasian Chalk Circle*. I had very little to do in this; it was produced in such a way that a lot of the actors were sitting on stage a lot of the time, so I spent much of it watching the older actors while simultaneously losing all feeling in my lower body. I have no memory of any line spoken; I was basically an audience member with a very good view.

The other production was *A Midsummer Night's Dream*. This was more like it; I played Starveling, one of the mechanicals who put on the play *Pyramus and Thisbe*. Steve Roberts played Bottom and was hilarious; my part was smaller, but was enlivened and enlarged slightly by my taking a dog on to the stage each night. It was decided that my character would have a dog on a piece of string and this at least meant I could engineer a few laughs from disparaging looks towards the bemused creature. It only became a problem during the special matinee performance for school parties, when most of the kids in the audience began calling the dog, whistling and clicking away at him to try to encourage him to break free from my clutches. He, in return, began to bark back at them. This was very funny for about a minute, and then it wasn't.

I suppose that I passed through my two years with the NYTW without ever displaying any great promise, or certainly none that anyone noticed. I can only remember the director Alan Vaughan Williams once commenting on my performance. It was after the last evening of *A Midsummer Night's Dream* and I ran into him in the corridor. He complimented me, saying that I had made something out of a very small part. This meant a lot and was enough for me to feel that my time there had not been entirely fruitless. It would have been nice to have played some more substantial parts, though. I suppose at that time I was still quite shy and hadn't learned to push myself forward.

When the organization had a tenth anniversary bash they produced a commemorative booklet in which were listed all the students who had been involved over the years. Some of the entries recalled funny moments, odd character traits and celebrations of roles past; a few of them ran to twenty or more lines. Mine read:

> **Robert Jones.** Robert was from Port Talbot and came twice on the course. Unfortunately he moved to Neath and was not eligible for a grant from his new authority. He is now at the Royal Welsh College of Music and Drama.

> I couldn't fault its accuracy.

7

While I was going from strength to strength at school (certainly in terms of the shows, if not academically), at home things were about to take a turn for the worse. The recession had hit Port Talbot hard and left many without jobs. The steelworks was far and away Port Talbot's largest employer and when the workers began a fourteen-week strike, the knock-on effect was huge. This, coupled with record interest rates of 17 per cent, was too much for Dad's business to take, and it folded. We sold the house and moved back to Baglan. We moved in with Nan, who was now living alone since Grandpa had passed away. This was of course a very difficult time for all the adults concerned, but I was wrapped up in my teenage life and much of the stress and strain passed me by.

While Pete changed schools to Glan Afan Comprehensive in Port Talbot, I stayed on at Porthcawl, to continue with my A Levels (ha, ha) and, more importantly to me, to carry on with the school shows. I now had to get the bus from Baglan to Porthcawl every morning, a journey that took an hour given its painfully circuitous route. Unlike the other sixty-minute special that I'd taken to Dumbarton, I made this journey without the company of any school friends. There was, though, a regular cast of characters that I would observe on the bus each morning, joining at their usual stops like clockwork.

A small group of what I considered at the time to be old ladies – although, I suppose now, they would have been in their fifties – would sit in a huddle in the first two rows of the higher section of seats at the back. From the moment they sat down, they would smoke like chimneys and sit there in their own hazy blue atmosphere, a self-sufficient nicotine-fuelled ecosystem, taking much of it with them when they finally disembarked, while always leaving enough behind so that we wouldn't forget them.

For a while I became friendly with an older man who travelled part of my route each day. He would have been in his sixties and wore a dark pinstriped suit; his hair was whiter than white. We got talking and one day it emerged that he was none other than Bonnie Tyler's father. There surely can't be any readers who need reminding that Bonnie was a familiar voice in the charts from the seventies onwards with hits like 'Lost in France' and 'It's a Heartache' – although, at the time of my daily journeys, she had been notable for some time by her absence from the hit parade. One morning on the bus, her dad, with some pride, told me how she had been in New York working with Jim Steinman.

'Do you know who Jim Steinman is?'

'Yes.'

'Who is he?'

'He wrote and produced *Bat Out Of Hell*.'

'That's right.'

'I know.'

'Well, she's been working with him and the new record is coming out soon, and I think it'll be a Number One.'

'Ooh.'

Deep down inside – in fact not that deep down, actually quite near the surface – I doubted that Bonnie would be enjoying a Number One hit. How wrong could I have been? A few months passed and before you could say, 'Turn around, bright eyes,' she was at the top of the charts everywhere with 'Total Eclipse Of The Heart'. Given my early-morning chats with her father, I've always felt slightly connected to the record; I feel that I should, to some small extent, be credited with having played a part in its success.

It was 1983, a good year for Number Ones: 'Billie Jean', 'Every Breath You Take' and 'Baby Jane' for Rod Stewart. David and I went to see him at Wembley on the weekend that 'Baby Jane' got to the top of the charts; we stayed at the flat behind the chemist's shop. When we got back after the gig we put Rod's album on loud and David walked into the bathroom to find me in front of the mirror, miming into a hairbrush.

Not long after Bonnie had been at Number One, David Bowie took the spot with 'Let's Dance'; everyone had the album and stayed glued to the television, hoping to see the video. I'd had a soft spot for Bowie since singing along in the car to 'Life On Mars?' at the age of eight.

It's a God-awful small affair . . .

To which my mother quickly replied, 'It may well be, but we won't have that sort of language here . . .'

And especially since discovering that his real name was David Robert Jones.

Years later, I was staggered to hear him being interviewed on Radio One and saying that, when on the tour bus, he liked to watch *Cruise of the Gods*. The presenter hadn't heard of it and Bowie said, 'It stars the guy from *Marion and Geoff* ... you know ... what's his name? Umm ...' The presenter not only hadn't seen *Cruise of the Gods*, he also had no idea who the guy from *Marion and Geoff* was.

The two of them spent a good minute stumbling unsuccessfully towards my name while I shouted at the radio, '*It's me, it's me!*'

My cries went unanswered by the Thin (Forgetful) White Duke.

Ground Control was unable to make contact with Major Tom ...

I could go on.

Cruise of the Gods was a curious melting pot of talent; new, established and undiscovered. Written by the splendid Tim Firth it tells the story of Andy Van Allen, former star of sci-fi series *The Children of Castor*, who has now fallen on hard times and accepts a booking to appear on a fan cruise where he will mingle with and answer questions from a collection of fanatical devotees of the show. While on the boat he comes into contact with his old co-star from the series, who is now a huge star in America. I played Andy and Steve Coogan played Nick Lee, now a big star. The head of the fan club was played by a pre-*Little Britain* David Walliams; a relatively unknown James Corden played the fan who turned out to be my son, and Russell Brand was an extra. We shot at what appeared at first sight to be an idyllic though, on closer inspection, turned out to be a mosquito-ridden beach resort a few hours from Athens and then on a cruise ship for a couple of weeks as it sailed between Athens, Venice, Dubrovnik, Santorini and other Mediterranean beauty spots.

This was the first time I had met David Walliams, and we hit it off from the start; he was a very appealing combination of Frankie Howerd, Kenneth Williams and a Pet Shop Boy, making us all laugh as he minced around the ship, camping it up. He did something very funny, though it's hard to explain. As he walked around a room he would reach out and touch various pieces of furniture – a table top, a door frame, a vase of flowers. It doesn't sound like much, but it had me in stitches.

We began to form a little double act, two old queens cruising the seas in their retirement, one minute affectionately calling each other My David and My Rob ('Ooh, My Rob's enjoying that ice cream' 'My David's loving it . . .'), the next bickering and mercilessly savaging each other in front of our fellow cast members ('Ice cream? You don't know the first thing about ice cream!' 'I'll ice cream you in a minute!' 'I wish you would . . .').

All the while that we were on the boat, David's main topic of conversation was the pilot that he was going to be making with Matt Lucas once we got back to the UK. 'Me 'n' Matt are making a pilot of *Li'l Britain* . . . *Li'l Britain*, me 'n' Matt . . . me 'n' Matt, *Li'l Britain* . . .' It was a constant bubbling in the background; he was fantastically focused.

Midway through the cruise the ship ran aground and ripped a hole in the hull. All the guests were taken off the vessel by lifeboats that evening, slowly chugging towards land as, behind us, the brightly lit cruise ship shifted further away. It's a tad obvious to say it was like something from *Titanic*, but it was. After a couple of hours waiting on the dockside, David and I shared a cabin on a rough and ready overnight ferry to Athens and kept up our old queens act as we struggled to get to sleep on hard bunk beds in a tiny cell, obviously too close to the engine room for comfort. David would call out in the night from the bottom bunk, 'Oh, My Rob! This constant pounding, it's incessant – will it ever stop?'

When we eventually got back on the sister ship of the stricken original there were not enough cabins to go around so David and I said we'd share. Joining ship again at Athens, we were shown to our quarters by a smiling young stewardess who took us into the room and pointed to the beds, two singles pushed together to make a double. 'Ooh, My Rob!' squealed David with delight. Sometimes I would wake at night and make my way through the darkness to the loo, assuming David was asleep, until, mid-flow, I'd hear, 'Ooh, My Rob!'

We had such a laugh together; each night before dinner I'd take a bath and he'd arrive in the bathroom with a glass of champagne, which he would hand over like an inappropriately intimate butler, a butler gone bad. In Athens we visited the Acropolis together, very Kenneth Williams and Joe Orton; then, on the island of Santorini, David, Steve, James and I rode donkeys from the port up the steep hill to the town, all the while David wailing like a demented Frankie Howerd, 'Ooh, yes . . . well, hmm . . . It's a big donkey, I'll give it that . . .'

This trip was also the first time I'd met James Corden,

an eager young pup of a boy, who loved to tag along with Steve, David and me and join in any banter that might arise, often starting it off himself and encouraging us to get involved. On one occasion we were in Istanbul and James came along with David and me for a look around the town. He says now that we were forever trying to give him the slip; I don't remember it like that, but I do remember thinking that he was always around, a few yards behind us, puffing and panting as he caught up. In Venice he joined a group of us one lunchtime in the famous Harry's Bar and we were asked to leave when our singing (in my opinion, our rather beautiful singing) disturbed some of the other customers.

The first time I noticed his talent was when we were filming the scene where I realize that he's the son I didn't know I had. We were in a cabin, the windows covered up to simulate night, and I vividly remember playing the rather intimate, two-hander scene and thinking to myself, *Bloody hell, he's good! I'd better pull my socks up.* Just at that moment the boat lurched violently one way, then the other, and a loud scraping sound was heard. We looked at each other in shock. *That can't be normal, can it?* It wasn't – we'd hit a rock. Opening the cabin door revealed crew members, normally the model of composure, panic-sticken and running through the narrow corridors. Within minutes, we were all up on deck wearing our life jackets. The official term is 'mustering', and we mustered with some degree of anxiety until being told that, while the boat wouldn't be going anywhere any time soon, we were in no immediate danger of sinking.

One night, while filming at the infested beach resort,

we were walking back from a taverna together along a dusty road in the darkness. James was telling me how he wanted to write, but didn't know how to start. I told him to just get on with it. I wonder if he did?

The last notable in this remarkable cast was a very young, slightly chubby and entirely unknown Russell Brand, playing one of the fans on the boat – more or less an extra, with maybe two lines. He was a remarkable boy even then, and would hold me spellbound on the deck each morning as he recounted his adventures of the previous night when he'd ventured off the ship and explored the seamier side of Istanbul.

'Her hand shot out from the darkness, a finger beckoning me onward . . . Should I enter hither? Behind me, gunshots filled the night air . . . I leapt on to a nearby canopy and began my escape across the rooftops of Istanbul . . .'

Listening to him tell these wonderfully vivid and absorbing tales, as the ship chugged on around the Mediterranean and the wind blew through our hair, was like watching Peter Pan flying around the rigging of Captain Hook's *Jolly Roger*. Although he was just an extra on the shoot, I took the unprecedented step of predicting that he would one day be a big star. Well done, me.

Nineteen years earlier, I was continuing my mammoth daily bus journeys to school right through to the end of my time at Porthcawl Comprehensive, an occasion marked by spectacular failure at A level. This didn't matter, as I'd really been staying on solely to enjoy more school shows and to keep on resitting O levels until I had the five required for a university grant. The A levels were never really needed. Academic historians might wish to note that I eventually walked away with O level passes in English Language, English Literature, Drama, Economics and Maths.

Throughout these long-distance commutes I was involved in the various unrequited yearnings detailed earlier in this book, and it was while on the bus that I would build up a modicum of confidence and belief that I might be in with a chance. This was due to the darkened plastic sheet that hung behind the driver's cab, a device originally employed solely to separate the driver from his passengers but nowadays primarily used to *protect* the driver from his passengers. When sitting in the seats closest to and facing directly this large piece of darkened plastic, the reflection that came back was an altered image of oneself, as the plastic was slightly curved. This had the effect of squashing whatever it was reflecting, and so a fat person would appear fatter, making the seat something of a no-go area for the tubby. Long-faced horse whisperers like me, though, were able to see a far more solid fellow staring back at them, someone who had been working out for a while, and with some degree of success (to the point that, at the height of my state of denial, I became convinced I looked a little like Christopher Reeve, star of the *Superman* films).

I can't help wondering now whether my romantic history would have been different if I'd managed to strap any of my distantly adored beauties into the front seat of the Neath-to-Porthcawl bus. As it was, I ploughed on bus-less and living in hope of romance that was never to surface.

Every year as Christmas approached, I would dread the Christmas Disco, which for us would take place at the now-vanished Stoneleigh Club, just along the road from the record shop in Porthcawl and not far from Fulgoni's ice cream parlour. Here it was that I would chat happily with a variety of girls; dance with them, even. But come the end of the night and the dreaded slow dance to 'Merry Xmas (War Is Over)', I would be left at the edge of the dance floor wondering how so many of my mates had managed to find themselves wrapped around a girl. Each year it was the same, John Lennon taunting me, reminding me that it was Christmas and asking me what I'd done. The answer, when it came to girls, was an emphatic 'nothing'. He'd bang on, reiterating that another year was over and that we were about to begin a new one. He'd then add insult to injury by cheerily informing me that he hoped I'd have fun. No one was hoping more than me, John, no one.

Several of my teenage years ended like this, drunken friends getting off with drunken girls while Sober Bob strolled home mystified by the unfairness of the universe.

The Stoneleigh was one of the very few nightclubs at which I spent any time as a teenager; the other was the Troubadour in the Aberavon Shopping Centre, where I worked weekends while in the sixth form. Seeing the name of the place in print is a little misleading, lending it an undeserved air of sophistication when you bear in mind that the glasses were made of plastic. If readers are at all familiar with a nightclub called the Troubadour, it's more likely to be the one found on Santa Monica

Boulevard in Los Angeles, a legendary venue famous for the role it played in launching the careers of, amongst others, Elton John, James Taylor and Carole King. To really appreciate my memories of the Port Talbot Troubadour, it's vitally important that you clear your mind of any thought of the Los Angeles venue. They were very different.

I worked behind the bar of the Port Talbot branch, handling the plastic glasses on Friday and Saturday nights, during the last summer before leaving home and heading off to college. In doing so I joined a group of regular employees who would have been a scriptwriter's dream, so clearly were their characters defined; had it been a sitcom that was being written, then a convincing argument could have been made for their individual and collective entrapment (the state in which, we are told, all successful sitcom characters find themselves).

There was the single mum, Julie, who I'm guessing would have been in her early twenties, with lots of make-up but the perfect skin of a porcelain doll. Then the young lovers, Sandy and Andy. Sandy worked behind the bar and Andy helped the DJ. (Did he? I don't know how anyone writes an autobiography without a team of helpers.) And then there was Barbara, the older, matriarchal member of the team. (Was she forty? Was she younger? I don't know! I was nineteen, it was ages ago.) I do remember her regarding me with amusement as a nice boy who'd lived a pretty comfortable life up till now and had perhaps not experienced much of the earthier side of life. I can't remember what it was exactly, but one evening she responded to something I said with an emphatic, 'What you need is a good fuck.' Perhaps I'd asked her what it was she thought I needed?

The resident DJ at the club was a jovial fellow with the violently heterosexual name of Roger Knight. He worked on a raised dais, from where he enjoyed a panoramic vista that encompassed the entire dance floor and most of the rest of the club. From his lofty eyrie he had control of the sound system and lights. Not just the flashing and spinning disco lights as they pulsated in a never-ending festival of colour (red, blue, green . . . ooh, purple) but the house lights too. When one of the not infrequent fights broke out, Roger would press a button – like Christopher Lee's Scaramanga reaching under the table to fire his gun – switching on the ceiling lights nearest to the affray, and calmly point to the newly illuminated offenders so that the bouncers would know where to go. He did all this without breaking a sweat, still managing to mix seamlessly from KC and the Sunshine Band into something new from Level 42.

If you've ever worked in a bar or 'disco', as I suppose this was, then you'll know that the running of the place is a curious blend of show business, the hospitality industry and a hint of the underworld. It has to be said that some of the clientele would have struggled to keep up with the etiquette requirements at the Henley Regatta and could be quite direct in their responses to what was going on around them. One chap to whom I served a pint of something or other screwed up his face in disgust and spat the mouthful of liquid straight back out at me, saying, with admirable economy, 'That tastes like piss.' Thus expressing in four words what even the most gifted food critic would struggle to contain within a page.

The many scuffles and fights I witnessed while working at the Troubadour weren't limited to the boys, although it was usually the young men that started them. The girls would often get involved too, in the traditional 'leave it, Wayne, he's not worth it' manner, pulling at the mid-eighties-fashion-clad arms of their beloved before getting a taste for the action and piling in themselves.

Fans of the macabre will be pleased to hear that the bloodshed wasn't confined to the dance floor. One of the most disturbing sights I have ever witnessed was revealed to me all those years ago in the Ladies' toilets after an especially unpleasant mishap. Earlier that evening, I'd noticed a bit of a scene developing around the entrance to the conveniences, and the subsequent appearance of an ambulance crew. Once the club had closed and we were clearing away the plastic glasses, one of the bouncers came over to me, gesturing towards the toilets and smiling, 'Come and have a look at this, Rob . . .' The bouncers were always very friendly to me, huge, hulking, brick outhouses of men, often with children's faces. They seemed to take to me. There was something of Androcles and the Lion to our relationships, although I can't honestly claim to have ever removed thorns from their toes. We went into the Ladies toilets, to be met by a sight that wouldn't have been out of place in Brian De Palma's *Scarface*.

A toilet was lying in pieces within its cubicle; there were pools of blood on the floor, and blood splattered over the walls. It was all I could do not to be sick. The bouncer told me what had happened, shaking his head and tutting as he recounted the story. Apparently, a girl had been standing on the then unbroken toilet, looking over the cubicle divider to chat with her friend, one booth along. The toilet had given way under her weight and split open. As she fell to the ground, the jagged porcelain of the shattered toilet had sliced into her leg and, hey presto, 'Say hello to my little friend.'

It wasn't a bloodbath every night, though, and I had many good times amongst the regular staff whose number I was swelling during the busy summer holiday period.

As I look back now on these few months of work, which would lead up to my leaving home and going to college, the whole episode takes on the air of a Neil Simon play. Me, the young innocent, taking my first faltering steps into the adult world, bumping up against all sorts of characters who, in light of my age and the setting in which we found ourselves, related to me for the first time more as an adult than as a child. Substitute Brighton Beach, New York for Port Talbot, and Eugene Jerome for me, and my story could remain roughly the same without any impairment of the audience's enjoyment.

All the staff welcomed me and made me feel as though I was one of the team – although, looking back, I was more than a little wet behind the ears and I'm sure, for this reason alone, a great source of amusement to them all. I was yet to be initiated into the ways of the fairer sex, with no sign of a girlfriend on the horizon despite many efforts on my part to woo my classmates at Porthcawl, all of whom seemed to have taken a vow of abstinence when it came to anyone answering my description. But surely, you protest, working in a nightclub must have presented you with some opportunities to explore new possibilities? Hmm, you'd think so, wouldn't you? If I might be permitted to employ the terminology of the football fan for a moment, perhaps I can relay to you an episode in which it can be said I missed 'an open goal'.

It was Hawaiian Night at the Troubadour, an exciting prospect for staff and locals alike. I remember arriving for work in an optimistic pair of colourful shorts and a suitably Hawaiian shirt, to be met by a wolf whistle from Barbara. Ironic, I've no doubt. Julie would have treated me to a sympathetic 'aww . . .' and Sandy probably joined the chorus with a giggle.

There were two bars at the Troubadour: the big main bar, which would be staffed throughout the night by three of us and, around twenty-five feet away to the left, in the darkness on the edge of town, a smaller facility, which would be manned solo. For this reason I always referred to it (rather wittily, I thought) as the Millennium Falcon. It would not be the last time I would find myself explaining a joke. On the night in question, after a period on the big bar with my colleagues, I was sent over to man the Millennium Falcon. This gave me a great sense of pride, to be handed such responsibility so soon into my tenure at the club, and as my short white legs crossed the floor space, clad only in my colourful tropics-suggesting shorts, I was determined not to abuse the trust that had been placed on my young shoulders.

The thing to remember about the smaller bar was that you were on your own, and the till was your sole responsibility; if there were any mistakes or discrepancies at the end of the evening, they were down to you and you alone. It was expected that you would make good any shortfall, a serious proposition given the modest wages that the job provided. With this in mind I was extra careful to give the correct change and to always keep an eye on the till, which was positioned behind and to the right of me, lest someone attempt to dip their fingers therein. With hindsight, this overly cautious approach cost me an evening of delights which would, I've no doubt, have altered the course of my future relationships with women. At the very least, I would have started the race at the same time as the other runners, rather than chasing desperately behind them, baton in hand. It's fair to say I handed over my baton much later than my friends . . .

But back to the little bar. There I was, working away diligently in a Hawaiian style when at some point I found myself talking to two girls as they leaned against the bar. I can remember absolutely nothing about their appearance. I remember a great deal about their actions. As the conversation progressed (what were we talking about? I have no idea . . .), it occurred to me that the girls, and certainly one of them in particular, were becoming increasingly fruity, the one leaning in ever closer as her friend looked on approvingly. I remember them urging me to come out from behind the bar and join them so that we could familiarize our young selves. I was hesitant, my lack of success with girls at this point leading me to believe the only rational explanation for such interest on their part was their being involved in an elaborately planned sting, the design of which was to separate me from my beloved till. At which point their stripy-shirted accomplices would drop from the ceiling, SWAT-style, and empty the till of all the carefully counted money I had collected thus far.

To encourage a positive response on my part, the more forward of the two, while her helper looked on offering encouraging glances, began to suck my finger. *She was sucking my finger!* It may have been two fingers; it may even have been three. It was all I could do to stand upright and not pass out. In between slurps she would keep imploring me to come out from behind the bar. I wanted to. God knows, I wanted to. I think it's fair to say that I had never wanted anything more in my entire life. She had managed to wangle out of me the fact that my mother's red Datsun Cherry was parked outside, and suggested it would be the perfect vehicle for the three of us to drive off in towards her warm and cosy flat on the nearby Sandfields Estate. I pictured this beautiful abode as she sucked and licked my fingers ever more salaciously, while simultaneously glancing nervously over my shoulder to check on the till.

By now, there were two things stopping me from leaving the safety of my post. One was the till, the other was the risk that my flimsy shorts, robbed of the shielding properties of the bar, might give too clear an indication of my conflicted state. I have to say that nowadays in such circumstances I would probably leap up onto the bar and demand a spotlight, but in those long-gone times of fantastically frequent and often unaccountable downstairs developments, I usually found myself reacting with great self-consciousness. And so it went on, the freshest stalemate known to man, until, bewildered and defeated, the two of them sloped off in a highly aroused state of defeat and I was left, standing proudly next to the till – still intact.

On many occasions since that day I have played out in my mind the events of that most anti-climactic of evenings, struggling to remain true to the details as they unfolded. Rather like a screenwriter adapting and altering a much-loved book for the cinema, the only thing I change is the ending. In all my nights at the Troubadour, this was the one and only time that sex – or, at least, the faint possibility of sex – reared its head. This and the ever present, 'can't rule it out' scenario lurking in my overdeveloped adolescent imagination that one evening, quite without warning, Barbara, in the manner of a short, Welsh and slightly aggressive Mrs Robinson, would take me in hand and teach me the ways of the world.

She never did.

The Troubadour was the first job I ever had, unless you count washing cars for Dad's sideline, a car valeting business in a lock-up in Port Talbot. There's not a great deal to report about my time with the sponge – in fact, it's no exaggeration to say that my only memory is of washing away one day and hearing the DJ on the radio announce that the new single from Shakin' Stevens was entitled 'Green Door'. I can remember that with sparkling, high-definition Blu-ray clarity. I must have spent hours there, washing, polishing and buffing; yet that's all I can remember. Perhaps it's Shaky that makes it memorable. I was a huge fan, with an exhaustive collection of his record-breaking singles, stored neatly and safely in one of those little plastic carrying cases that we all had in those days. I would cycle to Port Talbot and purchase the discs on the day of release, at Derrick's, the record shop favoured by Port Talbot's more discerning young hipsters.

I eventually met Shaky many years later, when he came on *The Keith Barret Show Christmas Special* and we sang together. Almost. He had a throat infection, so we ended up doing a peculiar version of his big festive hit, 'Merry Christmas Everyone', where we'd sing a couple of lines each, he miming and me singing live. It hadn't been easy, booking him; I had to call him personally and reassure him that we weren't going to take the mickey. We weren't. I couldn't have been more excited than at the prospect of singing with my childhood hero. When I finally got to speak to him on the phone and make my pitch, I probably scared him a little with my knowledge of his back catalogue, listing obscure album tracks and 'B' sides to convince him of my sincerity.

I wasn't the only one excited at the prospect of Shaky's appearance. I remember singing away on the night of the recording, as the fake snow fell all around us, and seeing that most edgy of actors, the King of Credibility, John Simm, who was standing on the studio floor behind the cameras, jigging around and singing along. I'd met John while filming *24 Hour Party People*, Michael Winterbottom's retelling of the Factory Records story, all about Joy Division, Happy Mondays and New Order. Here he was now, dancing along to Shaky and me.

If someone had told me when I was back at school,

or sitting up in my bedroom playing Shaky's records, that he'd one day be standing next to me on my TV show miming his heart out, I wouldn't have believed them. As it turned out, I would go on to meet and often work with many of my heroes in the years that followed – but of course I didn't know this at the time.

As a result of the school shows, I had a quiet confidence that I would go on to find success as an actor or a performer of one sort or another; it was a confidence that would be put to the test, but for now it was intact. With that in mind, the first step was to find a place at drama school.

PART TWO

'Working on a Dream'

8

In my final year at school, assuming that I'd somehow manage to pass the five O level exams necessary for a grant, I began filling out the forms required to apply for auditions at drama school. I chose the Royal Academy of Dramatic Art (or RADA, as it is famously known), the Central School of Speech and Drama, both in London, and finally, closer to home, the Royal Welsh College of Music and Drama, in Cardiff. As far as I can recall, applicants were told to prepare a piece of Shakespeare and something modern. Something modern tended to mean Pinter, and so I set about learning a piece from *The Homecoming*. It was the bit where Lenny is talking to Teddy about his misappropriated cheese roll, and it's full of unpleasant undertones. I'm not sure that I managed to convey the darkness and unbearable menace that is so obviously there; I suspect I came across more as David Jason's Del Boy in a bit of a bad mood.

Many, many, many years later I would meet Harold Pinter at a restaurant in London. My wife and I had been for dinner with friends, one of whom was on good terms with Harold and his wife Lady Antonia Fraser who, we discovered, were seated two tables away. At the end of the meal our companions went across to say hello, and so I drifted over to join them, admittedly a little intimidated by the thought of the great playwright whose words I had failed to do justice to, twenty-three years previously.

To my surprise, he recognized me as I approached. 'Ah, you'll know . . . We're talking about laughter, different forms of laughter.'

I affected a look of confidence, as though casually chatting with Harold Pinter in a West End restaurant (it was the Ivy – there, I've said it) was something I took in my stride, an occurrence of almost monotonous regularity. Meanwhile I was searching for something to say that would show me to be a bit of a thinker.

He was looking up at me, and waiting for my response.

'Well,' I said, 'there's a great difference between the laughter you hear from the studio audience on an old *Morecambe & Wise Show* and the laughter you hear from the audience at a modern television recording,' and I made a face to indicate that in my opinion things were better in the days of Eric and Ernie.

'Oh yes,' he replied. 'Yes!'

Emboldened by Harold Pinter agreeing with me in the Ivy, I went further. 'Harold,' I said, 'I'm glad to have met you. In 1984 I auditioned for RADA with a piece from *The Homecoming*. I didn't get in . . .'

He waited.

I debated whether to carry on along my intended path – I could, after all, fall flat on my face. Then I remembered something Anthony Hopkins had once said when interviewed by the remarkable James Lipton on *Inside the Actors Studio*. He had been asked if he had any advice for young actors, and replied that all actors should leap into the abyss and trust their talent. I decided to chance it.

I continued, 'I can't help thinking that if you'd tried a little bit harder with the writing, things might have been different.'

Silence.

He looked at me quizzically and an eternity passed as a chill wind blew through the Ivy.

Then he laughed, long and hard. Without pausing.

I breathed out.

So, as I was saying to Harold Pinter at the Ivy, I failed to get into RADA. I had found the whole experience of auditioning there to be pretty intimidating; it was as if I knew in my heart that I wasn't good enough, or what they were looking for. Or maybe I just wasn't ready. I like to think that if I auditioned now I'd get in. But then – no chance. The whole place spooked me; the other kids who were there to audition on the same day all seemed so much older than me, so much more mature. They all seemed to be wearing long flowing coats and had wild Byronic hair, which danced on their heads like a shampoo commercial as they strolled confidently along the corridor outside the audition room, text in hand.

These auditions at the London drama schools were hugely significant staging posts in my life and yet I only have the vaguest of memories of the actual RADA audition itself, a hazy image of a panel of judges united in their cosmopolitan disappointment at what had just been presented to them in such a provincial manner. I slunk away from the imposing building on Gower Street and walked, defeated, along the London roads, sure that I wouldn't need to be looking for digs in the capital any time soon.

The audition for Central was a similar experience, and the whole business of coming to London in the hope that the schools would recognize they had the next Richard Burton on their doorstep was destined to be a failure. With hindsight, I was never going to be accepted at either of these prestigious establishments; on the wall at RADA is a beautiful wooden board listing the school's medal winners through the years, including Gielgud, Kenneth Branagh, Albert Finney, John Hurt. These are serious actors, and the would-be students waiting in the corridor with me seemed serious also; they looked to me as if they were concerned with acting as an art form that could explore the human condition. I wasn't.

I was always looking for the laugh; there was no place in my mind for subtext or layers, beyond classic misdirection in the setting up of a joke. It amuses me, on reflection, to think that when I finally did break through with *Marion and Geoff* and *Human Remains*, I was very much involved with examining the human condition. That's really what the shows were all about.

I travelled up to London twice for the separate auditions, and the intervening years have meant that I can't really differentiate between the two trips much beyond a hazy memory of an abundance of glass at Central. But I do know that my chosen treats while up in London were hardly those of the serious drama student.

For one of the stays I went to see *Run for Your Wife*, the Ray Cooney farce, in its original West End production. I had a last-minute seat in the Gods and laughed till I cried at James Bolam dashing between his two wives. On the other visit I went and watched *Live from Her Majesty's*, the

ITV variety show hosted by Jimmy Tarbuck. If I had been there a week later, I would have witnessed the death of Tommy Cooper. I'm glad I wasn't. *Run for Your Wife* was excellent, the timing of the ensemble cast was perfect (as it has to be, for a farce to work).

I saw the play again a few years later when a new cast toured and visited the Grand Theatre in Swansea. This time the lead role was taken by the mighty Les Dawson, and as a result the play became *The Les Dawson Show*. He would break off in the middle of a scene and cross the stage like a gorilla, pretending to pick fleas from the hair of his fellow actors. Now and then he'd make eye contact with audience members and raise his eyebrows suggestively, causing not just the audience but also the cast to burst out laughing. It was still funny, just a different kind of funny.

One of the auditions, I forget which, took place at ten o'clock in the morning, meaning that I would have to stay in London the night before if I was to get there in time. Money was tight and so finding accommodation was something of an issue. Luckily Dad was in London that week on a course, staying at a hotel next to Heathrow airport, and he came up with the idea that I could stay with him, at the company's expense. Knowing that he finished each day at around four thirty, we decided that we would meet at Heathrow, more specifically *at the terminal*, where Dad would pick me up in his car and we would go on to the hotel. I think the last time Dad had been to Heathrow there had only been one terminal; I'd never been to Heathrow before (all my flights up to that point had been from Cardiff/Wales Airport or, as it was known at the time, Rhoose Airport). While never enjoying the reputation of a Charles de Gaulle or JFK, Rhoose Airport was nonetheless a glamorous location for South Walians in the 1970s. I even had a birthday party there.

Given my limited airport experience, I was shocked on arriving at Heathrow to find that a) there was more than one terminal and b) no one had baked me a cake. By a stroke of luck which, had it been featured in a film would have preceded me being accepted by the London drama school, Dad just happened to drive by as I was wandering lost outside one of the four terminals. I hopped in the car and we headed off to the hotel together.

As I say, in a film I'd have stormed the audition the next day.

In life I didn't.

In the spring of 1984 the Royal Welsh College of Music and Drama represented the last of my attempts to win a place at drama school. It appeared a far less intimidating building at which to audition than its London counterparts, and on the day of the audition itself displayed a welcome lack of long-haired and long-coated applicants strolling through the corridors, text in hand. It felt cosy and attainable, helped I dare say by the wonderful times I had spent just up the road with the National Youth Theatre of Wales. Whereas the audition panels of the London schools had seemed to view me with a mixture of no curiosity whatsoever and a soupçon of sympathy, I got the impression that the Cardiff panel felt they were looking at someone who might have a talent. I instantly worried that it might be a Welsh thing, that people would only 'get' me in Wales, where so far I'd been met with almost universal praise and encouragement. Maybe the Severn Bridge was made of kryptonite and, once across it, I was no more than a bumbling if well-meaning Clark Kent.

The audition pieces were the same as for RADA and Central, but this time when I sang the 'My Little Girl' section from Carousel's 'Soliloquy' it elicited warm smiles and a collection of appreciative glances. Maybe it's easier in the provinces. It's been my experience while touring my live show around the UK that London crowds are often harder to please than their country cousins. Partly this can be put down to the capital's culture seekers being spoilt for choice. London has an embarrassment of riches when it comes to options for an evening of theatre or comedy, and all stand-ups will surely recognize the almost palpable sense of gratitude that a more provincial audience can exude as they welcome their comedian of choice to the stage. London audiences also lack the sense of community so evident within the auditorium of King George's Hall in Blackburn, or some such lovely old northern venue.

When playing the West End for three weeks in 2009 I soon developed a technique of repeatedly referring to that night's audience as 'London' in an effort to force them into a single identity as a recognizable group, rather than a large crowd made up of many individual, disparate audiences. This was the complaint I'd hear from comedians who had become stuck on the Jongleurs comedy club circuit, that the crowd would be made up of many groups, often stag parties, hen nights or office dos. This is always harder for the comedian to control, as each group has its own dynamic, although it can be argued that it's excellent training. (The 'excellent training' argument is only good, of course, if the Jongleurs experience is just a stage of your career and you move up to theatres filled with your own audience.)

Discovering that I had been accepted at the Royal Welsh College of Music and Drama was a relief. I had no Plan B waiting in the wings and don't know what I would have done if they'd said no; luckily, the problem never arose, and in the September of 1984 I set off for Cardiff and the beginning of a new chapter.

It didn't feel like a new chapter. Things never did in those days, although now, looking back, it's almost impossible not to see one's life in chapters – some more readable than others. To start with, given that Cardiff was not that far from Baglan, and because we hadn't sorted out any accommodation, it was decided that I would commute to college each day until suitable digs had been found. I felt like a young Reggie Perrin: 'Morning, Joan. Fifteen minutes late, escaped panther at Bridgend . . .'

Digs were found sooner than expected. On the first evening, at a 'getting to know you' event at the college bar, I got to know a music student who told me there was a room going in a house he'd found in Roath, a mile and a half or so away from the college. I would imagine that the 'getting to know you' evening involved many of the young students getting to know each other in a far more interesting way than I got to know the accommodating music student. (Indeed, there were rumours during my time at the college of very exciting student-tutor she-nanigans going on.) Needless to say, I never witnessed any – not even a sniff. I was too busy clutching my little piece of paper with the details of the house belonging to Mrs Williams, in Oakfield Street, Roath. I duly presented it to my parents and then sat back as they took over.

The next evening, Mum and I drove to Cardiff and visited the very nice Mrs Williams. She and her husband lived with their daughter on the ground and first floor of a large Victorian terraced house. My new musical friend took a room on the first floor; the top floor had a small cold-water kitchen fit to burst with empty milk bottles that previous occupants had been too lazy to carry downstairs and, off a small landing, two bedrooms in the eaves, each with romantic, sloping ceilings. The room nearest the cold, tiny kitchen was taken by another musician, a composer with appalling personal hygiene yet an almost Olympic ability when it came to sexual encounters with fellow students. Many was the time I'd be woken in the middle of the night by the sound of his exertions, accompanied by the familiar smell of yet another curry wafting from his oversubscribed pleasure dome. For a rather naive chap from Baglan, who'd never had a girlfriend – or even properly kissed a girl, for that matter – it was a bit of an eye-opener.

Looking back now, the room at the top, as indeed it was, lacked some of the creature comforts enjoyed by my fellow students in their set-ups. There was no central heating, just a small gas fire attached to the wall, so that during one particularly cold winter I would go to sleep each night wearing pyjamas, a tracksuit and socks. I would sleep until about five, when I would be woken by the cold. I would creak frostily out of the bed and walk the two paces to the fire, which I would light with a match before returning to the relative warmth of the duvet. By the time I woke properly at seven thirty the room had a semblance of heat and I would sit on the floor cross-legged in front of the fire, eating my breakfast of Ribena and two Tracker bars while watching early-morning television on the portable set.

This hearty breakfast was in keeping with my general culinary outlook at the time, which might best be described as 'limited'. My cooking, such as it was, consisted of emptying a tin of Goblin beefburgers into a large saucepan. Any potatoes would be tinned too. In many ways I was doing my bit to keep the British tinned-food industry in business; my meals soon assumed the appearance of an exhibit at a Second World War museum.

The walls of the room were decorated with images of my heroes on pages ripped from magazines. Richard Burton as Hamlet in Gielgud's New York production of 1964, taken from an original vintage copy of *Life* magazine. There were various shots of Elvis and Springsteen and a front-of-house poster for Al Pacino's Broadway production of Mamet's *American Buffalo*, performed in London the year before I came to college and the subject of much inner debate on my part. Shall I go? Can I afford it? How will I get there? I didn't go. I wish I had. Towards the end of my time at college my room was graced by a huge, half-complete, billboard-size image of

Bruce Springsteen torn from a wall near the National Theatre while on a college trip to London.

It was my first ever visit to the National. We'd gone to see *The Duchess of Malfi*, but on arriving at the South Bank I noticed that Anthony Hopkins was performing a matinee of David Hare and Howard Brenton's play *Pravda* that afternoon, so I bought a standing ticket and saw that instead. It was, at that point in my young life, the finest piece of theatre I had ever seen. I can still remember the scene on the moor/heath as Hopkins circles Tim McInnerny like a shark. I remember thinking to myself, *Good God, I haven't taken my eyes off him since he came on the stage*. It was a stupendously good performance.

The Springsteen image, an advert for his latest single, 'Cover Me', was wrenched off the wall on the way back to the coach. As it came down it brought with it not just the previous four or five adverts that had been pasted underneath but also a small portion of wall, which lent the piece some weight (both literally and figuratively). I clutched it proudly all the way back to Cardiff on the coach, as though it was some kind of religious artefact, before hanging it proudly on the wall of my tiny room in Mrs Williams's house. Here it served a dual purpose: on the one hand it announced my love of the Boss, and on the other it covered up a patch of damp.

This would not be the only time that a college trip to London took a slight detour from the planned itinerary. It was the mid-eighties, the miners were striking, Margaret Thatcher was threatening to impose tuition fees and many of my fellow students were actively political, joining picket lines and holding meetings. I'm a little shamefaced to say that all this passed me by. In my state of naive ignorance – or was it indifference? – I learned that there was a trip planned to London, where we students would join forces with others from around the country and march en masse to the seat of power in Downing Street and, in so doing, effect some change. I signed up for the outing, happy to play my part in this positive action.

It was unprecedented and quite out of character. I'd like to tell you I was undergoing a political awakening, but the reality is I was probably thinking of Al Pacino in *Dog Day Afternoon*, whipping the crowd outside the besieged bank into a frenzy with his cries of, '*Attica! Attica!*' At this stage I still had enough hair which, at a distance (some considerable distance) and with a good following wind, to my mind you could confuse me for a young Al.

On the allotted day we all climbed on to the coach and wove our way out of Cardiff towards the M4 and our chance to be heard. While on the coach somewhere between the service stations of Leigh Delamere and Membury, I glanced at a copy of the *Guardian*, brought along by one of my edgier friends, no doubt to get the latest on the planned march. As was my wont when faced with a broadsheet newspaper, I went straight for the culture section and the theatre listings, curious to see what was on in the West End. My eyes settled on the National Theatre's offerings, always more interesting than its commercial rivals', if only by virtue of its three separate performance spaces. The first, the Olivier, was obviously named in honour of the great actor that I knew from *Marathon Man* and *The South Bank Show*. Then there were two other mysteriously named venues: the Lyttelton and the Cottesloe. Were there actors named Lyttelton and Cottesloe? I'd certainly never heard of them. Why weren't these theatres named after Gielgud, or Richardson? Or, better still, Burton?

Scanning the current productions, I was delighted to see that Barry Humphries was giving a 'platform' that afternoon at two. I had no idea what a 'platform' was; surely it wasn't simply a platform? Although, if it had in fact been no more than Barry Humphries standing on a platform, I would still have wanted to go. He was one of the comic delights of my childhood – Dame Edna and Sir Les Patterson first and foremost, but I was aware also of his slightly lesser-known creations Sandy Stone and Lance Boyle (although in blissful ignorance of the double meaning of the latter's name).

On stepping off the coach in London, I made straight for the National Theatre and bought myself a ticket for what I discovered would be Barry talking about Sir John Betjeman. Let's say it was due to begin at two o'clock; by ten past the hour the stage was empty, save for a small table, a chaise longue and an oriental-type screen, the sort that saucy ladies disrobe behind, draping their silky undergarments over the top as they go. The audience began to get a little restless, when suddenly a doddery old figure shuffled on from the wings and took centre stage. The immediate reaction to his appearance was laughter, as we were sure that this was Barry Humphries in disguise. The laughter came to an abrupt halt once this old chap started to speak and it became apparent that it wasn't Mr Humphries trying to pull the wool over our eyes, but simply someone connected to the organization of these events who had come out to brief the audience on future happenings. We squirmed in our seats in embarrassment, as he must surely have heard the laughter while crossing the stage. I felt more than a little guilty at the poor chap's predicament.

He pressed on, undeterred. He was not a natural performer, rather flat and dull in his delivery, and after a while began to stumble a little with his words. Finally, introducing Barry Humphries, he announced him as 'Brian Humphrey'. It was then that the wool was pulled away from our eyes. The laughter began as this doddery old fellow stepped behind the screen and, like Clark Kent emerging from a phone box as Superman, walked out the other side to reveal himself as Barry Humphries. How can I communicate to you just what a shock it was? He had taken us in completely. I was bowled over by his ability to come onto the stage and completely fool the audience, making us feel guilty for ever doubting him. He went on to give a marvellously entertaining talk on Betjeman, telling us how the poet had been an influence on his own writing and then performing a Sandy Stone monologue, involving the recital of a shopping list, by way of illustration.

I would finally meet Barry Humphries many years later at a party held at the home of a friend. Given the acerbic nature of Dame Edna, I was surprised to find a rather sensitive man. Vulnerable, even. We got into a conversation with Ronnie Corbett about the delights or otherwise of performing at corporate events, and it was reassuring to hear these two legends of comedy relating tales of dying in front of pissed-up businessmen and women.

Towards the end of the night, Barry and I were part of a group of guests standing round a baby grand piano singing tunes from the Burt Bacharach songbook. Whenever Barry hit a line or a note that pleased him, he would let out a high-pitched squeal of delight, and it was as though a little door to Dame Edna had been opened. We made our way through the book, eventually arriving at 'Alfie'. A rumble of excitement spread through our ramshackle choir, partly because it's a popular song but mostly because there, just ten feet away, sitting at a table and chatting, was none other than Michael Caine.

I had hovered near him at various points during the evening in the hope that he might strike up a conversation – being, as I was, far too nervous to initiate one myself. It didn't happen. He spent most of the evening talking to friends, and as I passed his table I would strain to hear the conversation, hoping for a brief glimpse into his exciting international world of glamour. Stories beginning, 'So, I said to Roger Moore . . .' or, 'Anyway, as I stood there with the Academy Award . . .' This wasn't to be; he seemed to be involved in a heated discussion about his local council's unreliability when it came to collecting the rubbish. Hearing this sort of mundane conversation not just in Michael Caine's voice but actually spoken by Michael Caine himself is an uncommon delight. If he were to release a recording, I'd buy it.

Meanwhile, back at the piano, Barry and I looked at each other, uncertain of the protocol in a situation of this kind.

Barry had a mischievous glint in his eye. 'Dare we?' he whispered, '*Dare we?*'

We didn't dare. I wish we had.

What's the worst thing that could have happened? Sir Michael rising angrily to his feet, pointing in our direction and shouting, 'You're only supposed to sing the bloody songs that have got nothing to do with me! And, by the way, what about these bins?'

Although the college was considerably smaller than its neighbouring Cardiff University, there were nonetheless many clubs and societies up and running and in the first few weeks new students were encouraged to join up and get involved. Larry Franks was entertainment secretary of the Students' Union and one day, at a lunchtime meeting, stood up to address the crowd. He talked about the various events he hoped to see us at and his easy, relaxed style elicited a few laughs along the way. On the hazy stage of my unreliable memory he looks like a young Julian Sands. He was another student who seemed older than his years, and something he said has stayed with me. He was talking about the third-year performances in the main theatre space at the college and how we 'first years' should make an effort to come and see them. The performance began at seven thirty, he informed us, but why not get there early at seven and 'soak up the atmosphere'. That was the line, 'soak up the atmosphere'. I just loved it. It struck me as very grown-up, very dry, very understated and made me think that I was now in a different environment altogether from the one I'd known at school.

I've never been a great joiner of clubs or societies. As a small boy I briefly joined the Cubs. This involved going with Mum to the outfitters and getting kitted out in the uniform, complete with woggle, and then setting off for my first (and, as it would turn out, last) Cubs meeting. It was a cold, black, Ivor the Engine night as I entered the warm and buzzing scout hut, full of excitement at the prospect of undiscovered knots and a world of bob-a-jobbing opportunities. All I can remember of the evening now is one game inflicted on us by the Scoutmaster that involved the boys all standing in a line in our short trousers and having to jump over a thick, grizzly knotted rope being swung a foot or so off the ground. This wasn't what I signed up for; it was terrifying. Once collected and safely home, I managed to convince my parents that Cubbing was a barbaric activity and one that posed a clear and present danger to their beloved son. They accepted this with good grace, and the brand-new Cubs uniform was folded away, never to be seen again.

Perhaps this episode has had a bearing on my continuing reluctance to join any clubs. It was while at college that I made a notable exception to my rule when I joined the Swansea Camp Society. In 1984 it could be argued that Perry and Croft's popular holiday-camp sitcom *Hi-de-Hi!* was at its hi-de-height. Especially popular was Ruth Madoc's character, Gladys Pugh, who would address the campers every morning over the tannoy in her thick Welsh accent. It became a popular pastime amongst Britons of a certain inclination to mimic her lilting tones, and it was this that prompted a handful of students to form the Swansea Camp Society, an organization whose only purpose was to encourage speaking in a camp Swansea accent. This was, and still is, something at which I excel and so I didn't hesitate to arrange an audition. That's right – you had to audition to join this club.

Potential members were required to perform a piece of Shakespeare, a modern text and a song, all to be delivered in a camp Swansea accent. I rose to the challenge with ease, basically using my drama school audition pieces but with the subtle twist of the Swansea accent. So we had Pinter's *The Homecoming* and Cassius from Julius Caesar ('Oh, Caesar! The mighty Tiber was raging!') both delivered thus. For the song I chose Lionel Richie's popular ballad of the day, 'Hello'. While I could never hope to evoke the emotion of the video – in which Lionel helps a pretty blind girl to listen to and enjoy his singing, even though she lacks the power of sight – I was confident that I'd raise a laugh. I sang the first verse tentatively, ending on, 'I sometimes see you pass outside my door . . .' I then paused for a short eternity before smiling and loudly proclaiming, 'Hello!' in the slightly questioning manner of a person greeting a friend they've not seen for a while. It worked and I was ushered into the society.

Twenty-five years later I performed the same routine on my tour of the UK, often to some acclaim, and in so doing remembered a quote from the great Steve Martin. Early in his success he had been a guest on *The Tonight Show*, the hugely popular and influential talk show, hosted by the hugely popular and influential Johnny Carson. In the course of his interview and much to his surprise, he'd found himself juggling as he sat on the guests' sofa, to the delight of the audience. This wasn't something he'd planned to do.

During the ensuing ad break he leaned across to Carson and said how shocked he was to have juggled on television.

Carson replied, 'Kid, before you're done, you'll do everything you ever knew.'

When my ridiculous Small Man in a Box voice took off and became one of the things people would associate with my name, I was quick to recall the words of Johnny Carson.

9

I settled easily into my new life at the Royal Welsh College of Music and Drama, at no point mounting a challenge for my relinquished title of Loneliest Boy in the World. It was everything I had hoped it would be; we basically spent the whole day doing what I'd enjoyed doing at school, acting. There were other classes too – movement and dance, for example, a discipline with which I struggled. These were the days of *Fame*, the hugely popular television show spun off from Alan Parker's film and while we never ran singing and dancing from the college, leaping and pirouetting around the traffic, we did master the art of wearing the leg warmer. Our dance teacher, Tim Hext, who had appeared on television in *The Black and White Minstrel Show* and onstage with Topol in *Fiddler on the Roof*, must have despaired of some of us and our complete lack of anything approaching a desire to dance. If you're reading this, and you were there, and you felt you were standing on the threshold of a career in dance, only to be held back by lumbering oafs like me, then please accept my apologies: I cannot remember anyone with anything other than a comical lack of aptitude when it came to dance. In my eyes at least, the dance and movement classes were tolerated as little more than an anthropological experiment, albeit an enjoyable one. Imagine scientists trying to teach a room full of monkeys to walk upright and you'll have a fair idea of the standards we achieved.

Speech was another subject altogether, and perhaps my favourite. The classes were taken by a wonderfully dry and erudite man named John Wills. Imagine a blend of Kenneth Williams, Gore Vidal and Stephen Fry, who could captivate a group of students with just his voice and who possessed that most important of qualities for a teacher, the ability to inspire confidence in his students. John had the added cachet of having once taught a young Robert Lindsay, who at that time was enjoying enormous success as Bill Snibson in the revival of *Me and My Girl*. One of my finest moments under John's tuition was being told that I had a stillness that reminded him of Robert. Moments like this, when a teacher goes out of his way to praise and encourage, are so important in building self-belief. I remember quietly thinking to myself that this was more like it. It seemed to me that these classes had a very practical usefulness to them, in as much as we would be asked to memorize pieces and then perform them for the rest of the group (as opposed to struggling to commit to memory the moves of a dance routine). I had no intention at that stage of my life of embarking on a career in the cut and thrust of the professional dance world, and so the dance lessons could never really be entered into with any sort of gusto.

As I sit here now, reflecting on those long mornings spent flexing and pointing in front of a floor-to-ceiling mirror, I feel vindicated. 'See? I *told* you I wasn't a dancer!' The speech classes were different, though, and here was an area where I felt I could compete, maybe even win. We were taught the now rather quaint concept of 'RP' – received pronunciation – what you might think of as Queen's English (i.e. speaking without a regional accent). It was the sort of voice that you might hear on a television commercial in the 1970s or 1980s extolling the virtues of just about anything. Whereas now, of course, the regional accent rules. Having always had an easy knack for voices and accents, I found this task a doddle; for others it was an ordeal and one that, frankly, they needn't have been too worried about. We were, in 1984, at the very tail end of the notion of received pronunciation being of some practical use to an actor; I can't imagine any hopeful young acting student today being told to disguise his or her accent.

On my first proper day at the college, I noticed one of the other new students across the crowded common room. He was loud, extrovert, slightly camp and very posh. A cross between Gyles Brandreth – who, oddly enough, he would later go on to work for – and an upper-class Timmy Mallett. I took an instant dislike to him and made a mental note that I would not be spending much time in his company. His name was James Lovell, and he became my best friend.

James came from Hampshire – as he put it, 'the land of milk and honey'. He was confident, outgoing and had the energy and enthusiasm of a puppy. He loved Noël Coward, Cole Porter and soon, thanks to my intervention, Bruce Springsteen. He also loved showing off, parading around the college in sweatpants, leg warmers and an authentic Second World War flying jacket that his father had worn while piloting Spitfires. He seemed to already know many of the other students, and to be living college life to the full.

His first impression of me was of a boy in a big jumper with quite a lot of acne, who was rather shy. He remembers noticing the range of voices I could summon up in John Wills's speech classes, lessons in which he also shone. John would listen to James reciting a piece in his loud plummy tones and then delight his student by predicting that in no time at all James would be starring in the West End, making his entrance through French windows, upstage centre, in a production dreamed up by John entitled *Tons of Jelly*. We would all chuckle in agreement; John's approval was a most desirable commodity.

For one of his classes I memorized and performed the opening page or so of *The Catcher in the Rye*. I sat, or maybe leaned, against the classroom wall and stared down at my feet and out of the window, taking a while before I began, 'If you really want to hear about it, the first thing you'll probably want to know . . .' I was pleased with how it went; I'd tried to make it as naturalistic as possible, a low-key performance like those of my cinema heroes. I was thrilled when John said how much he'd liked it, and that a sign of how good it had been was the fact that he didn't know I'd started. I don't think I gave another performance that natural and unforced until *Marion and Geoff*, fifteen years later.

Alongside James I became very friendly with another student, an altogether different type of personality. Dougray Scott was not Dougray Scott in those days; he was Stephen Scott (the name was changed out of necessity when he joined the actors' union, Equity). Dougray was an intense young man whose natural talent, drive and good looks marked him out to me as winner of the 'most likely to succeed' competition. We bonded over a shared love of that holy trinity of actors, Hoffman, Pacino and De Niro, and an appreciation of Arthur Miller's masterpiece *Death of a Salesman*. Like my dad, Dougray's father had been a salesman, and the play resonated deeply with both of us. We would read it to each other and talk of one day playing the sons, Biff and Happy, together on the stage. It never happened – and now we're too old. I'd still like to do the play, and so would he; it'll be interesting to see who's first to show their Willy. Forgive me.

Dougray was very much a devotee of 'the method' and by his own admission went through college 'like a tortured young artist' while I 'breezed through it, destined to make people laugh'. In improvisation classes our different approaches to our craft were evident. When asked to observe an animal and then present our interpretation to the class, Dougray spent all his spare time in the park, notebook in hand, studying the pigeons. He arrived in class and gave us his pigeon; it was a very intense, beautifully nuanced pigeon. It may have been one of the pigeons from *On the Waterfront*, with maybe just a slight hint of one of the doves from the wedding scene in *The Godfather*. I had done no preparation at all, but entered into a lively impersonation of our dog at the time, a Yorkshire terrier named Purdey. I jumped up and down, yapping excitedly, much to the delight of our teacher, who praised my diligence and remarked that I'd obviously spent many hours studying the creature. I nodded sagely in agreement, while making a mental note that you can indeed fool some of the people some of the time.

Along with James and Dougray, my main friendships were with David Broughton Davies and John Golley. Dave was a Welshman from Wrexham and, at twenty-six, a little older than the rest of us. This age difference gave him the air of a man who had already lived his life and had come to college as a project to see him through his retirement. He had begun his working life as a civil servant for nine years, before turning his back on the security and heading off to drama school. He shared my love of Springsteen and had his own collection of bootleg cassettes, which we would listen to religiously. Dave stood out for many reasons: his age, his ever-so-slightly-portly frame, his generally upbeat nature, and the fact that he owned a car. It might have been the worst car I've ever known – an appalling black Fiat Panda that seemed to be made of the material used to make fizzy-drink cans. It was also the best car I had ever known, by simple virtue of the fact that it was there and Dave was very generous in his use of it. Dave was very generous, full stop. He was always encouraging me and making me feel that I was a little bit more talented than was necessary. He seemed to love college life too – partly, I'm sure, because he'd known what it was to work in an 'ordinary' job. College must have seemed a breeze by comparison.

Dave also had a girlfriend, a fellow student called Debbie. My memory of Debbie is that she came from London and had quite a hard, cynical edge. The three of us were in a pub one night talking about another student when Debbie said, 'Yeah, well, he's all right but I wouldn't part my legs for him.' As ridiculous as it sounds, I was rather shocked by her remark; I'd certainly never heard a girl speak like this before. If I'd been holding a cup of tea to my lips, it would have been the perfect moment to pay tribute to Terry Scott and spit it out.

Dave lived in a big house on Llandaff Road, which he shared with James and also John Golley. John is a very easy man to describe. Picture David Bowie in his Thin White Duke period and you're almost there. John was the epitome of cool, and his room, as was the case with all of us, was the perfect representation of his personality. It was an eaves room at the top of the house with little or no clutter. A row of carefully arranged cassettes, a hairdryer and a vintage Gretsch guitar are all I can remember. As wonderful as the guitar was, I don't recall ever seeing him play it. He would laugh at my jokes with the easy air of an indulgent uncle whilst, in the corner of his mind, calculating the details of his next sexual conquest. Thinking again of his room, I would describe it as a Zen temple of benign narcissism and sex.

Number 186 Llandaff Road was a welcoming environment. It had a sense of community that my own digs in Oakfield Street lacked, with their strictly enforced immersion heater rules and cold-water kitchen facilities. It turned out that the music student who had brought me there in the first place was a practising Christian Scientist. This only came to light when he went down with a very heavy cold but refused to take any kind of medication. He survived, although he was very poorly for some time (during which I went in his place to see Level 42 at the university with his girlfriend, so the tickets wouldn't go to waste).

Llandaff Road was always buzzing. James had an electric keyboard, as well as an upright piano and a toasted sandwich maker. This splendid machine was never off. James would pile in as many ingredients as the thing would take, most notably ham and cheese. James's cheese of choice was Edam, a new experience for me; until then my cheese life began and ended with Dairylea. It was while eating toasted sandwiches that I introduced James to Bruce Springsteen, an artist whom he had yet to encounter, content as he was with Noël Coward, Cole Porter et al. After munching the sandwiches, we would sing together. James would work out the chords to songs by Bruce and Elvis, and I would wail away to my heart's content.

As time went by, these evenings became more frequent and eventually we would find ourselves slipping away during free periods at college up to the top floor where the music department's practice rooms were to be found. These were tiny cells, just big enough for an upright piano and a chair; there was certainly no way they could accommodate the circular transit of a dead cat. James and I would walk along the corridors and glance in through the little oblong window in each door until a vacant room was found. Then we'd slip inside and work through our favourite songs. Anyone walking past would have been perplexed at the sudden change from Elgar to Elton John. They would have considered

A friend had a camera.
I had delusions of James Dean.

Sky Masterson in
Guys and Dolls.

*'I've never been in
love before . . .'*

Rhian and I compete to
see who can wear the
most make-up. I win.

An Oscar for 'Sweet Charity'?

FOUR out of ten places in the National Youth Theatre of Wales were awarded this year to pupils of Porthcawl Comprehensive School.

The school has earned a reputation 'second to none' with success following success in drama productions.

Tonight is the night when this reputation will be tested. It is opening night at the Grand Pavilion of 'Sweet Charity'. The cast of over 100 has been rehearsing for months and it is rumoured to be 'the best ever'.

Debbie Nelson plays 'Charity' and Robert Jones 'Oscar' — it is certainly a show not to be missed.

Debbie Nelson and Robert Jones — see 'Sweet Charity'.

Me and Nicola Ball in *Carousel* (1984). Look at those heels!

Amanda Trimble, Robert Jones, and Ruth Jones lead the cast of 'Carousel'.

Join the Carousel

THIS week the curtain rises on Porthcawl Comprehensive School's production "Carousel".

It was probably easier to get tickets for Saturday's international than for "Carousel".

Certainly every seat in the Grand Pavilion for Wednesday, Thursday and Friday, was booked within three days of the tickets going on sale.

Last year I said the school could never top "Guys and Dolls" . . . but

I have a sneaky suspicion I was wrong.

The "Gazette" will publish a page of pictures and a full review of

Carousel next week . . . if you didn't manage to get a ticket at least you will be able to see what you missed.

Press intrusion. Why won't they leave me alone?

A good luck card from Pete.

Peter Wingfield . . . 'would soar past, cape flapping in the breeze, en route to Planet Sex'.

Steve Speirs, at the National Youth Theatre of Wales, aka the evil dermatologist.

The Caucasian Chalk Circle, National Youth Theatre of Wales, 1983.
'A lot of the actors were sitting on stage a lot of the time, so I spent much of it watching the older actors while simultaneously losing all feeling in my lower body. I was basically an audience member with a very good view.'

At home with Pete.

Darkness on the
Edge of Duvet.

A trip to Bute Park
with Jacque.

Born to Jump.

From left to right: Nanny Margam, Me, Cousin Jayne and her husband Steve, Mum, Aunty Margaret, Pete and Dad.

With Dougray and James in Cardiff. I appear to be searching for my keys.

On the town with Jacque and James.

With James, evoking the spirit of a young Stallone.

The soon-to-be-liberated poster.

Sylvester Springsteen.

the college to be rather progressive – or perhaps catering for children with learning difficulties.

As we pressed on with our practices, they began to take on the feel of rehearsals, and so we decided to put on a show. The 'show' consisted of a big, overblown, over-generous, expectation-raising introduction from one of our fellow students followed by James and me, under the title of Rob and James, rattling through a collection of songs. James banged away at the piano while I cavorted with the microphone, hoping to summon the spirit of Jim Morrison as I writhed and spun amongst the assembled crowd in the student bar. It's safe to say that the Lizard King's spirit remained unevoked – beyond, perhaps, an irritable turning in his grave. The performance was not so much Jim Morrison as Jim Carrey. I suspect I brought to mind a mid-period Bruce Forsyth. And yet despite or perhaps, to be fair to Brucie, *because* of this, we went down a storm.

We were soon known as a double act, spoken of throughout the college with some affection, and with almost indecent haste we landed our first broadcast gig. We were called into our head of year's office one day and told that BBC Radio Wales, based just up the road in Llandaff, were looking for local acts to take part in a live radio show, in front of an audience. Would we like to give it a go and try out for a spot? It amazes me now to think that we didn't hesitate for a moment; we jumped at the chance. We can only have done two or three public performances at this point, but that didn't stop us from taking the bit between the teeth and trotting on towards potential humiliation.

It transpired that we had to complete not one but several auditions to win a spot on *Level Three*. It was a magazine-style show on BBC Radio Wales, which was broadcast live each Friday morning from the recently opened St David's Hall in Cardiff. In a classic example of the psyche of the performer (years later, an agent would enlighten me with his opinion that all performers are in possession of high ego and low self-esteem) I was simultaneously overawed and tremulous at climbing the steep and imposing steps that led to the mighty BBC Wales, and appalled that we were having to audition more than once for what was essentially a local radio show.

My memory now projects a sepia-tinted silent movie of James and I playing and singing our hearts out in a vast, cavernous studio along the lines of the fabled Abbey Road. I think I've fallen victim here to the *Vanilla Sky* scenario whereby Tom Cruise's memories (or manu-factured reality/lucid dream) are made up largely of the pop-culture influences he has absorbed during his life-time, as opposed to any actual reality. I now know that the studio wasn't all that big; my memory has allowed all the biopics of struggling artists, and the documentaries on the making of classic albums that I've seen, to seep in and corrupt my consciousness. This must explain why, when thinking of our audition for Radio Wales, I can remember Paul Simon in a far corner of the room, becoming increasingly irate with Ladysmith Black Mambazo.

We decided that we would audition in character, with

me playing the role of Tony Casino. Tony was a Welsh nightclub singer who thought of himself as Tom Jones but in reality was sadly lacking in every department. I can't claim that Tony was a masterpiece of observational comedy or, for that matter, a stinging satire on the state of light entertainment; he was basically me with a more pronounced Welsh accent. We went through our collection of numbers: an upbeat 'Amarillo', a ludicrously French-accented 'She' (a nod of recognition here, surely, to Kenneth Williams and his 'Ma Crêpe Suzette') and finally, fresh from its success at the Swansea Camp Society audition, my moving interpretation of Lionel Richie's 'Hello'. We played them again and again for the producer of the show, Caroline Sarll, and her assistant, Siân Roberts, until finally we were given the nod and told that we'd made it onto the show.

I'm playing down its significance now, but at the time this was a very big deal indeed – a live radio show, a live audience not made up of friends but of real people who would judge us entirely on merit. The Friday morning of the broadcast duly arrived. With time off from classes we set out for what was to be, for both of us, our first paid gig. I'm not sure how it is today, when it would seem that any sixteen-year-old with the slightest inclination towards performance can stick themselves up on YouTube with a potential audience of millions, and at the very least secure a regular role in *Hollyoaks*. In 1985, things were very different. Short of bellowing out of your bedroom window, you couldn't broadcast yourself; you were always in the hands of others, and so the radio held an air of exotic inaccessibility. To my twenty-year-old self it represented a fair chunk of my dream pie.

I had for a long time held an above-average interest in the medium of radio, listening to it avidly and even hoping that one day I might myself become a disc jockey. My heroes were disappointingly predictable; when grouped together they effortlessly formed a list of solid, middle-class BBC-approved respectability. Names like Ed Stewart, Tony Blackburn and Noel Edmonds would have been high up the chart, although I also possessed a slightly more risqué (if that's not too misleading a word, and I'm fairly certain that it is) fondness for some of the present-ers on whistling and whiney Radio Luxembourg.

Enjoying Radio Luxembourg required a certain dedi-cation and tenacity on the part of the listener. My memory tells me that it only broadcast in the evenings, although I'm prepared to accept that may not have been the case; it may have been that I only listened to it in the evenings, when its medium-wave crackle and hiss made it seem so far away. Never mind another country, it may as well have been broadcasting from another universe; it sounded so distant, the signal weakening as the night progressed. It was home to a variety of characters: the flamboyantly titled and curiously voiced Emperor Rosko, Tony Prince (famed amongst we Elvis fans for having once actually met the King, in Las Vegas), Stuart Henry (who basically sounded like the more outgoing brother of Radio Two's Ken Bruce) and my own favourite, Rob Jones. I'm not sure what it was that I liked about Rob Jones, beyond the fact we shared the same name – it was reassuring to know that someone with my name could, and had, become a success in radio.

I actually met him once, on a summer's day in the late seventies at the West Wales seaside town of Saunders-foot, just a few miles away from its more celebrated neighbour, Tenby, as he hosted the Radio Luxembourg Roadshow at Wiseman's Bridge. It's an accurate reflection of the comparative status of Radios One and Luxembourg that while Rob was announcing, 'Hello, Saundersfoot!' to a relatively modest crowd, just down the road a far larger name, possibly with the initials D. L. T., was yelling, 'Hello, Tenby!' to a far larger and I dare say more enthusiastic crowd. I happily supported both ventures and the thought of visiting either roadshow would have filled me with excitement. The likelihood of bumping into the Hairy Cornflake while attending the Radio One offering would have been a million to one but, arriving early for the Luxembourg effort, Mum, Pete and I came across Rob Jones as he sat in a nearby café. We had a chat, the details of which have been mislaid, though I imagine that Mum would surely have told him of my thespian leanings and my desire to get into radio, and it's likely that he would have offered words of encouragement in return. My only clear, strong recollection of the encounter is that he possessed two remarkable forearms, which at that early stage of my existence were the hairiest I had ever seen.

My love of radio was not confined to just listening to it; I would spend much of my time performing and recording my own little programmes on to cassette, the celebrated format of the day. Setting up a mini studio in

David Williams's bedroom, awkwardly jumping from vinyl to tape and back again, from Abba to ELO to David Soul, we produced our own miniature shows.

I was in my element.

I would go on to have a long, brief career as a radio presenter some years later, although before that there were two encounters with the inside of a radio studio that would serve to whet my appetite for the medium.

On Saturday the 3rd of April 1982, the day after war was declared against Argentina, I found myself at the BBC in Cardiff for a topical discussion programme. A group of us from school had travelled from Porthcawl on the minibus, and I can remember the excitement I felt at first glimpsing the BBC. Once in the studio we were soon live on air in the midst of a discussion regarding the grave news of the previous day. The subject of conscription came up and the students, given their age and the obvious implications, were asked for their views. So it was that I made my national radio debut, confidently and calmly sharing the opinion that, as far as I was concerned, 'subscription' was neither a good nor a bad thing. This was more than just an embarrassing malapropism on my part; it spoke volumes about my unworldly nature and complete lack of insight and awareness when it came to world affairs. I was just a happy chap, content in his own little world.

However, this wasn't my first radio appearance; that had occurred four years previously in 1978 when, aged thirteen, I appeared on our fledgling independent local radio station, Swansea Sound, as their 'junior DJ'. This involved sitting in with one of the station's regular presenters and helping to play the records, voice the links, etc. The station's familiar jingle rang out: *Two fifty-seven, Swansea Sound!*

'So, our junior DJ this week is from Baglan, near Port Talbot, and it's Robert Jones! So, Robert, what about girlfriends?'

The bastard. Of course I didn't have a bloody girlfriend. I was thirteen! I shuffled uncomfortably, insecure in the knowledge that every family member within the broadcast range of Swansea Sound (i.e. every family member) would be listening intently as I revealed my startling lack of progress in the trouser department.

'Uh, well, no, not really, uh, no . . .'

'What, none at all?'

'Uh, no, not really . . .'

'So, you're just looking around?'

Oh God, please make this stop.

'That's right, just looking around . . .'

Still requiring a little more humiliation before he could rest, Steve – yes, he was called Steve – got me to introduce the next record: 'And it's Captain and Tennille . . . and what's it called, Robert?'

'Uh . . . "You Need A Woman Tonight"?'

'That's right!'

For God's sake, none of my friends had girlfriends at thirteen. There was a boy in my year at Dumbarton, Glenwood Evans, who went out with Helen Williams at a spectacularly young age. Glenwood was the boy – I dare say every class has one – who seemed remarkably more mature and advanced than the rest of us. It wouldn't have surprised me to learn that, although he managed to pop into school every day, he was actually in his mid-forties with a wife, two children and a successful scaffolding business. I've not seen him since the late seventies, but if he carried on at the rate he was going he must now pass for a hundred and ten.

My spot as this week's junior DJ was deemed a success and, to ensure that it was preserved for the family archives, a friend of my dad's taped it from the pristine FM broadcast (as Steely Dan rightly said, 'no static at all') on to a stunningly clear Maxell chrome cassette. At the time, this represented cutting-edge, space-age technology. I still have the tape – in fact, if you're currently enjoying the electronic e-version of this book, then you may well be able to press, prod or even swipe an excerpt into life right now. The majority of you, though, the late adapters of this world, will have to simply use your imaginations and conjure up the hits of the day.

Alongside Captain and Tennille we heard Gerard Kenny, Mick Jackson (I'm not being overly familiar with Michael – Mick had a hit with 'Weekend'), Billy Joel (another hero of mine who, at the time of writing, has recently undergone a double hip replacement . . . sigh) and an advert for Dial-a-Disc, featuring the voice of Nicholas Parsons. When I first came into possession of the recording, I would listen to it repeatedly, hoping to detect the seeds of a career in broadcasting. At the top of the show the DJ played Bruce Springsteen's 'Born to Run'; this would, I'm sure, have been the first time I heard the man who would go on to be a huge part of my listening life and an influence on everything from my dancing 'style' ('Dancing in the Dark' video), to my resting gait (inner sleeve of *Born in the USA*), and even to the way I dressed.

It was said that I bore a slight resemblance to the Boss – due largely, I suspect, to our prominent jaws and generally handsome features. I found this quite uplifting. Before long, in a barely subconscious effort to morph into my loved one, I would be dressed most days in jeans and a checked shirt. Cowboy boots, often favoured by Bruce, were a tricky proposition for a man of my height, on whom they could be interpreted as a cry for help. A compromise was reached with the purchase of a pair with very modest heels. These were pre-*Born in the USA* times, so Bruce had yet to adopt the headband. I like to think that even if he already had I would have had the presence of mind to resist. Of history's great headband-wearers – Borg, Springsteen . . . shall we include Rambo? – only one, Mark Knopfler, has been of UK origin. And when it comes to the Sultan of Swing's fashion sense let's be honest, the jury is still out.

As far as resembling your heroes goes, I have a pet theory. So many of my acting friends, when asked who they admire from the world of film, will proffer someone who isn't a million miles away from themselves in terms of physical appearance. I always liked short, dark, brooding actors – Hoffman, Pacino . . . Corbett – partly, I think, because I could see myself in them. It's a curious mix of narcissism and wishful thinking, a bit like couples who resemble each other, both revelling in seeing their own reflection each day. As far as Bruce goes, and his inclusion on the tape of my radio debut, it's funny to recall that at the time I would always fast forward through this never-ending dirge, which sounded to me as though it was sung by a grumpy Australian with a sore throat.

Thirty-two years later I would finally meet my hero in an encounter of heartbreaking awkwardness, which involved my gripping his hand a little too tightly, staring a little too intensely into his eyes, and uttering the following:

'Bruce! It's really, really, really . . . *really* good to meet you.'

He did his Little Billy Goat Gruff laugh. 'All right!'

To make sure that he would leave our meeting convinced he'd just met an idiot, I followed up by thanking him for, and I quote, '. . . the moments.'

Glory Days, indeed.

Back in 1985, Bruce was at the height of his *Born in the USA* fame. James and I would go on to Wembley on the 4th of July to see The E Street Band and their Boss onstage in a show that seemed to last the whole night. But now we had other things on our minds.

On the morning of the live broadcast of *Level Three* on BBC Radio Wales we would, I'm sure, have arrived early at St David's Hall. We would also, I'm sure, have been bloody excited. I seem to have a memory of last-minute shirt-buying. My dad slipped away from work and came to see his son explode on to the radio. The main guest on our edition of the show was Sir Jimmy Savile. Jimmy was something of a hero of mine. Like Basil Brush, he was someone who turned a lot of people off, but to whom I was drawn. And, like Brush, he had a very distinctive appearance and an easy way with a catchphrase. I can remember, as though it was last week, James and I sitting with Jimmy after the show and listening to him dispense his wisdom. I don't say that in a sarcastic way; I've remembered his words to this day.

'Look at me,' he said. 'I can't sing, I can't dance, I can't act. I can do fuck all. But, I turn up at places, I smile, I wave. The punters look at me and say, "Jim's having a good time, therefore so are we."'

He told of how when he was giving an after-dinner speech he would walk around each table in the room during the meal and have a brief chat with everyone, something along the lines of, 'I'm here to arrange the washing-up rota,' before returning to top table and preparing for his speech. 'By the time I get up on my feet, everyone in the room thinks they're my friend and they all want me to do well.'

The most telling piece of advice or observation that he uttered that day, though, was this: 'It's very hard to get to the top in this game, but it's a damn sight harder staying there.' That has never been far from my mind, from that day to this.

So, why such a fan of Sir Jim? Well, he's a one-off; there's no one else like him, and that surely should count for something.

I loved his radio style too. How about this (he's just played 'Way Down' by Elvis)?

'Elvis. "Way Down". But . . . way . . . up . . . in . . . the . . . minds . . . of . . . his . . . many . . . fans.'

Then he played the next record. That was the link. Brilliant.

*

Our debut radio performance went well, the audience liked us, and we were deemed a success.

Hurrah!

I very much liked the atmosphere of the broadcast, the efficiency of the team as they bustled around preparing the programme and completing last-minute checks before the audience was allowed in and the show began. Rather like when I auditioned for the Royal Welsh College of Music and Drama, this felt within my reach. Far from feeling especially daunted by it, I saw it more as a challenge at which I was fairly confident I would succeed.

Buoyed by this success, I would revisit St David's Hall every Friday lunchtime and loiter around the production team in the hope there might be something to do. There often was – basically, in the form of providing a silly voice for an announcement or sketch, which I was more than happy to supply.

I was, quite unknowingly, taking the first steps towards my subsequent career. At the time, it simply felt as though I was going with the flow, taking an opportunity as it arose.

10

Back at college, James and I were flushed with our success and decided to take the band on the road. We secured a booking at the Wyke Regis Working Men's Club. This was in a small town near Weymouth, of which I had up to that point been unaware. James came from Hampshire so I suspect it was his idea, although I doubt he had any personal knowledge of the place, coming as he did from the other end of the social spectrum. The gig provided a modest fee, which we never saw; it failed even to cover the cost of renting a car to get us there in the first place, to say nothing of the petrol. So we were down on the deal before we started, but it didn't matter. We weren't in this for the money; that would come later. We were in this for the experience. And that's what we got.

We arrived at the venue after our long drive to see a list of the week's attractions pinned to a board in the foyer. We scanned it with ill-concealed excitement, keen to see our names in print. It was a roll-call of the sort of acts you see advertising their services in the back of *The Stage* newspaper – the foot soldiers of show business, toiling away in the trenches of low-paying, hard-graft entertainment. Still, our names were going to be on there and that meant we had arrived. Admittedly, it was only Wyke Regis Working Men's Club. But for us it was an arrival nonetheless. Finally spotting our billing, it would appear that we hadn't in fact arrived; rather, it was someone who sounded almost but not quite like us. There on the board under tonight's date was the name Robin James. Hmmm, there'd evidently been a breakdown in communication and somewhere along the line Rob and James had matured into Robin James. *Not to worry, it doesn't really matter*, we told ourselves as we set about lugging the equipment in from the budget-breakingly expensive rental car.

A couple of hours later, we launched into our act to a room that was filled to perhaps a quarter of its capacity. The inhabitants seemed, to our young eyes, to be on the other side of old, and we set about assaulting them with 'Crocodile Rock', 'Hungry Heart' and other foot-tappers of a similar ilk. The crowd, if it could be called that, seemed unimpressed but we carried on gallantly with our collection of upbeat tunes performed to the simple accompaniment of an electric piano, no percussion in sight. Our elderly audience grew less impressed by the minute; these people didn't have time on their side and were livid at the prospect of it ebbing away in our company.

After a very long period of us singing inappropriate songs into an empty void of nothingness, a blue-haired lady edged towards the stage, crossing the vast desert wilderness of the empty dance floor before coming to a faltering halt right in front of us. She smiled sweetly, but underneath the smile was a steely undercurrent that told us she was not to be messed with. Like Brian Dennehy's redneck sheriff telling John Rambo that he wasn't welcome in this town, she said, 'We don't want this kind of music. We like waltzes, you should play a waltz . . .' Of course we didn't have any waltzes in our set list, or even up our sleeves. We were strictly rock 'n' roll. Pop, perhaps. But certainly not waltzes. Necessity being the biological mother of invention, we came up with a solution – one which still impresses me now, twenty-five years later, for its sheer guile and cunning. We had with us *101 Easy Hits for Buskers*, a huge groaning book of sheet music within which was 'Can't Help Falling in Love'. Now this may already be in 3/4 time – I don't know, I'm not a proper musician – but what I do know is that we hammered the hell out of the song in a strict 3/4 rhythm, snapped out by my fingers as they conducted the dancing.

'Wise [*boom, boom*] men [*boom, boom*] say [*boom, boom, boom*] only fools [*boom, boom*] rush [*boom, boom*] in [*boom, boom, boom*] . . .'

It worked. The disappointed dancers, to their credit, slowly shuffled on to the dance floor and gamely supported our last-ditch effort at entertaining them. With a quarter of the available floor space bulging to capacity we sang and played on until there was no more 'Can't Help Falling in Love' to give and we couldn't help stopping.

'Well, that's all from us, ladies and gentlemen. Thank you very much and good night!'

We left the stage to applause best described as angrily polite, and collapsed into a couple of chairs at the side of the dance floor in a heap of nervous exhaustion. We looked at each other. There was nothing to say. We had survived – just. Let's leave it at that. While we were sitting there trying to comprehend the scale of our humiliation, we noticed a gentleman heading over to us. It was the chap who was in charge of the evening; we'd spoken to him briefly on our arrival when, for all he knew, he'd stumbled on the new U2. We were sure he wouldn't have been overly impressed, but perhaps he'd admired the way we pulled the Elvis song out of the bag and almost turned the audience around. He stopped a couple of feet away from us. He didn't smile.

'You've got another ten minutes to do. Get back on.'

A recurring fear in my professional life has been not having enough material for my designated slot. Whether it's been the West End, a tour, or a spot on a charity show at the O2, it is something that has dogged me for as long as I can remember. Only now does it occur to me that this may have been the birth of my condition. Thank you, Wyke Regis Working Men's Club social secretary. Thank you very much.

We dragged our feet back to the stage and managed another ten minutes of faux waltz music to an audience giddy on a heady cocktail of anger, pity and contempt. When the ten minutes were up, we looked over to the social secretary. He gave the cold, steely nod of the professional executioner ('Goodbye, Mr Bond . . .'), a thin smile spreading imperceptibly across his lips. We trudged back to the chairs at the edge of the dance floor and sat staring at our feet, scanning the floor tiles for a silver lining, when a pair of comfortable shoes entered our view. They belonged to a man, perhaps in his seventies, with a soft friendly face and a kindly disposition. He looked at us and thought for a moment. We knew he was about to tell us that it hadn't been as bad as we'd thought and that he'd enjoyed it anyway, so what do *they* know?

He began to speak.

'Boys, I've been coming here for a long time, seen a lot of acts come and go over the years, but I have to say, you were the worst I've ever seen. You were crap.'

He turned and was gone.

We packed up our equipment in next to no time, jumped into the 'never more expensive than now' car, and began the journey home. These were the now-forgotten days before satellite navigation so I have to assume that we would have conversed at some point regarding the best route back to Cardiff. Try as I might, though, I can't recall a single word being spoken the entire length of the journey.

It's an odd thing about performers, artistes, 'turns', call us what you will – and it will, I'm sure, become a recurring theme throughout this book – that no matter how bad the beating, how great the humiliation, we always dust ourselves down and get back in the ring. So often, comedians are told by friends and family, 'I don't know how you do it.' This is to miss the point. All the successful comedians, actors or musicians that I've known have had one thing in common. Their job is a calling, not a choice. It's something that I'm sure annoys the hell out of people with a degree of contempt for those whom they view as self-absorbed luvvies, but it's true nonetheless. It's something the person feels compelled to do, as opposed to a choice made while chatting to a careers officer on a wet Tuesday afternoon at the local school.

It's a feeling of having something to say, of wanting to get something 'out', and it's what carries you through the traumas of many hostile audiences.

We experienced a few more, James and I, in those early days with everything ahead of us and no guide-book to consult along the way. There was a nightclub in the centre of Cardiff called Jacksons, which in the mid-eighties was a fairly upmarket, sophisticated sort of place. It was a step up from Bumpers, another celebrated haunt for nocturnal Cardiffians, which had a more down-market feel. Jacksons seemed the sort of place for young people on their way up; if a soap star was in town for an opening of a shop or an envelope, Jacksons was where you might find them relaxing after a hard day's smiling. It had a touch of glamour (to my Port Talbot-trained eyes, anyway) and was undoubtedly a step in the right direction, a little further up the evolutionary ladder of sophistication than the Troubadour, sitting snugly as it did in the shadow of Cardiff Arms Park. It even had a dash of showbiz thrown into the mix with the presence of a manager who had recently appeared on *Blind Date*. Cilla Black's massively popular dating show was huge and, although a little racy at the time, now of course appears positively Edwardian in its values.

James and I somehow landed a try-out at the club. We were to perform early one evening, before too many of the paying customers had come in, and we had the added excitement of knowing that a coven of the company's directors would also be in attendance, judging our fledg-ling performance. I don't remember if we were nervous. Maybe we were. As I've said, there were some situations that I just didn't get nervous over; I felt I was better than them, and therefore they were lucky to have me. This may have been one of them. What I do remember with alarming clarity is the sight of the celebrated blindly dated manager, one and a half songs into our try-out, walking hurriedly towards us from the huddle of directors while making a cutting motion across his throat.

We were to stop. Immediately. No ifs, no buts. And, more importantly, no more songs.

This was embarrassing on many levels, not least because a small group of friends from the college had gamely come along to support us, amongst them a very young Hugo Blick (with whom, fifteen years later, I would go on to make *Marion and Geoff*). Sadly, my lack of fortune-telling abilities meant that the prospect of awards and plaudits fifteen years down the road was of little comfort. So, with no other option open to us, we did as instructed and left the building, our metaphorical tails tucked metaphorically between our very real legs. The evening ended with James and I sitting on a bench on Cardiff's Queen Street, contemplating our inability to entertain. It was dark now and the gloom of the night was easily matched, if not outdone, by the gloom we felt at another failure.

As has been the case on so many occasions, the start of a new day brought renewed hope. And so we trudged on undeterred and determined to prove the naysayers wrong. We had a few successes; a gig at a golf club on the outskirts of Cardiff went very well, as did a twenty-first birthday party in Hampshire. At both of these outings we performed under a new name, as Tony Casino and the Roulette Wheels (the wheels in question being our backing singers). One of the Roulette Wheels was a girl named Jacqueline Gilbride.

Jacque was from Glasgow, the daughter of a pharmacist; she was taking a one-year postgrad acting course, and had recently been awarded the title of My First Girlfriend. My initial sighting of her was in a student production of Alan Bennett's *Habeas Corpus*. I felt she was the most naturally funny member of the cast and thought it would be nice to tell her so, which I did when we met in the bar later that evening.

That was all.

Most people, when writing of their formative college years, particularly with reference to their early romantic endeavours, often explain things away by reminding the reader that the events being recalled occurred during 'my drinking years'. With me, the opposite is true. I didn't begin to drink alcohol until my early to mid-thirties, so all these episodes came to pass without the liberating assistance of a drink. I take an odd pride in that now. Anyone can walk up to a girl and begin chatting her up if they've had a drink; I was going into battle, not without a sword – if you'd said I was entering the fray without a sword, I would have taken great offence – but certainly without a shield. The mind-boggling thing for me now is to think that, at the time, I was entirely unaware of the difference this would have made to my prospects. How could I not have realized? Well, sober as the chair of a judicial review I made my first faltering steps on the road to romance – a road which, let us not forget, is often described as 'rocky'.

I would not rush to oppose that view.

*

It was during the winter of 1984, my first winter away from home, that I had taken a job at the New Theatre in Cardiff, selling programmes and ice creams during the run of that year's pantomime. *Robin Hood* starred Ruth Madoc and *Crackerjack*'s Stu Francis (at that time on top of the world with his uncompromising catchphrase, 'Ooh, I could crush a grape!') alongside a still relatively unknown double act from Rotherham, the Chuckle Brothers. I was not toiling alone; both Dougray and Dave also had jobs there. The three of us would stand in the foyer of the theatre wearing our Robin Hood hats and holding little wooden toy bows and arrows above our heads as we sang our own little ditty, to the tune of the kids' TV show *Robin Hood*.

> Bows and arrows, bows and arrows, only 90p,
> Bows and arrows, bows and arrows, buy them
>   all from me.
> They're made of wood,
> They fire really good,
> Bows and arrows, bows and arrows,
>   bows and arrows . . .

Anyone who works front of house in the theatre will tell you that it's the best way to see beyond the supposed glitz and glamour of show business as you watch the same performance night after night after matinee. For an actor, it's an invaluable education.

The New Theatre was a receiving house and played host to dozens of touring productions which Dave, Dougray and I would watch, often standing high up at the back of the gods, sometimes weighed down with trays full of ice creams, drinks and chocolates. No greater incentive was needed to shift these overpriced refreshments than the fact that the more you sold, the lighter the tray became. Having shifted the programmes, we would head back to the office and hand over the cash, carefully counting out the remaining unsold items to ensure fair play, before loading up again for the interval. In between these duties you could just stand and watch.

I saw Tom Baker, Tony Haygarth and Dora Bryan in the National Theatre's tour of *She Stoops to Conquer*, was put off opera by the rudeness of the audience at an interminably long production of Wagner's *Ring Cycle* and also watched Ayckbourn's *Way Upstream*, which featured in its cast Norman Rossington, an actor of great interest to me as he had appeared alongside not only The Beatles in *A Hard Day's Night*, but also Elvis in *Double Trouble*. One afternoon, between the matinee and evening performances, I cornered him in the corridor and asked him the question he must by then have been well and truly sick of: 'What was he like?'

Solo acts came too. I remember yawing at the prospect of two nights of Max Boyce. I couldn't have been more wrong; he was astonishing, putting on a show somewhere between stand-up and a rock concert, on both nights performing as though it was the last show of his life. After one performance I happened to pass him on the stairs as he came off the stage and made his way to his dressing room. He looked like a man possessed, drenched in sweat, staring straight ahead. It was a glimpse into a distant world I would inhabit one day. But not yet.

The Cardiff pantomime had an annual tradition it shared with its neighbours at the Grand Theatre in Swansea and across the River Severn at the Hippodrome in Bristol. Each year the three casts, crews and front-of-house staff would hold a huge party in one of those cities. As that year's productions drew to a close, it was the turn of Cardiff to host, and so Dave and I made preparations for the big bash. Unbeknown to me, Dave had his eye on Jacque and had invited her as his guest, telling me that she would be bringing her friend Lisa. Lisa enjoyed some celebrity status within the college, having already appeared in a film with no less a person than Richard Gere. If you watch his Second World War movie, *Yanks*, towards the end as the aforementioned Americans begin to leave the Yorkshire town and travel home, a girl is seen crying and waving from a railway bridge. That was Lisa.

The four of us poured into Dave's tinny little black Fiat Panda and crossed our fingers that we would make the journey unscathed. We headed across Cardiff and arrived at the hotel, quickly and effortlessly mingling with Ruth Madoc, Stu Francis, Barry and Paul Chuckle and even Alfred Marks, recently arrived from Bristol, before getting some drinks and finding a table. I was seated next to Jacque and we began to talk. We talked and we talked and we talked. We really did talk a great deal; we got on like a house ablaze, its occupants running screaming out on to the street. I thought I might have noticed a few disgruntled looks from Dave, but couldn't be sure. He seemed happy enough, chatting to Lisa, and even happier when, towards the end of the evening, the DJ called out the number of the winning raffle ticket as

Jacque and I made our way to the dance floor. Lucky Dave was sole winner of a beautiful, extremely limited-edition plate, celebrating another successful year for the triumvirate of pantomimes. As he carried his commemorative crockery proudly back to our table, he looked across the room to the dance floor, to see Jacque and me entwined in each other's arms, kissing. He wasn't happy, even with his plate – which, in light of recent events, had taken on the role of consolation prize.

We left the do in Dave's car with the placatory plate and, if I'm being honest, a bit of an atmosphere. It would have made sense, geographically speaking, to drop Jacque off last. I was against this as it would have meant leaving her alone in the car with Dave once Lisa and I had been jettisoned. I somehow managed to convince our hard-done-by driver that it would make much more sense to drop her off first. In so doing, I ensured that she remained beyond the clutches of my dear friend. And so it was that Jacque and I began to see each other. Tentatively, at first.

It was a week or so later that we went back to her place, a room in a shared house on the prophetically named Colum Road. I stayed the night – rather nervously at first, although I got the hang of things after a while. Jacque's room was at the back of the ground floor; at the front was a room taken by her friend Tracey and her boyfriend Gary. If either of them wished to use the loo during the night they had to come through Jacque's room; this gave the proceedings a bit of an edge (and, I suppose, must at times have resulted in what can only be described as an early form of dogging).

As I've said, I was tentative. With the light turned off we slipped out of our clothes – quite quickly, I recall – and jumped into bed, where Jacque soon discovered that I'd kept my trousers on, just to be sure. She expressed her surprise at this, and I reacted as though it was something of a shock to me too: 'Where did they come from?' I got out of bed in the dark and returned, trouser-less.

As the situation developed, Jacque was surprised once more to discover that, while my trousers were now languishing in a crumpled heap on the floor, I nonetheless still had my pants on.

I explained that I was just being careful, before submitting to full disclosure . . .

The following morning I borrowed her bike and cycled back across town, along the pedestrianized Queen Street and down on to Newport Road, a huge smile on my face as I pedalled. I looked at the people as I rode by and laughed out loud at the thought of them having no idea where I'd just come from or what a momentous night I'd enjoyed. When I play the moment back now, it has a joyous, filmic quality to it; the sun is shining, birds are singing and music fills the air. I think I knew then, in a rare case of self-awareness, that a milestone had been reached – one which I would never forget.

In the fullness of time Jacque was enticed up to my top-floor sub-zero love nest and managed, with admirable foresight, to see past the cold-water kitchen and its collection of empty milk bottles, the damp-stained walls and the tinned-food diet to the handsome young man beyond. The house had a strict 'no girlfriends' policy, which Mrs Williams made no secret of. I'd already got on the wrong side of my perfectly reasonable landlady earlier that week when I openly flouted her hot-water rota by turning on the immersion heater one afternoon for an impromptu bath. I further angered her one morning when Jacque, having stayed over the night before, was sneaking down the stairs and out of the house. She quietly slipped through the front door, closing it carefully behind her before silently turning the handle on the door of the porch. It wouldn't budge. Mrs Williams had cunningly locked the porch and hidden the key, leaving any unwelcome sex maniacs trapped in the tiny glass cell with only a local property paper for comfort until it pleased her to release them. Nothing was ever said regarding this breaking of the rules, although I did suffer an icy stare as I returned home that evening.

This whole wonderful 'having a girlfriend' experience was all new to me. Most of my fellow students had had girlfriends prior to coming away to college, and some of them were already working their way towards personal bests when it came to bedposts and notches. I, on the other hand, slipped happily into a new world of doing things together and having someone else to share thoughts and experiences with.

We stayed together for two years and lived in a variety of flats and houses. When my time with Mrs Williams came to an end, I moved to an appalling *Young Ones*-style student house in Grangetown on a busy main road where heavily laden lorries and trucks charged past at all hours. We slept on a mattress on the floor while the architecture student in the room below worked to the sound of heavy-metal music turned up to eleven. I would wander downstairs bleary-eyed, knock on his door and ask him to turn it down, while he stood there looking as though playing music that loud at that time of night was the most reasonable thing anyone had ever done. The windows rattled through the night from the vibrations of the passing traffic, and I sellotaped cling film around their frames to keep out the cold. We'd stay up late and huddle under the duvet, listening in the darkness to Tom Waits and Crystal Gayle on the soundtrack album *One from the Heart.* The trucks rumbled by and the noise from the room below seeped up through the floorboards, but we were wrapped up and safe in our own little world. 'It's got to be love, I've never felt this way.'

II

Meanwhile, college life went on. With the exception of the more academic classes, like Theatre History, it was a doddle. Being able to make people laugh made everything that much easier, and already knowing what I wanted to do once I left college also helped. I knew that I wanted to be involved in comedy in one form or another, and I had a naively comforting belief that everything would be fine and that work would somehow come along for me. It's virtually impossible, when studying acting as a student, to have any grasp of what life will be like in the outside world. There are always a few lucky ones who fall into work straight away, and some, luckier still, who find fame and fortune. But for the vast majority it is a dispiriting, endless slog of letters sent, CVs posted and auditions applied for – usually with very little coming back in the way of encouragement.

While in college, students are given the opportunity to play a wide range of parts. This is excellent experience, allowing them to stretch and test themselves, but it's very unrepresentative of the real world. Having left the comfort of the college walls, actors are generally cast in accordance with how they look. Perhaps it would be more accurate to say that they are cast in relation to how they are perceived. I wouldn't learn this for some years yet, as my hoped-for career as an actor would have to wait while I took a few unexpected detours.

After our success on the *Level Three* radio show, I had become known to the Powers That Be (Powers That Were? Powers That Beed? *Powerful Bees?*) at BBC Radio Wales, and wasted no opportunity to make a nuisance of myself and remind them that I was eager and able when it came to radio. This persistence paid off one day when David Peet, the Director of General Programmes at the station, asked me to come in and audition for the role of holiday relief presenter on a twenty-minute mid-morning quiz show called *Bank Raid*. The programme involved a host talking to contestants on the phone and asking them questions about general knowledge. Successful answers helped the contestants progress towards the 'vault' where more successful answers would lead to an eventual winner, announced through the cunning deployment of a pre-recorded sound effect – in this case, the sound of coins showering down from a great height, signifying the sudden acquisition of not inconsiderable wealth. In reality the contestants won a book token.

The audition went well, and the job was mine. I replaced a staggeringly confident and capable young man named Mark Wordley, who flew abroad to his honeymoon. Were it not for this honeymoon, I might never have begun my career at BBC Wales where I stayed, on and off, for the next six or seven years.

Hosting *Bank Raid* was not a difficult job. The production team did all the hard work, finding the contestants, sourcing the questions and grouping them into categories.

All I had to do was chat to the callers in a cheery manner, ask the right questions and play the correct effects cartridges. I managed this with ease and was eventually offered the job of hosting the show permanently. This would mean leaving college early, pretty much halfway through my three-year course, and without a qualification in the form of the diploma we were all studying for. I didn't spend too long weighing up my options; it seemed clear to me that there was only one. It was a *job*, paid work, and in radio, which I had always loved. Surely it wouldn't be difficult, once established as a broadcaster, to move across into the world of acting?

Hmm.

Readers familiar with the popular ITV game show *Family Fortunes* would do well at this moment to conjure up the distinctive sound of a wrong answer.

'Rob says it would be easy to slide across into acting after being a radio presenter. Our survey says . . .'

I didn't know it at the time, but it would prove very difficult indeed to make the leap. For now, it didn't matter. I was working; I had money coming in, and life looked good. I had to tell the college that I was leaving and worried enormously that, when doing so, I would see a look in their eyes that told me they thought I was making the biggest mistake of my young life. I sat across a table from a couple of the senior staff members and told them my decision. In replying, one of them made the point that they were worried that I was drifting towards light entertainment. *Nonsense*, I thought to myself. Within two years I was bounding down a stairway in front of a studio audience, my hair bouffant, my jacket blouson, as

I turned grinning to camera and welcomed viewers at home to a Saturday teatime quiz show called *Invasion*. Touché.

I don't know if the cautionary words of my tutors were a real concern to me; I was too excited by the prospect of work, by the idea of getting out there into the real world and paying my way. I rented a large ground-floor flat on Cathedral Road. I'd coveted these huge, bay-windowed, high-ceilinged abodes for some time and moved in as soon as I could. It was only once tied into a contract that I realized that I would be sharing the place with a large family of confident, outgoing slugs. The road runs parallel with the River Taff and, I was told later, this was the reason so many slugs wanted to make friends with me. You wouldn't see them during the day – they were busy, I suppose, or sleeping off the excess of the previous night – but come the evening they treated the place as their own. They would climb the walls of the bathroom and creep slowly across the bedroom floor under cover of darkness, only to be discovered when my bare foot came down unknowingly on their soft jelly-like form and ended their short life.

Aside from the slugs it was a good place to live, mid-way between the city centre and the BBC – where I found it possible to spend a large amount of my time, quite disproportionate to the length of the show I was hosting. *Bank Raid* was a small portion of a longer, mid-morning magazine programme called *Street Life*, hosted on alternating days by folk musician and broadcaster Frank Hennessy and rugby legend and broadcaster Ray Gravell. The brilliant Ray had played for Wales and the

British Lions, as well as being part of the Llanelli team that had famously beaten the All Blacks of New Zealand by 9–3, back in 1972. (The town's Wikipedia entry proudly notes that the score would have been 10–3 in today's scoring system.) Ray was one of the loveliest people you could ever hope to meet, a huge gentle bear of a man who made everyone he spoke to feel that they were the most important person in the world. He was a very honest man and enjoyed our handovers, when we would switch from his show to my little section.

I once asked him, on air, 'How's it hanging?' I honestly had no idea what the phrase meant; I thought it was a figure of speech.

There was an awkward pause, a moment's dead air, before Ray responded with admirable frankness, 'Well, since you ask, to the left.'

I stayed in touch with Ray right up until the end of his too-short life. Years later, when I had achieved some success and had begun to make a name for myself, he would phone me out of the blue, for no other reason than to tell me he was proud of me and to congratulate me on how things were going. People often call out of the blue once you've found success, to wish you well. While I don't doubt their sincerity, the conversation often ends with something along the lines of, 'Oh yes, I know what I meant to ask you; we wanted to go and see Peter Kay, but it's sold out. You couldn't get hold of any tickets, could you?' It's fine – I do it myself – but Ray never once had any such epilogue to his calls. He really was just calling to say well done.

Ray particularly liked it when I insulted him. While we

worked together at Radio Wales, I would make him laugh with my impressions of Al Pacino. These, in essence, amounted to no more than me pulling a vaguely Pacino-esque face and shouting, 'Oh, Ray! You piece of shit! Fuck you!'

He loved it. 'Aw . . . crikey! Tell me to fuck off! Tell me to fuck off!'

In 2000, at the age of forty-nine, Ray was diagnosed with diabetes, which eventually resulted in him losing his toe. This was followed by the loss of his foot. I saw him a little while after the amputation, when we both appeared on a television show hosted by our friend Max Boyce. Ray now had a prosthetic lower leg, on which was emblazoned the crest of his beloved Llanelli Rugby Club. He had lost weight, but was full of beans; he moved quickly on his new foot and, as usual, was only concerned with how I was doing, how I was feeling.

Two weeks later, he died after suffering a heart attack while on holiday in Spain. He was a truly great man, and the world was a better place with him in it.

I hadn't been at Radio Wales for long when I was offered the opportunity to take over the early-morning slot: six thirty to seven thirty. To start with, as had been the case with *Bank Raid*, I sat in for a week while the regular host, Roy Noble, took a break.

This would have been 1985 or 1986; compact discs were beginning to emerge but, like many radio stations, BBC Wales was still using mostly vinyl records. Each day I would pick up the programme box. This was a sturdy black case, big enough to hold about twenty or thirty long-playing records, with a large and – to me, at least – strangely intimidating BBC logo stamped on the front. It contained the records and the running order for the next morning's show. The running order was a script of sorts, which listed the sequence of the records along with any other features within the programme, such as news, sport and weather. Next to the title of the record was printed its duration and the length of the introduction, also whether the record 'ended' or faded – essential information for any disc jockey serious about his craft.

Once back at Slug Towers, I would sit at my record player and practise my links, i.e. what I planned to say in between the records. In the very early days I even used to script these seemingly off-the-cuff and certainly inconsequential bits of chat. Frankly, it terrified me. Most people getting to host a national radio show would have risen up the ranks of hospital or perhaps local radio. Their on-air personality would have formed gradually, at its own pace, away from the pressures of such a relatively large audience. Here I was, thrown in at the deep end.

On my very first morning, as I approached the Greenwich Mean Time pips at seven o'clock, I trotted out my pre-written line.

'You're listening to BBC Radio Wales, I'm Rob Jones, it's seven o'clock . . .'

Nothing.

Silence.

I'd peaked too soon.

I started again. 'I'm Rob Jones and you're lis–'

BEEP, BEEP, BEEP, BEEEEEEEEEP.

Oh God.

Those early shows were a very bumpy ride; I would get quite worked up and panicked at the prospect of making a link run to a specific time. For a long while, as ridiculous as it sounds, the sight of a needle three-quarters of the way across a forty-five rpm single would bring on a mild but effective bout of anxiety.

If we're going to talk about anxiety, I should tell you that all through my broadcasting years I would suffer the radio equivalent of the classic actor's nightmare where he or she is struggling to reach the stage and can hear their cue being delivered in the distance. Or they arrive onstage in the wrong costume. Or they don't know the play they are meant to be appearing in. I've subsequently enjoyed the delights of all these types of an actor's nightmares since working onstage with my stand-up tours. Back in my radio days a good night's sleep would often be hijacked by vivid images of me sitting in front of the mixing desk, a turntable at each side of me, as I frantically searched the programme box in vain, unable to find the next record. Scarier still was the one where I had the record in my hands but couldn't cue it up as the turntable was on fire. Meanwhile, on the other turntable, the needle was the dreaded three-quarters of the way across the disc.

These anxieties aside, I suppose I settled into radio pretty well. I bought my first house, on a new estate just minutes away from the BBC, a little two-bedroom starter home for the colossal price of £28,000. I felt like I was Elvis, taking hold of the keys to Graceland. This house taught me my first lesson in not believing everything an advertiser tells you. When walking around the show home, unless someone has told you otherwise, it's perfectly reasonable to look at the furnishings and take them at face value. Yes, this room really is big enough for a double bed *and* a chest of drawers. No, my friend, look closer. See how that double bed *looks* like a double bed, in many ways it *is* a double bed, but on closer inspection it's a pretty damn small double bed. If you're being generous, you might call it a huge single bed, the furniture equivalent of Al Pacino in *Dick Tracy*, where he played 'Big Boy' Caprice, the world's tallest dwarf. And that chest of drawers, you're right, is just that little bit smaller than a chest of drawers should really be.

But hey, it was a house, it was mine. And, as far as I could see, there were no slugs.

Jacque and I were together through these early days at the BBC, and we would get on the train on a Sunday and head home to Neath for lunch with Mum, Dad and Pete. I delighted in showing her parts of Wales: the Brecon Beacons, the Gower Peninsula and, closer to home, the Aberdulais Falls. We once went for a walk along the canal and found what I thought was a clearing, where we began to enjoy each other's company in a particularly enthusiastic manner. On reflection, I should have realized that it was a very long and narrow clearing; I suppose some people would call it a path. Certainly the man who came walking along it towards us would have done. The two of us ran, clothes in hand, away from the poor Welsh walker who probably still tells the story of the day he stumbled upon two lovebirds on the bank of the canal.

I went to Scotland for the first of several trips to meet and stay with Jacque's large family. It seems curious to me now that in honour of the visit – in essence, the first time I would meet the parents of a girlfriend – I bought some slip-on leather shoes to replace the trainers I normally wore. It was a mark of respect, I suppose, a desire to create a good impression. The family lived in Jacque's childhood home, a big double-fronted sandstone Edwardian house in the Pollokshields area of Glasgow. It seemed to me to be some kind of rambling manor house and was home to a variety of family members. There were her mother and father of course, as well as her brothers Andrew, John, Simon and Patrick. Aunty Eileen had a room on the ground floor and Uncle Michael, the priest, was an occasional resident with his own room on the first floor.

I got on especially well with Simon and Patrick, who were both on my wavelength when it came to humour. As I recall, Simon was a fellow enthusiast for the cinematic musings of my hero Sylvester Stallone. Indeed, it was in Glasgow and with Jacque that I went to see *Rambo: First Blood Part II*, having queued round the block to get in. I'd like to tell you that I considered it inferior to *First Blood* and indicative of a general decline in Mr Stallone's output. But I can't. I loved it.

Jacque's brother Patrick was great, with a superb dry wit. He had been born with arthrogryposis, a congenital disorder that had left him with a curvature of the spine, and so he moved around the house in an electric wheelchair. There was no trace of the 'Does he take sugar?' syndrome here, though, thanks to his lovely self-effacing but also stinging wit. As he was transferred into or out of his chair, he would cry, 'Dignity! Always dignity!' (This was a quote from Gene Kelly's character in *Singin' in the Rain* who, having found fame and fortune, then glosses over his slightly dubious past with the cry of, 'Dignity!') This derived from the many occasions when Patrick was left rather undignified – perhaps shoved in a luggage rack when his wheelchair was attended to, or being manhandled by a taxi driver. He and his brothers greatly enjoyed the evening when we all sat down to dinner and somehow Jacque's polite Welsh boyfriend managed to sit on his food, the plate having mysteriously found its way on to his chair.

I think it was on that same weekend that Jacque and I cunningly decided to spend the Friday night together at a hotel in Glasgow before I would arrive at the house on the Saturday morning, claiming to have travelled up the night before on the sleeper train. Jacque's absence was explained by her having attended a friend's party and slept over there. Her brothers were of course aware of the scam, and greatly enjoyed almost letting the cat out of the bag at dinner.

'So, Rob, you look a bit tired. Were you up all night on that train?'

'Well, I was a bit, yes . . .'

'It must have been hard to get your head down?'

'Well, no, I managed to in the end . . .'

'I suppose the train, it just keeps going all night, does it?'

'You could say that, yes.'

If Jacque's parents were aware of our transgressions,

they didn't let on (though I suspect they were far more knowing than I realized). As was always the case, I got on splendidly with Mr and Mrs Gilbride and looked forward to welcoming Kathleen to Cardiff when she came down to Wales to see her daughter in a play. This would also be the setting for her first meeting with my parents.

The play was *The Hard Man* and took place at the Sherman Theatre, scene of my tiny roles with the National Youth Theatre of Wales. It concerned the story of the infamous Jimmy Boyle and much, if not all, of the action was confined to his prison cell. Jacque played his wife and – much to my alarm, dismay and embarrassment – on the occasion of my parents meeting Jacque's mum for the first time (with me sitting between them in the darkness of the auditorium), we witnessed the lovely spectacle of the lead actor stripping naked and indulging in what can only be described as an enthusiastic dirty protest. He slapped his hopefully substitute doo-doo around the walls of his cell with gusto, like Rolf Harris in the grip of a breakdown. My poor parents. Jacque's poor mum. We went out for a meal after the play; it was very nice, though as I recall, when it came to dessert, we skipped the chocolate.

Jacque was my first girlfriend, and first girlfriends are only around for so long. We split, saying that the parting was only for a while. She was struggling to find acting work in Cardiff and I was thinking that I was settling down too soon. She sensed that I was getting a bit twitchy, and her older head was wise enough to be the one to say that we should break up for a while and then see what happened. Although it was what I wanted, I was still broken-hearted as I drove away from Euston station after putting her on the train back to Glasgow and her old life.

We hooked up again six months later to go on holiday to Spain with her brother Simon and his in-laws. But on our return, we called it a day.

Meanwhile, my six or seven years at BBC Wales had begun. It's a period in my life about which I've often been a little dismissive whenever asked how I began my circuitous route to here. I have to say that, at the time, I enjoyed it for the most part very much. I did a huge amount of work on a wide variety of shows, both radio and TV. As a presenter I hosted radio shows at various points of the day and week; I also worked on radio as an actor, usually in sketches that called for a range of voices and impressions. On TV I hosted the aforementioned quiz show *Invasion*: two teams competing to win county-sized chunks of a large flashing map, hindered only by my appalling pronunciation of many of the Welsh place names. There was one in particular that I struggled with.

Have a go yourself, see how you fare . . . Glyndyfrdwy.

Quite.

Even the most cunning linguist would surely have to concede that the word represents a challenge. Time and again I pronounced it Glyn Duvrudwee, much to the visible annoyance of the fluently Welsh-speaking floor manager, when I should of course have been saying Glyn Duverdoy. If you'd like to see this humiliation for yourself, and have had the foresight to purchase the electronic version of this book, then press here now and enjoy my rolled-up, blouson-jacket-sleeved embarrassment at your leisure.

My problem with the Welsh language was that I'd never managed to get to grips with it at school (where learning it was compulsory), and at home it had always had dreadfully dull associations. Whereas now I think it is something to be celebrated and hung on to – so obviously a vital part of our cultural identity – back then it was the language spoken on the news programme in Wales shown in place of *Batman* or some such glamorous TV show. To have grown up an English-speaking Welsh child in Wales in the 1970s was to know the befuddled agony of staring at the screen as the continuity announcer declared, 'Now on BBC1 *Batman/Star Trek/Land of the Giants*, except for viewers in Wales . . .' and a newsreader began, in his native tongue, bringing us up to speed with the latest developments in our homeland (a high proportion of which seemed to feature reporters in rainswept fields addressing the camera as a herd of cows lolled around behind them).

Missing *Batman* was a body blow. It seemed, on the rare occasions that I did get to see it, to be impossibly colourful and glamorous, a world away from a cold wet field just outside Carmarthen. I went through a period of becoming fixated on the show, dreaming of one day owning a house with a study in which a bookcase would slide back to reveal two poles, down which I could slide to my hideout. Hiding was a recurring theme during my childhood, with a dream I kept having in which I sat concealed in a small submarine, possibly yellow, parked on the grass at Woodside. From inside my vessel I could see what was going on around me via the periscope, while I remained invisible. This was a most agreeable state. With the benefit of hindsight, my fixating on poles and submarines seems worryingly Freudian. Let's move on.

Alongside *Invasion* I played a few odd comedy characters on a pop-culture youth show called *Juice*, became a roving reporter on a Sunday-morning magazine programme, *See You Sunday*, and made an ill-fated cinema commercial for a local jewellery firm. All this was going on while I noticed contemporaries of mine from college begin to make progress as actors. Several of my friends found work at varying levels, but it was only two who achieved what I'd call real success on a large and noticeable scale: Dougray and Hugo Blick. Dougray found theatre and television work with quite indecent haste, while Hugo bagged the role of the young Joker in Tim Burton's wonderful though pole-free *Batman*.

During my time at Radio Wales, I spent a couple of years on the early show, and several on a Saturday-morning youth programme, which I absolutely loved doing but hated listening back to (I sounded like such a buffoon). It was a laugh though. I was earning money and living an easy life with little responsibility, breezing in and out of the BBC at my leisure and, in the process, building friendships that would last for years. I became very friendly with Mark Wordley, for whom I'd originally stood in on *Bank Raid*. He continued to present and produce shows at the station and was responsible for my first TV presenting role on *Invasion*, which he produced. I also at this time met the man who was to become my best friend, Rhys John.

Rhys was working with Mark, and I clearly remember

my first sighting of him as I was being shown around the offices on the second floor of Broadcasting House. I popped my head around the door of his office and there he was, in his leather jacket, unshaven, with mountains of long black hair; he looked like he was enjoying a day off from his main job as a roadie for Motörhead. Just as I had when first sighting James, my best friend at college, I thought to myself, *Hmm, we're not going to be spending much time together*. Rhys, like Mark, was both a presenter and a producer and would go on to take charge of my Saturday morning show, a job which allowed us acres of time to do very little in the way of work. We would slope off in the middle of the day to play golf, go tenpin bowling or loll around in the health club at the recently built Holiday Inn where I was a member.

We were two young men in our early twenties, living the life of someone in his sixties who has retired through ill health and is slowly rehabilitating himself after a heart-related incident. Looking back on this period, I get a little cross with myself when I think of all the time I wasted, when I could have been more focused and working on an act. But I think I was such a late developer that it could only ever have happened the way it did.

Once I'd been a regular presence on the radio for a while, I began to gain enough of a name to receive the odd invitation to attend or host local events. These requests would come straight to the office at the BBC as I'd yet to find representation. Rather than deal with potential employers myself, I invented an agent and would play him on the phone.

Richard Knight was part of Knight and Day Management and spoke with a gruff London accent, a kind of Arthur Daley figure who could demand more money than I would have been able to ask for with a straight face. I'm ashamed to say that he would sometimes manage to get a modest fee from societies who'd asked me along despite obviously not having much spare cash knocking around. I remember one time calling a very nice, rather timid-sounding lady who wanted me to host an evening for underprivileged kids. I managed to get a fee for what I now realize was a charity evening.

'Is that Mrs Jenkins?'

'Yes.'

'Hello, Mrs Jenkins, this is Richard Knight of Knight and Day Management. I'm calling about your letter to Rob.'

'Oh yes –'

'Now I've had a look at the date and I think we might be able to manage something, but I've got to bring up the sordid subject of money.'

'Oh well, the thing is, Mr Knight –'

'Please, call me Richard.'

'All right, Richard, the thing is –'

'Let's go for Dick.'

'Ooh –'

'Can you go for Dick? Are you comfortable with Dick?'

'Well, I suppose so . . . Dick.'

'Now the thing is, Bobby is a saint, he'd do it for nothing, but I wouldn't be doing my job if I didn't try and squeeze a little bit out of you.'

'Right.'

'So, how about this? And I'm not going to squeeze you tight.'

'No.'

'We won't say a pony, we won't say a monkey. 'Cause you're both Welsh, let's call it a sheep. Can you handle a sheep?'

'How much is a sheep exactly?'

'Oh, that's very generous! A hundred it is . . .'

What appalling behaviour.

While at Radio Wales I became friendly with the teams on the various programmes I was involved with. My producer on *Bank Raid*, Tessa, had a younger sister who would come to stay with her at weekends. Martina and I first met in a pub on Queen Street that she and Tessa would frequent when she was in Cardiff. In those days, the Vaults was a smoky kind of place. On this night in question I had a cold, and was sitting there at the table amongst our crowd of friends feeling a little withdrawn and detached. In an echo of my first meeting with Jacque – although without, this time, the presence of even a solitary Chuckle Brother – Martina and I talked and talked and talked.

When she came back down to Cardiff a few weekends later, I contrived to muscle in on things and just happen to be around her. This second meeting prompted us to begin a correspondence, on paper of course (email was still the stuff of *Star Trek*), in which I would send her Opal Fruits and, eventually, in a more provocative gesture, a single Rolo. Younger readers will be blind to the significance of such a bold, sensual act – unaware, as they undoubtedly will be, of the advertising campaign of the late eighties in which viewers were asked to consider whether they loved anyone enough to give them their last Rolo.

The letters became more frequent and I began to search for a reason to find myself in London, where Martina was working at the time, so that I might be able to say, 'I just happen to be in the area, shall I drop in?' The opportunity arose thanks to the Brit Awards when the radio show I was hosting on a Saturday morning managed to get a ticket to the event, held that year at the Royal Albert Hall. I went up on the train, feeling very important indeed. The ticket had come via a record company and I wondered how close to the stage I'd find myself. As it was a record company ticket, I imagined my seat would be rather well placed, right in the thick of it. As it turned out, I was way up high – about as far away from the stage as it was possible to be while still remaining in the building. As the crow flies in a straight line, some of the surrounding houses were closer to the stage than I was.

Noel Edmonds hosted, and there were live performances from The Who and the Bee Gees. But all I could think about was the fact that, once the show was over, I was heading to Fulham to see Martina at the house where she was working as a nanny. In the end, my excitement at the prospect of romance won out over the excitement of being in the presence of Barry, Robin, Maurice et al. I slipped away early, got into a taxi and headed over to Fulham. Just as in my first digs in Cardiff,

Martina had a room at the top of the house, although this was a slightly posher, very Fulham house. One of her employers was a Right Honourable; I took against them on hearing that, when the new baby was six weeks old, the parents went to the West Indies for two weeks, leaving Martina with the three-year-old and the new-born with a maternity nurse. They didn't phone home once.

This wasn't on my mind as I wove through the London streets in the back of a black cab before slipping into the house and up to the top floor in blatant disregard of the 'no gentlemen callers' rule. Two hours and one kiss later, I was back at the Regent Palace Hotel in Piccadilly. I went to sleep in complete ignorance of the fact that I had just kissed my future wife.

The next day I had returned to Radio Wales, and was regaling Rhys with my exciting news – although, to him, seeing Noel Edmonds in the flesh was not that big a deal. I was soon heading up the motorway at every opportunity, excited both at the prospect of seeing Martina and at the added bonus of getting to hear Radio One in FM. I remember in these pre-satellite-navigation days getting lost in the traffic around Fulham; the sun is shining, and Aztec Camera are singing 'Somewhere in My Heart'.

Martina's visits to Cardiff became more frequent, and after a time she moved into my little house by the roundabout in Llandaff.

I was coasting along nicely when my time with the station came to an abrupt and rather ungainly end. A new boss was announced and, in the manner of all new bosses, this one wanted to make some changes. I had known Megan Emery a little already; she was the wife of Chris Stuart, long-time host of the breakfast news show on the channel and sometime Radio Two presenter. When she took over at the top, everyone was a little nervous with regard to the security of their position. In his capacity as producer of my show, Rhys went off to meet her for a chat about the future. He breezed back into our office twenty minutes later and uttered the words that still make us laugh, 'Rob, you're safe.'

Within a week Megan told me that my contract was not being renewed. She did, however – and this has foxed me every day since she said it – ask if I would like to make a documentary about lawns. Well, I wasn't happy. I took it very personally. I had a month or so of shows left to run and I'm ashamed to say that my anger got the better of me one Saturday morning when talking on air to a caller whose words were being obscured by the sound of a dog yapping in the background.

'Sorry, Rob, that's our dog.'

'Oh, really. What's it called?'

'She's called Megan.'

'Really? We've got a bitch called Megan here too.'

I know. Unbelievable. She didn't deserve that.

And off I went, never to return – until Megan eventually moved on, and a new editor took her place.

Within a few months of leaving Radio Wales, I was running out of money. I put my car up for sale, a brand-new VW Polo bought a year or so earlier from the Volkswagen garage in Swansea where Dad was working. I went to meet a man at Red Dragon, the local independent radio station, handing him my demo reel and trying to appear simultaneously nonchalant and keen. It came to nothing. I was sending off dozens of letters in response to programmes mentioned in the *Guardian*'s 'Media' section. (I still have a ring binder full of rejections. Perhaps they form part of the e-book – press the screen and see what happens.)

Eventually I wandered across the corridor at the BBC to the Continuity Department and managed to wangle a try-out as a continuity announcer. This job basically involved getting up at five o'clock in the morning, sitting in a darkened room surrounded by television screens and waiting until the time came to say, 'Now the news where you are . . .' Or, more excitingly, 'Let's catch up with goings-on in Ramsay Street . . . It's *Neighbours*.'

The announcer was also responsible for the technical side of things – opting in and out of what was being broadcast on the national BBC network, and making sure that the people of Wales got the Welsh news and not the latest happenings in Bristol and the West. This was the very mistake I made on one occasion, just towards the end of my shift. I slunk out of the building like a murderer trying to leave the scene of the crime undetected, although deep inside I felt I'd done us all a favour. The Bristol news was likely to be considerably sunnier than the Welsh – which, in those days, I would have considered to be rainswept and concerned primarily with redundancy and illness.

This may have said more about me than about the state of the nation.

I began to work continuity shifts quite regularly on a freelance basis and was ready to sign a longer-term contract when the phone rang one afternoon. I was in bed recovering from a strenuous morning's announcements. It was my agent – my first-ever agent, Siân Trenberth, of Siân-Lucy Management – calling to tell me that I had an audition for a job in London. London! This was exciting. London was the Promised Land, the land of opportunities, the gateway to proper presenting work. Or even to some acting work.

What would this audition be for?

Theatre, television, maybe even a film?

It was none of the above.

Siân explained that there was a new venture starting up on the recently launched Sky TV, called the Satellite Shop. It was home shopping, as glimpsed occasionally on the kind of programmes Clive James used to host, where viewers were encouraged to laugh at some of the idiotic shows that had made their way onto the airwaves in America but which we Brits were far too smart to fall for. My initial disappointment soon gave way to excitement at the prospect of auditioning in London and the belief that the job, were I to get it, would at least be a job in London. It would be a job in TV, and it could be the first step towards bigger and better things.

I took the train to London and went to audition in a building just behind Oxford Street. The would-be sales people were set the task of talking to camera and selling a few items handed to them by the production team just minutes earlier. Then, just when they thought it was over, they were asked to sell anything that came to mind. Determined not to be thrown by this, I calmly took off my shoes and began to sell my socks. 'Well, if you're looking for something special between your foot and your shoe, you've come to the right place . . .' I made an exemplary job of spontaneous sock-selling and, within a few days, was given the joyous news that the job was mine. This was an instant fix on the money front; I went from £30 a day as a continuity announcer to £150 a day as a proud ambassador of home shopping.

The programme was broadcast from Sky's new head-quarters in Osterley, West London, and ran from eight in the morning till two in the afternoon. My parents back in Wales bought a satellite dish in celebration and watched as much of the output as they could bring themselves to. My grandmother even went so far as to buy something (no doubt in the hope of securing my position with my new employers). Initially, the producers built a set in the style of a house so that garden products were sold in the garden, kitchen gadgets in the kitchen and so on, all under the glare of harsh studio lighting. I suspect the lighting was brighter even than the usual television studio lights, so as to shine on the products and make them sparkle. Lighting this bright meant heavy make-up for the presenters; whenever I think back to my time on the shop floor, it's always accompanied by the smell of the make-up as it sizzled and melted under the lights.

The presenters would all wear earpieces through which we could hear instructions from the gallery where the director sat, choosing his shots. Usually this would be a calm voice saying something along the lines of, 'That's it, just hold the watch up a bit . . .' But when things went wrong, the challenge for the presenter would be to maintain a calm and collected exterior while all hell was breaking loose in their ear. On one occasion, I was selling a lawnmower – one of the old hover types – in the garden set. As I nattered away, scaling new heights of insincere inanity, I decided to turn the device over and show how easy it was to take the blade off and replace it. As I began to undo the big central locking nut with the handy plastic spanner, a chorus of doom built to a crescendo in my ear, '*Nooooo!*' It was too late; I was committed now. As the voices reached their peak, the nut gave way and fell to the bright-green AstroTurf floor, closely followed by around ten separate component parts, which clanked and jangled into an unruly heap on the ground. I of course had no idea how to put it all back together again, although I tried for a while and succeeded in making things look even worse.

Another time, again in the garden, I was joined by an expert demonstrator from Black & Decker who was standing behind me, showing the viewers how easy it was to use one of their electric sanding devices on our in-studio fence. As we chatted away about how this appliance had enriched our lives, I enquired as to its unrivalled safety record.

'Oh yes, Rob, this is one of the safest devices that . . . *Argh! Bloody hell!*'

He'd inadvertently used the thing on his hand. Blood began to gush forth on to our pristine set.

After several months of broadcasting what was essentially a magazine programme with a bit of selling stuck on the end, the producers decided it was time, in light of poor sales figures, to get tough and kick some retail ass. A home-shopping guru was brought over from Hawaii. Her name was Renée, and she was a diminutive powerhouse of selling. None of us presenters could be said to have lived for selling; we were doing the job because it was all we could get at the time, and it paid the bills. Renée taught us the basics: the importance of energy when selling; the importance of selling the benefit, not the product. Tell people what this product is going to make them *feel*, how it will improve their lives. We were told to tease the viewers with what was coming up in the show, not by telling them directly but by being vague.

So, rather than saying that we had a gold dress watch for men coming up, we would say, 'If you're looking for some really special jewellery for a big occasion, something that's going to make you look and feel great, we've got just the thing . . .'

It sounds silly, but I'm here to tell you it works.

The other thing was to hammer home the price. The

prices were always structured so as to give the appearance of being reduced.

'This wonderful item [that you've managed to live without] was seventy-five pounds, it's now just fifty pounds! A huge Home Shopping saving of twenty-five pounds!'

And to create a sense of urgency, 'If you don't order now, you're going to miss out. Pick up the phone! Do it now!'

Some of the other presenters considered Renée to be a little vulgar and crass; I thought she was great. With Dad being a salesman, it's probably in my blood. I was actually quite good at the selling – in fact, they told me I was the best. So there. Well done, me.

In spite of our newfound skills, the programme began to flounder and three of the presenters were let go. This left just four of us to soldier on until a month or so later, when we were told we could all take the week off while some restructuring took place. The restructuring was thorough and, within days, the whole enterprise folded. Although television shopping was never on my list of ambitions, and I now cringe whenever I see a clip or am reminded of it, the whole episode was an interesting time for me. It was my first introduction to London, to the media outside Wales, and while it was obviously on the extreme outskirts of the outskirts of where I wanted to be, perhaps comically so, it was nonetheless a move to London.

I was meeting new types of people; I remember the excitement of going shopping for clothes with the stylist. A stylist! I'd never heard of a stylist before, let alone met one. She was a tall, willowy, dark-haired girl and she whisked me off to Next on Kensington High Street. Although I'd already been lucky enough to have experienced Next on Queen Street in Cardiff, this felt different, the stylist gliding around the store as though she owned it, and I was naively impressed by the whole thing.

It was while on the Shopping Channel that I changed my name from Rob Jones to Rob Brydon. I had joined the actors' union, Equity, and there was already a Rob Jones treading some boards somewhere, so I took my middle name, Mum's maiden name, instead.

Now that I had a tiny, tentative foothold in the metropolis, I began to make cautious progress – one step up and two steps back – towards my destination: comedy, shining like a mythical Camelot on a distant hill. While at Sky I had left my Cardiff agent and joined the books of Jerry Hicks, who was based in London. Jerry represented one of my co-presenters, Sara Hollamby, as well as a few comedians, and he began to get me some presenting work and the first of a handful of warm-up gigs.

I had never warmed up before, and I certainly didn't have a stand-up act, but I went along regardless, Jerry somehow having convinced my prospective employers that my lack of experience made me the perfect candidate for the job. The show was *Jameson Tonight*, Derek Jameson's short-lived and long-forgotten chat show on Sky, and was recorded at the historic Windmill Theatre in Soho. The Windmill had been famous for its nude girls, who had to stand perfectly still to stay on the right side of the law, and later as the starting ground for comedians such as Tony Hancock and Peter Sellers. I hoped some of the Hancock and Sellers magic might rub off on me, but without even the most basic of stage acts to my name, this was unlikely.

I would arrive at the Windmill around teatime and do my best to entertain the tiny studio audience and put them in a receptive mood for Derek Jameson. Coming from his background in newspapers, he viewed the whole thing as a wheeze; it seemed he couldn't believe his luck. A young Shane Richie was Derek's sidekick, the Ed McMahon to his Johnny Carson. While there, I saw many comedians coming through as they plugged their latest project. Michael Barrymore leapt around the sofa, destroying bits of the set in the process, and I chatted in the wings with the very nice Joe Pasquale. It didn't matter whether the comedians were to my taste or not; I was happy to watch and see if I could figure out how they were doing what they were doing, and whether I would do it any differently.

Music acts visited the show too. A jet-lagged Dion DiMucci of Dion and the Belmonts fame promoted his new record, while Sheila Ferguson from The Three Degrees and Helen Shapiro both took the trouble to tell me they liked my act. Surely they were lying? I was awful. The house band was led by the drummer Pete Thomas (famous for being the drummer with Elvis Costello's Attractions as well as Jonathan Ross's house band on *The Last Resort*) and I always felt that he viewed my meagre warm-ups with a mixture of pity and contempt.

Money, or the lack of it, was now very much on the agenda once more. I was owed a fair amount by the Shopping Channel people and began sending endless letters and making telephone calls in pursuit of whatever I could manage to prise out of them. We were living rent free during the week in Hounslow, in a flat owned by my old school friend David Williams. Martina was working in London three days a week, and so we lived a rather odd existence where she would head off to work in the morning and my day would stretch out ahead of me. I would usually fill it with endless phone calls, chasing money and jobs, writing to prospective employers, killing time browsing in WHSmith, and making ratatouille for Martina's return. All alone in the flat I would imagine I was presenting a cooking show and gaze at an imaginary camera, speaking out loud: 'Now I'm just going to chop up the aubergine. I like to chop it to this kind of size, but it's really up to you . . .' On Thursday we would head back to Cardiff, where I had a half-hour radio show each Saturday lunchtime, *The Welsh National Chart*. Most weeks this would be my only source of income.

Things picked up slightly when a few more warm-ups came my way, most notably for a sitcom called *Heil Honey I'm Home!* It was an old-fashioned, sixties-style set-up which revolved around Hitler living next door to a Jewish family. As far as I'm aware, it has never been broadcast (although, I have to say, I thought it was pretty funny). In one of the episodes there was a recording break while the actor playing Mein Führer was taken away to have a bald wig fitted. In the intervening years I've had the misfortune to wear a few myself, and I now know that this is not a speedy process. My job as warm-up man was to keep the audience entertained and suitably 'warm' until the actor returned, a task I estimated would take ten minutes or so.

It took half an hour.

After five minutes I had run out of anything approaching what you might call prepared material and was reduced to just chatting to the audience, searching for laughs. Eventually, and in desperation, I asked one of the crowd if I could have a sweet from the packet resting on their lap. I took the whole bag and slowly, very slowly, shared them out around the audience. It was painful for all concerned.

Why I carried on as a warm-up man is something of a mystery to me now; I seemed to limp on from disaster to disaster. Rhys was now working in London and remembers being at a recording of *Wogan* where my name came up while chatting to Terry's warm-up man.

'Ah, yeah . . . Rob Brydon . . . I've heard about him,' said the comic. 'He's the one who doesn't do any gags.'

I performed one such gag-free warm-up for a show BBC Wales were making at the time, *The BBC Diet Programme*. This involved a studio audience made up of people all trying to lose weight together, who would return to the BBC each week and share with the viewers the latest news of their progress. As the audience stood queuing outside the studio, I had the fiendishly clever idea that I would conspire with one of them; I would hide a chocolate eclair in a handbag and then, once the audience was seated, I would take on the role of a wildly over-the-top evangelical minister from the Deep South, suddenly claiming to have sensed a sinner amongst us. After a great, time-consuming show of scanning the audience, searching for the transgressor, I would apprehend the lady with the eclair planted in her bag. She would reluctantly open the bag, revealing the cream confection to the whole room, and the audience would erupt into applause.

That was the theory.

With the suitably plump accomplice selected and the eclair secreted, the audience made their way in and took their seats. I began my usual stuff about enjoying the show, telling everyone where the fire exits were and other housekeeping matters, before launching, with some considerable gusto, into my southern evangelist.

'Do you believe in the healing power of weight loss?'

'*Yes!*' came the reply.

They were playing along; this was excellent.

'Do you *belieeeeve* in the power?'

'*Yes!*'

I was on a roll. This was the point where I began to milk it, to over-egg it, to take it too far.

'I can't hear you! Do you *belieeeeeve?*'

The reply was now a little weaker, not quite so enthusiastic.

'Yes . . .'

'Has everybody been good this week, has everybody been eating less?'

Maybe five or six kindly souls offered up a positive response, but I could tell that I was losing them. Best to cut to the chase and reveal my cake smuggler, then revel in the applause that would no doubt follow.

'*Wait!* Someone is not telling the truth!' I eyed the audience with shock and distrust, as though I had been betrayed. 'There is a *sinner* amongst us! I will find you!'

I made a great show of scanning the audience,

'searching' for the lapsed slimmer. I thought I'd take thirty seconds or so to ramp up the tension, before making my great revelation. But as the thirty seconds came to an end, I realized that I had no real idea where my accomplice was sitting. Not to worry . . . she can't be that hard to find . . . now let's just think . . . what did she look like? I had no idea. I could conjure up nothing whatsoever of her appearance, not one single detail.

'I know you're out there . . .'

The audience began to sense that I didn't know what I was doing.

'Come out, come out, wherever you are . . .'

They started to shift uneasily in their seats.

'I know there's a sinner amongst us . . . [*gulp*] somewhere . . .'

Surely my little helper, my co-conspirator, would make herself known to me? I was dying out there!

She didn't, she kept quiet – emboldened, no doubt, by the thought of the free chocolate eclair waiting in her handbag. By now I'd given up on the accent, I was just pacing the studio floor back and forth, searching for my betrayer. She was nowhere to be seen. At this point, after about fifteen seconds of silence, a slightly chubby man in the front row, squashed in next to his seat-and-a-half-wide wife, piped up.

'We've come to lose weight, not to a bloody pantomime.'

I gave up, introduced the host of the show and got off as quickly as I could.

Believe it or not, I went on to complete more warm-ups after this experience, one for an ill-fated pilot for an afternoon show hosted by Simon Mayo, and another for *Hale & Pace*. In chatting to me after the recording, they proved themselves to be thoroughly nice chaps. I can only assume they hadn't witnessed my warm-up.

Fast forward to 2004, and I'm standing in the wings at the BBC waiting to go out and welcome the audience to a recording of *The Keith Barret Show* while our warm-up man has the audience in stitches. It's a still-unknown Alan Carr, mincing around the set, and he begins to talk about women who have piercings in delicate areas. On the one hand I'm wishing he'd tailor his material to my audience a little more – we've got Mr and Mrs Ronnie Corbett waiting to join me onstage, and I don't want to put them off – and at the same time I'm thinking, *Damn, he's good . . . my warm-ups never went like this.*

Alongside these sporadic bookings as a warm-up man, Jerry got me an occasional job presenting a late-night show, *Pick of the Week*, up at Yorkshire Television in Leeds. The show was a round-up of the '. . . and finally' stories from various regional news programmes during the week. The presenter just had to sit there and link them, with perhaps the odd weak pun every now and then. When I say it was a late-night show, I mean it was a very-late-night show. It bumped around the schedules a little, but once it went out at five past three in the morning – so late it was early. I'd pray that an insomniac casting director might spot me and catapult me to success. The team that made the show – especially the producer, Maria Malone – were great, and the hotel I stayed at in Leeds had excellent butter. Other than that, it was neither here nor there.

I continued to write off for jobs: I auditioned to voice promos for Sky Sports, unsuccessfully ('It's a bumper Saturday of football on Sky! All the goals! All the action!'); I auditioned to become a continuity announcer at Channel Four ('Now on Four, we join Richard and Carol for another *Countdown* . . .') and got down to the last two; I was a roving reporter for a BBC Wales programme about the Tall Ships Race; I auditioned unsuccessfully for a Kellogg's No-Nonsense Oat Bran advert (I should have known I wasn't the type to advertise cereal); and I continued to send mountains of voice tapes off to agents, in the vain hope of finding representation and moving into the lucrative world of voice-overs, at which everyone told me I'd make a killing. In the process, I collected rejections from every voice agency of note in London. I made a TV pilot for BBC Wales, *Throw Another Log on the Cottage* – the splendid title was Jerry's idea – and I managed to involve Ruth Jones and Steve Speirs, but it didn't get picked up.

Earlier in the year, on the 3rd of January, I had noted in my diary:

I am currently £1,800 overdrawn. This is not good news as my current regular earnings are just £80 per week, of which 15% goes to Jerry and 25% to the income tax fund.

By 8th October the overdraft had increased to £4,000, although my earnings had also increased slightly thanks to a new editor at Radio Wales.

Gaynor Vaughan-Jones was more of a fan than her predecessor and chose me to host a Friday-night show that would link up with the new station Radio Five. Each evening, between ten and midnight, a two-hour show would be broadcast from a different region. We were the Friday-night slot; the Wednesday-night slot was taken up by *Hit the North*, hosted by the soon-to-be Radio One breakfast hosts Mark and Lard. Our show was called *Rave*, although if you were hoping for an Ecstasy-fuelled bout of loved-up arm waving in a field, you'd have been bitterly disappointed. I've no idea where the title came from, but it bore little relation to the content of the show, which began as a magazine programme with music and soon morphed into me doing lots of characters and playing a lot of music. I co-hosted with Alan Thompson, now one of the cornerstones of the station, and it was with Al that Keith Barret first raised his eternally optimistic head.

He began as a voice. A silly, high-pitched Cardiff-accented voice called Keith, who would bounce off Al's character Tony, who ran a mobile fast-food van. Tony was what's known in Cardiff as a 'chiefo' (as in, 'Arright, Chief, how's it goin'?'). Al had the proud boast of having once followed Tom Jones into the toilet of an Indian restaurant just so he could stand next to him at the urinal. When Tom had finished and left, Al turned to his friend – who, it has to be said, had also followed Tom Jones into the toilet – and remarked, 'He's a bit of a chiefo, isn't he?' With that they heard a flush and Tom's son and manager, Mark, emerged from a nearby cubicle, presumably having heard Al's detailed character study. Tony and Keith were friends ('Aw, Tony, I love you like a brother . . .') but what Keith didn't know was that, while he was out driving his taxi, Tony was enjoying the charms of Keith's wife, Marion. And so it went; each week we would expand their world to include more and more ridiculous adventures until eventually they would break into song, 'Grillin' and Fryin'' being especially popular with listeners.

When Keith made the move to television, his job as a taxi driver only arose as a way of making ends meet after Marion had left him for Geoff. In the original radio incarnation he drove a cab from the start, primarily because it made it easy for his friend to be cuckolding him, but also because it struck me as very funny for a man to be cheated on while driving round in circles. His name came about for two very simple reasons. Keith is a thin, sharp and, to me, very funny-sounding name, especially when spoken in an exaggerated Cardiff accent. It just is. Barret was chosen in deference to Shakin' Stevens, who was born and raised in Cardiff and whose real name is Michael Barrett – the idea being that he and Keith were cousins. The curious spelling, with only one 't', was not intentional. In *Marion and Geoff*, when Keith is on the phone to the Orange phone company representative he has to spell his name for security reasons. I got it wrong.

There is a small but loyal number of fans of *Rave* who remember all the characters we came up with. Dave Connors was the West Country businessman with his adverts for the Dave Connors Bathroom Wonderland, a bathroom furniture superstore that would get bigger each week, eventually including 'a full-size Formula One racing track'. The ads always contained the mention of 'a ball pond for the kiddies' and ended with the promise that it was 'all under one roof'. One week he tempted customers with the unexpected delights of a 'fully working slaughterhouse, come and see how the burger gets to the table. And the kids can administer the electrodes themselves!' There was Conrad Bolivar, the camp young German who loved to tap dance and talked incessantly of his one-man show, a tribute to the actor and raconteur Victor Spinetti. He would greet Al each week with the same cheery, 'Yoo hoo!' As the series progressed, we were introduced to Conrad's Uncle Claus, a sinister man who spoke in an ominous low whisper. He wore nothing but a full-length black leather coat, and his pronouncements were always backed by the impending doom of Prokofiev's 'Dance of the Knights' from *Romeo and Juliet*.

I played two presenters. One was the American Bob Goldentan, an aged Casey Kasem type, who proudly boasted of having been the host of *Lucky Lobsters!* (the only water-based game show for the over-sixties and a show which, in thirty years of broadcasting, had only suffered twelve fatalities). His British counterpart was Barry Shoulder, a late-night DJ who offered his listeners 'a shoulder to cry on' in times of personal crisis. I based his voice on the real-life DJ John Sachs, augmenting it with an extreme lisp. He would read out a letter from a listener each week, which would always concern someone meeting the love of their life, only to cheat on them when someone more attractive came along. The letter would end with '. . . and then I did something, I did something very stupid. Anyway, when we'd finished I looked up, and there was Dave . . .' Barry would then play 'Hard for Me to Say I'm Sorry' by Chicago.

Perhaps my favourite was Jeremiah Fanny, the gravelly-voiced lead singer of the Fine Fanny Four, Bodmin's finest trad jazz/folk group. He had previously been a member of Thru'penny Bit and would each week tell Al of his adventures, before attempting a song.

It was while working on *Rave* that I first met Sir Tom Jones. I had been a fan for longer than I can remember and, I hasten to add, long before he had come back into fashion with his performance of 'Kiss' on Jonathan Ross's Channel Four chat show. I was there during the dark days too, proudly coming into school with a double vinyl LP of his rarely celebrated Canadian TV series. In 1992 he made a very good series for ITV entitled *The Right Time*. During the following rounds of press interviews I was able to arrange a meeting, for which I travelled up to London.

He was staying at a small and rather exclusive hotel near Bond Street and I was ushered up to his suite, clutching my little tape recorder anxiously in one hand. I was keen to avoid a repeat of my interview at a nearby hotel with Michael McKean in character as David St Hubbins of Spinal Tap, when half my allotted time had been spent trying to get the tape machine to work. (As I nervously flicked switches and plugged and unplugged cables, Michael offered words of advice in character: 'Yeah, well, I suppose you've got to plug it in properly, you put garbage in you get garbage out . . .')

I sat down on the sofa to wait and could hear Tom in the nearby bathroom, whistling to himself as he finished his ablutions. All the while, I was sitting there thinking,

Wow, that's the sound of Tom Jones whistling in a bathroom. He came and joined me on the sofa, positively radiating energy and good health, happily going along with my questions and the odd silly request that radio presenters are prone to ask of their interviewees. At that time, Al and I had a thing we did on the show where we would ask each other questions along the lines of, 'Is a horseradish a horse or a radish?' This would be followed by a pensive, 'Mmm . . .'

I know. It was no coincidence that we never troubled the jury at the Sony Awards.

I asked Tom if he would record a few of these questions, and then sat there listening to Tom Jones saying, 'Hello, everybody, this is Tom Jones. Is a horseradish a horse or a radish?'

Once he'd finished, I asked if he'd mind also doing the little pensive, 'Mmm . . .'

He obliged, about five octaves lower than me, making the sofa reverberate as though a tube train was rumbling by below us.

Many years later, I recorded 'Islands in the Stream' for Comic Relief with Ruth Jones. I found myself standing in the desert outside Las Vegas with Tom Jones, shooting the video while pestering him for stories about Elvis. We were filming in the limo and I asked Tom if there were any stories about Elvis that he didn't tell in public.

He smiled. 'Oh yeah . . .'

I asked if he'd tell me one.

'Well, I was in the shower one time and –'

I jumped in and said that I'd already heard that one.

He calmly turned to me and said, 'You haven't heard the ending . . .' and proceeded to tell me the story with an ending that I indeed hadn't heard before.

And which I couldn't possibly repeat here.

13

I loved presenting *Rave* with Al, although by now I was living in London and had to drive back to Cardiff each Friday afternoon for that night's broadcast. When the last record was on, at around three minutes to midnight, I would have my coat on and be heading for the door ready for the 156-mile door-to-door trip. Staying awake so late was often a problem; I would sing along with the radio at the top of my voice with the windows wide open and cold air rushing through the car in an effort to avoid nodding off. The best trick for staying awake was an odd one – I'd pull into the services and buy some mini sausages. As I drove away, I'd place the open packet on my lap and begin to eat them. The sausages had tiny hairs or fibres sticking out, and I would tell myself that I was eating portions of severed human fingers. This would keep me awake.

Rave kept going until Radio Five became Five Live, and we were left without a home. I thought it would be a good idea for Radio Wales to keep it going, but this was not an opinion shared by anyone beyond Al and myself. *Rave* ran for just over two years, and it planted the seeds for much of the success that would come to me further down the line. In writing and creating the character spots with Al, I began to find my own comedic voice for the first time and to gain confidence as a writer – something that I'd always felt was done by other people, not me.

Much changed for me while the show was running. Most notably, Martina and I married in October of 1992 and moved to London. We sold the house in Cardiff after it had been on the market for an eternity and, one month, the bank had refused to pay the mortgage. With the money we made I cleared the overdraft, now at £5,000, as well as a loan I'd had to take out for £4,000. I suppose the bank had been patient with me over the years as my earnings jumped up and (mostly) down with worrying regularity.

I had been called in a year or so earlier to see the Branch Manager, David Walters, as he wasn't happy with the state of affairs. Until that point I'd only dealt with bank staff further down the ladder of importance and had always managed to sweet-talk them into ever more lenient measures as my debt racked up and up. As I sat down opposite Mr Walters, I suspected I might have come up against a brick wall. He was older than I was expecting, and quite authoritarian in his tone. While we chatted, I tried to soften him up with the odd joke, to no avail. I mentioned that I was going to work at Sky and he remarked that he had a satellite dish himself, for the German channels. I saw this as my opportunity to get on friendlier terms.

'Ooh, you dirty dog . . .' I said with a conspiratorial grin.

His face turned to thunder. 'My daughter is learning the language!'

*

The move to London was prompted by my getting a new presenting job at Sky, this time on a film show, *Xposure*. I had auditioned in July and felt it had gone well. A couple of weeks later the show's producer, Colin Burrows, called Jerry to say that from an initial 250 applicants I was down to the last eleven.

'Rob's very good,' said Colin, 'but it's a pity that his skin looks so bad in some light . . .'

I was furious – not with Colin, but with my face. My acne scarring had been an issue some months earlier when I'd managed to get a meeting with a casting agent who specialized in commercials. I'd sent him my demo tape along with a photograph, and he'd invited me to come along to his office in the West End. This was progress. I can't tell you how difficult it was to get past the secretaries and receptionists of agents and casting directors – it seemed virtually impossible – so I was feeling rather good about myself as I entered the office and shook hands with Nicholas Young. We both looked at each other with a degree of surprise. On my part due to the realization that this Nicholas Young was the same Nicholas Young who had played John in *The Tomorrow People*, one of my favourite childhood television programmes.

David Williams and I used to play *The Tomorrow People* on the grass behind his house after school. We'd place our hands on our belt buckles and run twenty feet or so with our eyes closed, not opening them again until we'd come to rest in a new spot. This was our DIY version of 'jaunting', the name given to the teleporting that Nick and his chums were so adept at on their hit show. I had often dreamed in those days of meeting the Tomorrow People and maybe hanging out with them in their secret headquarters, deep within a disused London Underground station. I had imagined chatting with them as they welcomed me into their gang and handed me my very own jaunting belt. *What would we talk about?* I wondered. Evidently we would have talked about my skin, which was now the source of Nicholas's surprise.

'Ah, right, your skin . . . It's not very good, is it? Hmm, it doesn't really come across in the picture. I'm afraid I'm not going to be able to help you. I mean, I could hardly put you up for a chocolate commercial, could I? Eat this and you'll look like me . . .'

I agreed with him; he had a point, I suppose. I thanked him for his time and walked out of his office and into the cold fresh air of the West End as people bustled past me, going about their business. I couldn't help wondering if they were looking at my face and deciding it was unlikely they'd ever see me advertising chocolate. Had they done so, they would have been wrong. Just a few weeks later, Steve Speirs and I were chosen to star in the new Toffee Crisp adverts. Stick that in your belt and jaunt it!

We went to Pinewood Studios and shot five beautifully lit commercials in four days under the direction of the big ad director of the day, Nick Lewin (I think he'd done one for Flake that had performed very well). Steve and I couldn't have been more excited. We took photos of ourselves standing outside the dressing-room doors that had our names written on them – this had never happened before – and talked of how the money would help us both out of a financial crisis. The ads were good too. Steve played a lumbering buffoon and I was his small, smart friend who at the end of every commercial took a bite from a pristine new bar of Toffee Crisp. *Mmm, tasty*. In reality there would be a chap just out of shot on his hands and knees, holding a bucket into which I'd spit my mouthful of chocolate as soon as I heard, 'Cut!'

We left Pinewood on a high and waited for the ads to air and the repeat fees to roll in. It never happened. For reasons that remain unclear the ads never aired and the money, beyond the daily session fee, stayed put. Was it my skin? I don't think so; I saw the ads, and they were so beautifully lit that I could have advertised soap. Hey ho. As Les would say in *Human Remains* many years later, 'Onwards and upwards . . .'

Having heard Colin's harsh but fair appraisal of my complexion, I assumed that I would soon be out of the running for the movie show, so I was very surprised when I was then asked to shoot a pilot for *Xposure* a week later. The pilot went well, and soon the job was mine.

It was – on paper, at least – an excellent job. The show was a magazine format devoted to the week's new releases and was presented from a different location each week. There was no film reviewing, which I wouldn't have been comfortable with. My role was just telling the viewers what was coming out, and often getting to interview the stars. My co-presenter, Nadia, and I travelled the world; we shot in New York for the opening of *Home*

Alone 2, in Los Angeles to cover the build-up to the Oscars and witness the filming of the opening to Stallone's *Demolition Man*, as well as flying to Berlin and Cannes for their respective film festivals. It was fun.

I met Quentin Tarantino at a film festival in Nottingham; after the interview we talked about Elvis. I interviewed Andie MacDowell while she was in London promoting *Groundhog Day*. If you ever see the footage, someone should have told me to keep my mouth shut. (I'm almost drooling – I look like a lascivious wolf from a Tex Avery cartoon.) I flew to Morocco to watch Robin Williams filming *Being Human* and got to meet him, briefly. It was on this trip, actually, that I realized this wasn't what I wanted to be doing. Robin was brought over to meet me and the small crew we'd assembled for the trip, and I was introduced to him as 'the guy who's making the documentary'.

Eurgh! That's not me, I'm not a journalist! I'm one of your sort – I want to do what you do.

I was getting the urge to perform more and more. Meeting all these actors and visiting their film sets was great. It was exciting. But I was always there on the wrong side of the equation, and it became increasingly frustrating. The team was splendid, though, and I got on particularly well with the producer, Colin Burrows, a thoroughly good bloke who remains a friend to this day.

We had a little thing we'd do whenever he'd come over to me and ask if he could have a word.

I'd always reply in a Dudley Moore posh voice, 'Is it bad news, sir?'

How we'd laugh.

Then, one day, he wandered over and it was indeed bad news. There was a new big cheese at Sky and, just as had happened at Radio Wales a few years earlier, I didn't cut the mustard. So I was out.

I always remember Colin's face as he said, 'And you've just bought the flat . . .'

Oh dear. This was a considerable blow and served as something of a wake-up call. I made a decision to turn down any presenting work and just concentrate on acting and comedy. If I was ever going to get anywhere as an actor and a comedian, I would have to stop all the presenting and focus on what I really wanted to do. To make money in the short term I started to search for voice-over work.

One day, I was walking back from lunch with Jerry and told him that I wanted to do comedy.

He replied, 'We *all* want to do comedy.'

I decided there and then to leave him.

This focus on comedy had been growing for the past couple of years, in part through the variety of characters I was creating and performing on *Rave*, but also through the work I was doing in Bath with an improvisational comedy group I'd joined, More Fool Us. I had seen the group advertised in *PCR*, which was (and possibly still is) a round-up of castings and new projects in theatre, television and film which hopeful actors would subscribe to. *PCR* arrived through the post each week, and the lucky subscriber would then pester the various directors and producers mentioned within its pages for an audition. More Fool Us was the only time that my subscription bore any fruit, although I do remember reading one week that Richard Curtis had written a film and that it was to be called *Four Weddings and a Funeral*. I raised my eyebrows in despair at the British film industry, thinking that a film with such a title was most unlikely to be a hit.

This particular posting, however, talked of a new improvisational comedy group being set up in Bath and gave the phone number of a contact with whom to arrange an audition. Off I went to Bath, my audition went like a dream, and I was asked to join the group. It was run by Paul Z. Jackson, a former BBC Radio producer who had already worked with Caroline Aherne, Paul Merton and someone called Steve Coogan.

Paul's idea was that we would train for a few months before any performances were embarked upon, learning the basics of improvisation and bonding as a team on the way. Paul taught me techniques that I still use today, the most basic of which can be summarized as 'yes, and . . .' Also known as 'accept and build', it boils down to responding positively to whatever has been said to you, before adding another piece of information to the mix.

For example, if a scene began with a teammate saying to me, 'Ah, Doctor, I see you've brought your penguin with you today,' I would agree and add a little something.

Possibly, though not necessarily, 'That's right, he's an expert on all things to do with the throat, although he's a little under the weather himself at the moment.'

Straight away we're building the scene, as opposed to blocking each other.

'Penguin? No, no, this is my briefcase. And I'm not a doctor, I'm a bus driver.'

Paul was also big on clarity, on little things that make a big difference, such as repeating the suggestions that came from audience members and always thanking them, which in turn made other members of the audience more inclined to offer suggestions. Having said that, the suggestions invariably revolved around toilets and sex. Perhaps it's a British thing. When asked for a figure from history, you could be pretty sure it would be Henry VIII who would be offered; when looking for a location, it would inevitably be a toilet; and the household imple-ment of choice was an egg whisk.

The weeks of workshop sessions that preceded the first performance were hugely enjoyable affairs; it was like going back to college. Working in radio and in local television for so long had given my professional life an almost journalistic feel at times, and this wasn't what I was looking for. When I was a roving reporter on a magazine show in Wales I came into the office once and the team was cock-a-hoop about having just secured an interview with someone who was in the news at the time. I couldn't share their excitement; it felt alien to me. I just wasn't interested in people – at least, not in that way. I was very interested when it came to watching them, studying them and then using these observations to build up a character, but not in the way that they were, which was essentially a journalistic way.

When I was working on *See You Sunday* for BBC Wales, I did a piece in Tee Pee Valley, near Llandeilo where a community has grown up in the countryside, living in tepees. I went into one, talking to the camera and describing my surroundings as I went. There was a row of cassettes on the floor and I began to focus on them, mocking the musical tastes of the tepee dweller. I thought it was quite funny.

The director called, 'Cut!' and suggested we try it again. 'Maybe not so much on the cassettes this time.'

I wanted to scream. I was in the wrong place.

In the improv workshops I felt like I belonged; this is what I should be doing. It was a good feeling, but it also reinforced my belief that I'd taken a wrong turn in becoming so wrapped up in radio and television presenting. Paul had gathered a strong team of performers and we went on to play some great shows in Bristol, Bath and beyond. Amongst the founding members was the excellent Toby Longworth, who had been part of a double act, the Rubber Bishops, with a then unknown Bill Bailey, and who would go on to appear with me in *Human Remains* and *Annually Retentive*.

After a while, a couple of new girls joined the group. Julia Davis and Jane Roth worked as a double act, The Sisters of Percy. I straight away sensed a connection with Julia and loved the times we would play scenes together in the shows. It would be some years yet, though, before we would work together properly and eventually make *Human Remains*.

Ruth Jones also joined the group; we were working on some radio ideas for BBC Wales at the time and I thought she'd enjoy the improv too. She took to it immediately. As well as being a splendid addition to the line-up, her arrival meant that I now had someone to share the journey to Bath with. We would drive along, singing all the way, usually to Barry Gibb and Barbra Streisand doing 'Guilty' and 'What Kind of Fool', harmonizing to our hearts' content. I loved it. Fifteen years later, we were on *Top of the Pops* with Tom Jones and Robin Gibb, singing 'Islands in the Stream', written by the Bee Gees. Our long journeys up and down the M4 made that eventual collaboration for Comic Relief all the sweeter.

I stayed with the group for a few years, even after moving to London, but once the job on the movie show went away, money began to get tight and I decided I couldn't afford the trips to Bath and so had to stop.

Once again, things were getting difficult financially. I had the odd bit of radio work in Wales and Martina had found a great nannying job with a lovely family in Barnes, but money was tight. For the first time in my life I had to look for a proper job. I scanned the *Evening Standard* and saw an ad for a position in telesales, based in Kensington. Dad was a salesman; I'm good with my voice. Maybe I'd be good at this.

Dressed in a suit and tie, I got the bus to Kensington High Street and went to the address given to me over the phone. I found myself in a holding room with a few other would-be telesellers and was given a form to fill in. I hated myself. It had come to this. I'd never had to fill in a form for a job before. I'd been on the radio, I'd been on the television! This was failure in a big way. Although I kept telling myself that it would just be a stopgap until something else came along, I still heard a nagging voice at the back of my head wondering whether this was it for me, if this was my future now. I filled in the form and came to the part where they asked if the applicant had any hobbies or pastimes. This was the worst bit; it felt like I was being patronized. I wrote 'breeding rabbits' as a way of laughing at the whole process, then handed in my form.

I was taken through to another office, where a rotund Liverpudlian in his mid-twenties asked me to take a seat and began to interview me. I'd never been interviewed for a job before; I'd never had to submit myself to this. I'd done auditions of course, and had undergone every humiliation known to man in the process, but this was different; this was so *ordinary*. But the man was very pleasant, very personable, and he seemed genuinely interested in helping me. I began to feel bad for despising him simply for what he represented, and so when he got to the part of the form detailing my hobbies I started to make up all sorts of rubbish about my love for rabbits, just so he wouldn't realize I was lying to him.

'So, you like rabbits, Robert?'

'Oh yes.'

'Go on . . .'

'Well, what can I say?'

'What is it about them that you like?'

'Um, you know . . . their ears, their little fluffy tails.'

'Their tails?'

'Yes, their tails. Just the joy of keeping them, really.'

'I see . . .'

'And looking at their tails.'

This was first thing in the morning. After twenty minutes with the very nice man from Liverpool, it was

Before the *Level Three* broadcast with Dad.

Prowling the stage like a promiscuous panther . . .

Level Three. 'Look at me,' he said. 'I can't sing, I can't dance, I can't act. I can do fuck all. But, I turn up at places, I smile, I wave. The punters look at me and say, "Jim's having a good time, therefore so are we."'

ROB and JAMES

Our publicity card.

At Radio Wales. Poptastic.

The *Rave* team, with Alan Thompson on the right.

Interviewing Michael McKean as David St Hubbins. In his immortal words 'you put garbage in, you get garbage out . . .'

With the mighty Ray Gravel – 'Tell me to fuck off! Tell me to fuck off!'

Rhys and I at BBC Wales. Despite the briefcases, we did very little work.

Rob lands a job with Sky

THE sky's the limit for a former student at the Welsh College of Music and Drama, writes Penny Simpson.

Cardiff-based actor Rob Jones has landed a job working for the new Sky Channel — hosting a home shopping show alongside ex-EastEnder Ross Davidson and Treasure Hunt's Kenneth Kendall.

Brought up in Porthcawl and in Swansea, Rob left college after just two years training when he was "discovered" by a BBC producer on the look-out for a new, young presenter to host Bank Raid for BBC Radio Wales.

'Best test'

He went on to present several programmes for the BBC, including the quiz show Invasion, before his successful screen test with Sky Channel.

The live programme goes out daily for seven hours and encourages people to shop from the comfort of their own homes. Rob commutes from

Rob Jones

Cardiff up to Sky's new HQ in Osterley, Middlesex, for the recording.

His agent, the Cardiff-based Sian Lucy Management, said: "We were told that Rob performed one of the best screen tests and he was subsequently offered a year's contract for hosting Home Shopping Television Network."

Oh. My. God.

See above.

ESSEX HOUSE

XPOSURE

In an innovative step, *Xposure* will take cinema reporting out of the studio and onto the street. A pair of hosts - **Rob Brydon** and **Nadia de Lemeny** - will present the show (in a Richard Jobson/Paula Yates fashion) from locations relevant to one of the week's main topics, bringing the show closer to the cinema-going public and, for once, allowing the public a chance to air their opinions. The verite shooting style, cutting-edge graphics and wide-range of subject matter means that *Xposure* is a refreshing up-lift to both movie channels. **Xposure can be seen on SKY MOVIES on Fridays at 5.30pm and The MOVIE CHANNEL on Mondays at 7.30pm.**

Travelling the world with *Xposure*.

decided that I had what it took to give telesales a try. I was taken through to a large room full of desks at which were seated the telesales staff, all chatting away to potential customers. On the wall was a big whiteboard on which were written in erasable marker pen the names of the current top sellers, along with the prizes up for grabs if sales targets were met. It was as if Mike Leigh had written *Glengarry Glen Ross*.

The whole room was geared around selling environmentally friendly industrial cleaning agents and each seller was given a list of contacts, or 'leads', and a script to follow once contact had been made. It went like this.

'Hi, is that [insert name of lead]? Oh, hi there, I'm calling from [name of company selling environmentally friendly industrial cleaning agents] and I just want to say thanks for helping us out with the survey –'

'What survey?'

'That's right. And I just wanted to let you –'

'I'm sorry, what survey?'

'Oh, the survey. We just had the results back and it makes pretty amazing reading –'

'I don't know about –'

At this point we were encouraged to have noticed something personal about the poor soul at the other end of the line and to comment on it, so as to make some kind of connection. I remember noticing that one of my leads had a German accent, and so I asked him where he was from. On hearing that he hailed from Düsseldorf, I professed delight at the mention of a town so dear to my own heart.

'I don't believe it! I spent my honeymoon there!'

I know. It's appalling, isn't it?

From here the script took us through to enthusing about the product and how, by ordering now, the customer/victim/new best friend could benefit from a fantastic deal etc., etc. All the time I was talking on the phone, if I got past the first paragraph without the lead hanging up, a supervisor would notice my progress and wander over to listen in and make encouraging faces and hand gestures. The aim was to get an order number – that was the Holy Grail. Once it had been obtained, the call could end and the triumphant salesperson got to ring a bell that would be heard by all the other sales-people. A little moment in the sun.

I managed one bell ring before coming over all pecu-liar. I suppose it was a panic attack of sorts, but after spending much of the day trying to force people into buying something they didn't need I suddenly felt quite peculiar, stood up from my desk, walked out of the room, down the stairs and out of the building. Stand-ing in the bright sunlight on Kensington High Street, I reached something of a nadir. I really couldn't believe that things had come to this. I went to Barnes to see Martina, still feeling shaken up by the whole thing. I sat in the garden of the house where she was working, and played with Fraser and Will, the two little boys in her care. It helped to calm me down and wash away the day.

That night, back at the flat, I had an epiphany of sorts. It sounds stupid, but it was this. I can do funny voices. Probably nobody else in the telesales office could do them. I can do something that most people can't; it's crazy to be trying for a telesales job when I can do something that pays good money – if I could just get an 'in'. I decided that the following morning I would go all out to get voice work. I would call every contact I knew, and see what I could get; there must be something.

And I would try again to get a voice agent.

It took me a long time to get an agent, but I still managed to find some bookings as a voice artist – thanks largely to my old college friend John Golley, who was now a promo producer at recently set-up Sky rival, British Satellite Broadcasting (BSB). I called him that evening, after I'd got home, and told him about my experience and how bad I'd felt at hoodwinking Helmut with my bogus honeymoon. He arranged some sessions almost immediately and also secured me an introduction for some continuity work at the station.

The continuity announcing on BSB was not the same as continuity announcing at BBC Wales, where the incumbent was responsible not only for making the announcements, but also 'driving' the fairly complicated desk, resulting in a job somewhere between a DJ and an astronaut. At BSB, everything was new and computerized; all that was required of the failed actor sitting behind the microphone in the windowless room was to lean forward in his or her chair every half an hour and say, 'And now on BSB . . . it's *Mrs Pepperpot*.' The shifts were eight hours long and dull beyond belief. But (and it was a big but) they were well paid – especially the evening shifts, which also came with a chauffeur-driven car to take you home. It was no wonder that the station didn't survive when it was throwing its money around in this manner. I had been there for a short while, working the odd shift on a freelance basis, when I was offered a six-month contract. Although I didn't want to be working as a continuity announcer – it was most definitely a step backwards – we desperately needed the money, and so I intended to accept the offer and sign the contract, which arrived in the post one Saturday morning.

As I opened the envelope, on the radio the newsreader was telling the nation the breaking news – that Rupert Murdoch's Sky television was to merge with BSB. 'Merge' was a rather soft, fluffy and altogether too friendly word for what was about to happen to BSB – it was really only a merger in the sense that Germany once merged with Poland. I realized it was highly unlikely that my soon-to-be-accepted post would survive this 'merger' and, as I did so, the phone rang. It was my soon-to-be boss at BSB, asking if I'd heard the news and explaining that there was obviously no longer any point in signing the contract, given what was going to happen to the company. Perhaps it was my recent experience with the telesales, but I'm afraid I didn't hesitate to lie straight back down the phone, saying that I'd already signed the contract and popped it in the post. I might even have asked him where he was calling from and then claimed to be unusually fond of it.

'Brentford? I spent my honeymoon there.'

A few weeks later, this uncharacteristic moment of thinking on my feet resulted in the arrival of a cheque for many several thousands of pounds, although I never set foot in the voice booth again.

*

During this stage of my career I would pick up the odd corporate job, and it was around this time that I won an engagement that must surely rank as one of the most embarrassing. No easy feat, given the competition.

When interviewing me, journalists often bring up my time as the voice of the television commercial for Toilet Duck as representing a low point for me, but it's really not the case. (It was an ad that ran and ran for a long time and was very lucrative indeed.) No, the low point was my booking, as an actor, for a corporate event in Glasgow centred around thrush. The condition, not the bird – fungal, rather than feathered.

I was flown up from London and took to the stage at a shiny new hotel by the docks, a conference planner's heaven. In front of an audience made up of employees of Bayer, the makers of Canesten, I brought to life a plethora of roles – doctor, salesman, pharmacist – and bravely acted out a range of situations in which Canesten promises to make all the difference.

I remember little of the event, beyond the sense that my career was a boggy marsh and I'd arrived without wellies. But the slogan of the night has stayed with me all these years. It refers, in this instance, to inconvenience in a lady's special place. But it could so easily be applied to life in general.

Treat the cause, not the itch.

Wise words.

14

The thrush job had come through my new agent, Ashley Boroda at Noel Gay Artists, who also began to put me forward for corporate videos and a few small television roles. More importantly, in the short term I had, after much pestering, been taken on by the voice department at Noel Gay. After putting together a new demo tape, I slowly began to pick up some work voicing radio ads.

My agent at Noel Gay Voices was Bernie Gaughan, who also represented Chris Barrie, star of *Red Dwarf* and *The Brittas Empire*. Chris had been one of the voices on *Spitting Image* and was in great demand for commercials. Sometimes this demand outstripped supply, and that was where I came in; many of my early voice jobs were ones that Chris was unable to fit into his schedule. My schedule at the time was less than packed, and I jumped at the chance to get a foot in the door.

I usually played a character role, as opposed to the silky-smooth voice at the end of the ad (the 'end voice', as it is known) who speaks the 'tag line'. This is usually something along the lines of: 'Thickly, creamily . . . you won't find a better butter.' The end lines are easier and quicker to do, but the character roles are more fun. In those days, the early to mid-nineties, it was not uncommon for the ad agency to have brought in three or four actors to play a scene together. This would change in the years that followed, as budgets tightened and everything became scaled down, but back then there was a very enjoyable social aspect to the job. You'd run into friends in the studios, and then hang out in cafés afterwards.

Another perk with this kind of work was that I'd sometimes find myself working with well-known actors, the celebrities of the day. I acted in ads alongside Martin Clunes, Neil Morrissey and Caroline Quentin (huge at the time with *Men Behaving Badly*), with comedy stars like John Thomson and Graham Fellows, and once with the actor Sir Donald Sinden when I played Noddy to his Big Ears. It was a radio commercial for an insurance company and the gist of the ad was a tea party hosted by Martha Monkey, here played by Pauline Quirke, at which Noddy and Big Ears enjoy Martha's mushroom soup. All is well until Big Ears realizes the reason the soup tastes so delicious is that it is made from the biggest mushroom in the forest, which also happens to be Big Ears's house.

Before beginning the recording, we all sat in the control room while the director of the ad, Steve Bendelack (celebrated for his work on *The League of Gentlemen*) went through the script. Sir Donald leaned forward in his chair, listening intently as Steve likened the moment that Big Ears realizes he's eating his own house to something from *Titus Andronicus*.

'It's a dawning realization,' explained Steve.

The great thespian's eyes narrowed in agreement, and he nodded his approval.

'I mean, it's Titus fucking Andronicus, Donald!'

This was music to Donald's ears.

'Mmm . . . Titus Andronicus!'

Satisfied that we'd got to grips with the complexities of the script, the actors gathered in the recording booth and we began the session with my line as Noddy: 'Mmm, great soup, Martha!'

The ad then continued until Big Ears reached his moment of truth: 'Was it a large mushroom? In the middle of the wood? With a white picket fence all around it? *Noooooo!*'

We stepped back from the microphone and awaited the response of Steve and his team.

'That was great. Just one thing . . . Could you make it a little bigger please, Donald?'

Sir Donald Sinden's eyebrows raised ever so slightly as he noted the request, and he whispered to Pauline and me, 'Bigger? Mmm . . . He doesn't know what he's asking for!'

The next take was very big indeed.

I was getting bookings for radio commercials for quite a while before I landed my first television job. I was beginning to think that it might never happen when along came my debut, playing a Ribena berry in an ad celebrating the advent of an exciting new kind of Ribena – a Ribena with no added sugar. I'd long prayed for the arrival of such a product, and now here I was, an integral part of its launching to the general public. I was a hardworking little berry, slaving away on the production line, where my job involved remembering not to put the sugar in. I accidentally did just that – I put the sugar in the No Added Sugar Ribena. This was when my first line in a TV ad came: 'Oh! I must remember to forget to put the sugar in.'

It might sound odd to you, but I really was terribly excited at the prospect of finally getting my first TV ad, although I would have to wait some time to witness the fruit of my labours. It's worth remembering that this wondrous product was new – it didn't exist in the shops when I recorded the voice – so I knew that I wouldn't see the ad on the television until the cartons started appearing on supermarket shelves. With this in mind, I would slope off to Waitrose in East Sheen and casually stroll down the fruit-drinks aisle while casting a sly glance in the direction of the Ribena. It was months before I spotted the object of my desire; when I did, I gave a little yelp of delight and bought two. I had broken my duck and the ad was soon on the television with alarming regularity.

From here on in, the voice-overs just built and built. I realized that what producers were looking for was, first and foremost, someone who could give them a good read of their script, although there were very many other factors that came into play and dictated whether you would pick up repeat business with individual agencies. These included how quick you were (how soon you could get to the good read) and how well you could take direction (that is to say, to what extent you could listen to what they were telling you they wanted to hear, and then say it back to them, just as they'd envisaged it).

It's surprising how many actors *can't* take direction. There was one chap I used to do quite a few ads with in the early days who, on being given the note, 'Could you do it a little quicker?' would reply, 'Yes, well, you did ask me to do it a bit slower last time.'

My approach was always just to give them what they wanted.

'Could you time the read to half a second . . . ?'

'Could you shave a second off without sounding rushed . . . ?'

'Could you stretch the read out, without sounding stretched . . . ?'

The third request is far less common than the first two; ads are often overwritten, and the challenge is to get everything in without sounding speedy. There are tricks to reading quickly – perhaps the most helpful one is to stop trying to project your voice (you can fit far more words in that way).

The final tip for getting more bookings was, quite simply, to be pleasant to work with. I'd always try to make the producer and her team laugh at least a couple of times during a session, for no better reason than that people like to laugh. I figured they would probably choose the voice-over artist who made them laugh over the one who didn't, all things being equal.

In my heyday, at the height of my powers, the mid-nineties onwards, I must have recorded zillions of commercial voice-overs. It would be silly to list them. But if I did they would include Sainsbury's, Somerfield, British Home Stores, Tesco, McDonald's, Tango, Toilet Duck, Nivea, the *Sunday Times*, the *Sun*, *Daily Mail*, Subway, Domino's, Nationwide, British Gas, Sky, ITV, Wild Bean Café, Kit Kat, Hula Hoops, The TrainLine, Bounty,

Renault, Ford, Fairy, Crunchy Nut, Philadelphia, Raleigh and Pot Noodle.

I was a voice-over machine.

In addition to the commercials, I also found work lending my manly tones whenever a voice was needed. Had you visited Beaulieu Motor Museum in the nineties, you may well have heard me telling you all about the history of motoring. I did a similar thing for a canal museum, and also provided voices for prank phone calls of the sort found advertised in the back pages of lads' mags (a tenuous arrangement with a chap in Wales, for which I was never paid).

Another area to offer me gainful employment at this time was the relatively new world of computer games. While I love computers and all things Mac (I'm looking at a lovely MacBook Air right now), I've never really been a big fan of games, though that hasn't stopped me adding my voice to them when the opportunity arose.

Discworld was based on the hugely popular books of the same name by the hugely popular Sir Terry Pratchett. The lead role of Rincewind was voiced by Eric Idle, and I played an assortment of other characters. It was deemed a success, and so a few years later I was asked to do a follow-up, *Discworld Noir*, this time playing the lead character Lewton and many, many, many others.

Voicing video games sounds like it's going to be a lot of fun, doesn't it? It isn't. Perhaps, if you're an aficionado of the games, it can be quite pleasurable. But, to the disinterested money-motivated layman like myself, it's far from a walk in the park. Number one, in common with most animation, you record your bits in isolation, alone in a little booth. My excitement at the prospect of meeting a real-live Python was a little premature; at no point did I come within ten miles of Eric Idle. I would go on to eventually meet one member of *Monty Python* some years later at an awards do, when the excellent Michael Palin spotted me and made my night by saying, 'Oh, if you're here, it'll be good!'

The second problem with recording voices for video games is the size of the scripts. In my experience, video-game scripts are almost unbelievably large – huge, slab-like, telephone-directory-dwarfing tomes that take several lifetimes to read, let alone perform. Something like *Discworld*, set in a bizarre universe from the imagination of Terry Pratchett, is full of the most peculiar lines of dialogue.

> 'Behold, the goram-jewelled anti-husk of Grint, once belonging to Aaangrin, son of Pottywretch and Nim. See how it glistens under the shimmering light of our three moons. Eh, Lolfop?'

The script didn't actually say that, but it might as well have done; in fact, reading it back, I think it's quite good. I might give it a go myself.

From the voice artist's point of view, the main problem with the scripts is that, given the nature of game play, they have to contain a ridiculous number of options and reactions for and to whatever the pale, lank-haired, social-skills-lacking player does. This leaves the voice artist stranded for hours in his padded cell delivering mind-crushingly dull variations on a theme, so as to be able to deal with whatever the player chooses to do.

'So, you've opened the cursed casket of Minge!'
'Ooh! You haven't opened the cursed casket of Minge!'
'Why haven't you opened the cursed casket of Minge?'
'Can I interest you in the cursed casket of Minge?'
'Behold, the cursed casket of Minge!'
'What's that? It looks like the cursed casket of Minge!'
'Hmm, a cursed casket . . . I wonder where it's from?'
'If you like caskets and you like Minge, you'll love . . .'

It feels as though I spent years recording the *Discworld* games, though in reality it was probably just a week or so. I believe they were successful, and the people at the games company couldn't have been nicer, but I think it's safe to say they're probably my last attempt at the oeuvre.

I believe it was Sean Connery who said, 'Never say never again.'

He obviously wasn't referring to voicing video games.

I was becoming a regular fixture at the more lucrative voice-over studios scattered around Soho. This small area of London's West End contains a mind-boggling number of recording studios and at my busiest I would spend whole days schlepping from one to another, from Zoo on Wardour Street to Jungle on Dean Street, up to Saunders & Gordon on Gresse Street then across to the Bridge on Great Marlborough Street, finishing off at the Tape Gallery on Lexington Street. The studios were all in competition, not just in having the best technical equipment and engineers but, more importantly to me, in how luxurious they could make their reception areas. There would always be plush sofas, with acres of magazines and drinks being offered on arrival, and most also had overflowing bowls of sweets and chocolates that were constantly being refilled. I got to know the girls on reception at all these places; we would chat while I stuffed my face with sugary delights. Those sweets that wouldn't fit in my mouth would always find a temporary home in my pockets.

There would be gaps in between bookings, sometimes of several hours, and I soon became a leading authority on the fine art of killing time. My destination of choice would be HMV on Oxford Street, their huge store near the top of Poland Street, where I could easily while away several eternities, browsing through the CDs, the books and the videos. I remember something the broadcaster Danny Baker once said about record shops, and how he was quite happy to look at records he already owned. I understood that completely; it was like checking in on old friends and seeing how they were doing. I had a little routine.

On the ground floor, I'd visit Elvis, Bruce, James (Taylor) and Paul (Simon). The Bruce section rarely had anything new to offer in those days, maybe a Japanese CD EP with an odd track listing. The same was true of James Taylor and Paul Simon, but the Elvis section was always a potential treasure chest that might throw up all manner of curios (although even the most fervent fan would have to concede that, at the end of the day, he was unlikely to have recorded any new material – it was always essentially old Coke in new cans). But, 'Hey, now,' as Hank Kingsley once said to Larry Sanders, 'that's good enough for me!'

After I'd satisfied myself that the ground floor had no more to offer I would make my way to the escalator and head upstairs, maybe pausing on the way to wave to Rod (Stewart, who else?) and Billy (Joel). Oh, there's Barbra Streisand – sorry, Barbra, didn't see you there. Upstairs was video, and DVD. I spent absolutely acres of time here looking for Pacino films, or Simon and Garfunkel television specials that might feature the brilliant Charles Grodin. If I'm being horribly honest, I also used to loiter by the comedy section and look to see where I'd live, if I ever managed to get a DVD out. It was a nice neighbourhood, not far from *Blackadder*, Bill Cosby and Billy Connolly. I would picture my face staring out from the racks of the people who had already made it. Coming back to reality, I'd search for Marlon Brando or Richard Burton movies and odd videos collating Elvis's 1950s spots on the Ed Sullivan or Milton Berle shows. These were the dark days before the instant access of YouTube; the vintage clips still had great rarity value, which could give their lucky discoverer a sense of Indiana Jones-like adventure.

I would usually have to buy something, anything, just to have the satisfaction of going up to the till and walking away with an item in a bag, which would then be carried down to the basement and the exotic, subterranean world of film soundtracks, opera, classical and jazz. The soundtracks were always a good place to kill a few hours, hunting for films remembered from childhood. I would search out old James Bond – Marvin Hamlisch's *Bond '77*, the soundtrack of *The Spy Who Loved Me*, seen at the Royal Playhouse in Tenby that titular year – or John Barry's score for the rarely celebrated Christopher Reeve, Jane Seymour weepie *Somewhere in Time*. I'd watched it on the television as a teenager and been left in floods of tears. I could get it now on DVD, but I'd be afraid to spoil my memory of it as being an excellent film (it's noticeably absent from the endless lists of the '100 Greatest Movies' compiled by busy editors to fill their magazines and papers).

It was on this basement level of HMV that I'd find a rotating stand of specialist magazines: Sinatra fanzines; glossy spreads devoted to Barbra Streisand; and, best of all, a little publication called *Elvis: The Man and His Music*. This came out quarterly, I think, and although I would sometimes splash out and buy it, more often than not I would just stand there for as long as it took to read from cover to cover.

My departure from the store would always include a forlorn glance towards classical and jazz, and a moment's wondering if I would ever be sophisticated enough to walk amongst the serious-looking types browsing the Shostakovich and Coltrane. I have since come to appreciate both these art forms, but back in my voice-over days they were still another country to me. While at school in Porthcawl I had once gone to the home of a friend, Jason Chess, a very bright, academically gifted boy. He lived in Cornelly, just west of Porthcawl, and I was shocked on entering his bedroom for the first time to find his shelves lined with classical and opera records – no space here for my buddies Bruce and Rod, not even Elvis. He'd gone straight to sophistication, not passing 'Go' yet still managing to pick up £200 on the way.

We were once together in his car, an orange Volkswagen Beetle, when he was giving me a lift back to Port Talbot. Bruce came on the radio, singing 'I'm Goin' Down' from *Born in the USA*. If you're yet to familiarize yourself with the song, a lot of it is taken up with the mantra:

> I'm goin' down, down, down, down,
> I'm goin' down, down, down, down,
> I'm goin' down, down, down, down,
> I'm goin' down, down, down, down . . .

Jason said nothing at first, staring intently at the radio. After a perfect pause, he raised a quizzical eyebrow and said, 'Well, he's going down . . .'

He's now a lawyer.

15

In 1994, although the voice-overs were flourishing, my acting career had stalled. With so much of my CV taken up with presenting, corporate and voice work, it was almost impossible to be taken seriously by any casting director of note. In desperation I asked my old friend Dougray Scott if he would mention me to anyone who might be able to help. Within days he had managed to arrange a meeting with Mary Selway, one of, if not *the* biggest casting director in Britain. She had cast, amongst others, *Raiders of the Lost Ark*, *Return of the Jedi* and *Out of Africa*. When I went in to see her she was working on the Richard Gere/Sean Connery Arthurian adventure *First Knight*.

I sat down in her office at Twickenham Film Studios and tried to look like a film star, struggling to contain my nerves in the presence of this legendary and rather formidable woman. We chatted for a bit about Dougray, casually singing his praises as I smiled in a relaxed fashion. Inside, I was shouting, *Give me a part in this film!* She looked through the casting breakdown, a document detailing the roles in the film that still needed filling, before glancing back at me.

'Now, then,' she said to her assistant, 'what have we got for Rob? A marauder?'

I liked this. I'd never thought of myself as a marauder

but Mary had obviously seen something in me, a hint of the uncaring, brutal savage that other, less imaginative casting people had failed to spot. I was going to be a marauder. How exciting! Her assistant looked unsure, though, and studied my CV with a furrowed brow before turning back to Mary and reminding her of my limitations.

'Five foot seven?' she said, with a degree of concern, perhaps even sympathy, in her voice.

'Mmm . . .' purred Mary.

I sat up as straight as I could in the chair.

'What about a villager?' suggested her assistant.

There followed a moment or two during which it was evidently decided that there was no height bar when it came to villagers, and so I was handed a sheet of paper on which were printed some lines belonging to First Villager. This, again, was a good thing; he wasn't Second or Third Villager, he was First Villager, the King of the Villagers, the focal point of village life, the big cheese of the community, possibly even Chair of the Neighbour-hood Watch.

There weren't many lines at all, and they seemed to involve this poor First Villager pleading with an unnamed baddie to spare his life, while all around him evil hench-men began to pillage his village as per the instructions of the chief baddie (who was to be played by Ben Cross of *Chariots of Fire* fame). No mention was made of my subordinates, Second or Third Villager, but even the most optimistic reader would have to suppose that they would be lucky to avoid a similar predicament. Sadly, as I scanned the page, I could find no mention of Lancelot or Arthur (the roles to be played by Gere and Connery). A video camera had been set up in the office and I was instructed to deliver my lines straight down the lens, after which the tape would be sent off for consideration by the film's director, the very hot Jerry Zucker, fresh from his success with *Ghost*.

Oh boy, this is it, I thought to myself as I looked at the little camera. *Get this right, and you're in films!*

I began my performance by allowing a worried look to spread at first imperceptibly and then very perceptibly across my First Villager's face, before uttering the line, 'No ... please, please no, I beg you, please ... Urgh!' This last word was not to be found in the script; it was my own invention and preceded a bold and ambitious mime, conveying to the viewer the arrival of an arrow in my young chest, at which point my eyes widened in horror and I slumped forward to a grisly death.

My performance over, Mary thanked me for coming in and promised to be in touch. I smiled a smile that I hoped she might recognize to be that of an as-yet-undiscovered film star, and left.

A couple of weeks later, Martina and I were at Wimbledon; her boss had given us Centre Court tickets. As Andre Agassi cruised to victory, my phone vibrated with a message telling me that I'd got the part.

Agassi won a point and I cheered as though he'd won the tournament.

Two days before I began my one week of filming, I was in the supermarket, filling my trolley with the gay abandon of a man on the brink of a career in movies, when the phone rang again. It was my agent with the bad news that my one solitary line of dialogue had been cut and Mary was therefore wondering if I still wanted to do it. Of course I did! It was a film with Richard Gere and Sean Connery; who wouldn't want to do it, line or no line? I would have paid them to let me be in the film. In fact, I almost did – the money was *terrible*.

If you see the film, you may spot me at the beginning when Richard Gere's Lancelot comes to my village and challenges the local men to swordfights in return for cash. Look out for the long-faced grinning idiot who urges Gere's eventual challenger to step forward. I managed to get a line too. My character runs around a burning barn as the baddies are closing in and in the excitement I blurted out, 'Shut the door! Shut the door!'

When we went to the Odeon Leicester Square to see the film the following year, I couldn't believe how bad I was. I overacted appallingly; I look like a Griff Rhys Jones tribute act. (I'm not implying for one second that Griff is anything other than excellent in his acting, merely that I evoked the spirit of him playing a buffoon in a sketch.) Remembering how I'd tried to sit up tall in Mary's office, as the film went on I now found myself sinking lower and lower in my seat.

But that was yet to come; at this point I had no idea how bad I was, and so I blustered on regardless. It was a remarkable experience for me, an actor who'd never been in a film before, to find myself in a scene with Richard Gere and his megawatt charisma, and I stared at him the entire time he was on set. He had been studying all kinds of sword trickery in the run-up to filming and was able to toss and twirl his blade with ease, all adding to the impression of a bona fide movie star. One of my problems was my complete lack of any sort of technique. I hadn't worked my way up slowly, learning how to relate to the camera as I went. Up to this point I'd done some work as an extra, plus a few corporate videos, some sketches and a lot of radio. I had no idea about judging the size of the performance; witness my humungous gurning while Lancelot scans the crowd for a challenger.

If you're looking for the ultimate rookie mistake, though, fast forward to the scene where the misplaced villagers arrive in the garden of Guinevere, played by Julia Ormond. There's a shot over her shoulder that takes in some of the bedraggled refugees as she addresses our leader. I was there, right at the front of our group. But you'll be lucky if you see me, as I positioned myself just so that Miss Ormond was squarely between me and the camera. I had yet to learn the truth of the saying, 'If you can't see the camera, the camera can't see you.' A couple of inches to the left or right and you wouldn't have been able to take your eyes off me. *Who's the little gurning chap?* you'd have asked yourself. *Does he have some sort of condition?*

As well as Gere and Connery, the film featured no less an acting legend than Sir John Gielgud as Oswald, adviser to Guinevere, and I was able to watch him as he filmed a short scene with Julia Ormond. It involved Oswald telling Guinevere that he thinks she should accept Arthur's recent offer of marriage. Please try to summon up Gielgud's distinctive tones as you picture the venerable Sir John standing in a long flowing robe and holding a stiff wooden staff, while delivering his lines with that wonderful voice.

'You know how I feel . . . An offer of marriage, from Arthur . . . of Camelot . . .'

Jerry Zucker would call, 'Cut!' and a folding chair would be brought for Sir John. His staff would be taken away, and he would sit down until the crew was ready to roll again, at which point he would stand up, the chair would be whipped away, the staff would return to his hands and . . .

'You know how I feel . . . An offer of marriage, from Arthur . . . of Camelot . . .'

'Cut!' and the chair would be brought again. A few minutes would pass as Sir John, who was at this point eighty years old, sat in silence on his folding chair until off we went again . . .

'You know how I feel . . .'

They must have shot his short speech seven or eight times, and each time Gielgud delivered his lines identically, not a pause or inflection's difference; it was mesmerizing to watch.

This scene has a special place in my memory as Martina had come to visit the set and was standing just off camera throughout the takes. She was pregnant with our first child; the baby was due in a couple of weeks, so I was slightly on edge as I didn't think Sir John Gielgud would be much help if she went into labour.

The pregnancy came to loom large over my involvement in *First Knight*, in a rather unfortunate way, when the production team set about trying to book our little band of villagers for an extra week or so of filming. As Martina's due date was so close, I was not keen to be away from home any longer than we'd originally agreed. And so, when the First Assistant Director mentioned that I'd be needed for a little longer, I said that I didn't think this would be possible. He brought it up a few more times over the next couple of days, and each time I said the same thing: I needed to be home and so I wouldn't be able to do any more work on the film. If I'm being entirely truthful, I resented the assumption that an actor in such a small role would have nothing else going on in his life that might prevent his continuing with the film. This made me more determined to stand my ground.

After each exchange, the First Assistant Director would relay my feelings to the powers that be, until one day, the film's producer, Hunt Lowry, wandered over to the village set where I was sitting on the grass with some of my fellow villagers.

'Where's the expectant father?'

I stood up. Hunt was a powerful man. He had just produced *The Last of the Mohicans* and would go on to make *Donnie Darko*, amongst many others.

'Let's walk . . .'

I was dressed as a peasant villager, with greasy hair and mud on my face, and followed him as he strode up the hill and away from the make-believe village. He began to chat with me in a very friendly way, telling me that he understood what I was going through and how it was only natural that I wanted to be there for the birth of my first child. I felt as though I was in a John

Grisham novel or a Scorsese movie, being taken away to be whacked by a smiling assassin. Luckily, that wasn't on Hunt's mind. Instead, he tried hard to accommodate the actor on his film who was, let's face it, little more than an extra. Here's what he was willing to do; there were options. He'd have a nurse outside our home while I was filming, and if Martina went into labour the nurse would take her to hospital and he would stick me in a car and whizz me there to join her. Or she could come to the set; they'd give her a trailer and, if anything happened, we'd both be taken to the hospital together.

All these years later, I can see that he was being exceptionally reasonable and generous, but at the time I just wanted to be at home and not take any chances; I also had absolutely no idea how films were made and what was expected of actors, so I said sorry, but no. He turned crossly and walked away, explaining, in less friendly tones that I should realize this was how movies worked and how he'd never have booked me if he'd known I'd behave like this.

He was right; I was wrong. If you do dig out the film, there's a moment about three-quarters of the way through when the villagers are rescued from a church where they've been hiding from the baddies. I should have been one of their number; it would have been a lovely opportunity to fit in some more over-the-top acting as I staggered out into the daylight, eyes blinking and mouth wide open in shock. I might even have managed to improvise another line.

The cinematographer on *First Knight* was Adam Greenberg, who had previously worked on *Terminator 2*.

This was a cause of some excitement among the largely British cast. So was working for an American director in Jerry Zucker. The crew was mostly British, and I was chatting to one of them one day and asking how they were finding working for an American director. They were loving it, I was told; they had never worked as fast or as diligently as they were doing now, in an effort to impress their US boss.

A few days later, I asked Jerry Zucker how he liked working with a British crew.

'Oh, they're great,' he said. 'I mean, they're a little *slower* than I'm used to, but . . .'

As it turned out, I could have filmed the extra scenes quite comfortably; our beautiful daughter Katie arrived on the 28th of August, nine days late, and I became a father for the first time.

While the acting jobs were few and far between – my only other role this year was a very small one in a BBC drama, *The Healer* – I was at least continuing to establish myself as a voice artist, and this brought in a steadily increasing income. I had an ongoing series of radio ads for LWT, in which I played a DJ and was encouraged to ad lib a bit, and I had also been chosen to take over from an unavailable Richard E. Grant as the voice of Long John Silver in the second series of an animated version of *Treasure Island* for ITV. This was great fun; it felt like a lead role and I got to work alongside Hugh Laurie, who also performed a voice in the piece. It's probably worth pointing out that this was a reimagining of the classic tale and my Long John Silver was a fox, while

Hugh's Squire Trelawney was some kind of unspecified poultry.

I became involved with a project from the *Spitting Image* stable, a show I'd tried to get on many times (eventually getting close to the gig on the final series, but falling at the last hurdle when the job went to the brilliant Peter Serafinowicz). *The Strip Show* was an offshoot from *Spitting Image* and took the form of a collection of animated topical cartoons. I attended a few studio sessions, and it was here that I met for the first time Alistair McGowan, Ronni Ancona and Rebecca Front. The programme made it to air on Channel Four as a pilot, but it wasn't picked up for a series.

Back in Cardiff, Rhys came up with an idea for a radio show and managed to get a commission. *Who Died Earlier Today* was a spoof obituary show he and I wrote together in six episodes, each recapping the life of a fictitious public figure. It's notable for providing another stage in the evolution of Keith Barret, who here became celebrated as the subject of a fly-on-the-wall documentary, hence his passing being marked by a radio tribute. Other characters included a poet, a showbusiness agent (a reincarnation for my old friend Richard Knight), a footballer and a pop star in the form of Jeremiah Fanny (briefly revived from Radio Five's *Rave*). If Penguin have got their act together and you've invested in the e-version of this book, then there's a fair chance that you can hear a clip by clicking, swiping or blowing here. If not, then please read on with regret.

The series was broadcast on Radio Wales, and we submitted it to Radio Four only to receive a letter, in

September 1995, from then Commissioning Editor Mary Sharp, who let us down gently with the judgement that *Who Died Earlier Today* 'was not sophisticated enough in tone for the tastes of our audience'. Ouch!

At the same time as all these voice jobs were happening, I was still trying to get myself a proper, established, connected acting agent. Ashley was doing his best, but simply didn't have enough clout to make any real difference, and so I continued to send out a barrage of letters on a daily basis. I was missing a very simple point, expressed quite beautifully in the film *Field of Dreams*.

It is this: *If you build it, they will come.*

I wasn't building anything. I was just sending out letters and tapes with cleverly edited compilations of indifferent material in the vain hope that the recipient would spot the potential I myself sometimes struggled to believe that I had.

At one point, I did get close to getting a proper, established agent. I'm not sure, but I think it was the actor and impressionist Alistair McGowan who gave me an introduction to Vivienne Clore. I duly went to meet her at her offices in the West End, where we got on like a house on fire and she said that she'd be happy to represent me. This was based solely on hearing the many voices I performed on my voice reel; she'd never seen any of my acting tape, but flattered me hugely with regard to my voices, telling me that I reminded her of Peter Sellers. If you ever want to get to the heart of a voice-over artist, tell them that they remind you of Sellers; they'll be putty in your hands.

I knew that she wanted me primarily for my voices

and the money that they would bring in; the problem was that I was perfectly happy with my voice agent at the time and was only looking for acting representation. I didn't want to risk upsetting my current voice agent by leaving, but at the same time really was quite desperate for a proper acting agent. I was concerned also that Vivienne had never seen me act, although she assured me that she had heard that I was very good. I said I'd be happier if she'd take a look at my acting reel, just so we'd both be singing from the same hymn sheet, as it were. I left the office, promising to send my acting tape as soon as I got home and secretly thinking that maybe I *would* leave my voice-over agent if it meant being represented by Vivienne.

As soon as I got home, I packed one of my trusty VHS cassettes into a padded envelope and trotted off to the Post Office. I assumed that I would hear from Vivienne within the next couple of days, we'd hit it off so well.

A silent week went by, then another. I heard nothing.

I tried phoning but always managed to call when she was very busy indeed or had just that minute popped out of the office. Eventually, using one of the voices that she so admired, I rang in the guise of someone else – I forget who – and got put straight through. On revealing my true identity, there followed an awkward pause and then an even more awkward conversation in which she repeated her praise for my many voices (I think the god-like Peter Sellers reared his head once again, though this time in a more placatory role).

Then came the killer line.

I was calling from the phone box inside the main entrance to Kew Gardens. Martina and I had gone there for a walk – she was standing a few feet away, waiting for good news – and I had Katie in a sling on my chest, fast asleep.

I listened as Vivienne continued.

'I love your voices, Rob. I really do . . . and I would represent you for that in a flash, you know I would. It's just that your acting . . . well, it's . . . It just doesn't do it for me, I'm afraid.'

It's quite unusual that someone is this honest when issuing their rejection; it's rarely person to person, usually done by letter, and fudged under a fog of multifarious reasons (none of which could ever be construed to imply any shortcomings on the part of the aspiring actor). I have two separate rejection letters from my current and, I hope, final agent, the splendid Maureen Vincent, dated February 1990 and September 1993, both times explaining that it was the fact that she wasn't in a position to take on any new clients that prevented her from offering me representation.

The artiste, when faced with this kind of stock letter, valiantly convinces himself that the agent is actually desperate to take him on and is now kicking herself in the depths of her plush London office, furious for having taken on so many clients. Yesterday she'd had to turn away Al Pacino, today Rob Brydon. If only she hadn't taken on so many clients in the first place!

We walked away from Kew Gardens under a little grey cloud of defeat and rejection, yet again.

Ho hum.

If there was a good side to the lack of acting work, it was that being busy with voice-overs allowed me to spend lots of time at home and meant I was able to take Katie to her various preschool activities. I was a regular at Tumble Tots, walking alongside her as she clambered over huge squashy platforms, and encouraging her to take chances and climb ever higher. I'd always liked being with the children Martina had looked after while she was working as a nanny, and now that I had my own child my happiness reached a new level.

Yet I was beginning to wonder if it would ever happen for me. I suppose I was becoming resigned to a life of voices and the odd tiny role on the television; I suspect that I was inwardly preparing myself to admit defeat.

How was I to know that I just needed to hang on a little bit longer, just make one more push . . . ?

PART THREE

'From Small Things
(Big Things One Day Come)'

16

As I did more and more voice-overs, I came to look on Soho as my second home. It was an easy, good life and I would often arrive early at a session to make the most of the very generous hospitality on offer, reading the news-papers and magazines and raiding the bowls of sweets and chocolates. Once I had munched my way through the free confectionery and wandered, slightly heavier, along to the studio, I would invariably be told by the people from the advertising agency (almost exclusively comprising a female producer and male creatives, giving the impression of an indulgent mother showing off her gifted sons) how much 'everyone in the office' had enjoyed my demo tape; they'd all been laughing their heads off.

What a funny guy!

For a while, this was sufficient. It was enough just to be doing the voice-overs; it sated the hunger I had for performance that wasn't being satisfied by any decent roles on television or film. And the praise from the ad execs was very nice too, thank you. After a while, though, it was as if I was outgrowing it and I began to have a tangible feeling – as strange as it sounds, not unlike the feeling I'd experienced when I first knew that I wanted children – of needing to go to the next level.

I had, in my own way, been making baby steps towards

stand-up for a while now. When I was working on *Xposure*, I would entertain the crew between takes with seemingly spontaneous bits of business which, in reality, I'd been trying out for some time on as many people as possible. The material was going down well, and I began to visualize myself performing it onstage, in front of a paying audience. As the demo tape was proving such a hit, it seemed perfectly logical to simply perform it live at a comedy club and wait for the wave of riotous laughter to begin.

The first step towards performing at a comedy club is to get what's known as an 'open spot'. This is a short, usually five-minute set on that night's bill, unpaid and most times introduced to the audience as just what it is, i.e. a new comedian trying to get a foot on the bottom rung of the ladder. This policy of full disclosure lowers the audience's expectations and, depending on the type of club, will encourage either a sympathetic ear and large helpings of the benefit of the doubt or a viciously cruel mob, baying (or in my case *baa-ing*, but more on that later) for blood. Pretty much every successful comedian you've ever laughed at will have gone through this terrifying process. Getting an open spot is not easy, especially in London where there are long waiting lists. At some clubs hopeful comics can be kept waiting for up to a year or more, just for the chance to get up on the stage and do five minutes. Being inherently lazy, I phoned the club nearest to my house, the Bearcat in St Margaret's, and was given a date some months down the line.

The next step was to learn my tape off by heart. It consisted solely of impressions. I've since lost the cassette, but from memory they included Mark Little from *The Big Breakfast*, Chris Barrie in his *Brittas Empire* incarnation, Hugh Grant, Rolf Harris, Arnold Schwarzenegger, the cast of *Red Dwarf* and a little routine featuring Henry Kelly on his daytime television quiz, *Going for Gold*.

'Gunter, Helmut, Jean-Pierre and Dave . . . Who am I? Born in Ireland, I'm an annoying twa—'

Buzz!

'Helmut?'

'Err, you are Henry Kelly, no?'

I learned it quite easily – by now it was very familiar to me – and when the day finally came round, I set off confidently for the club. The Bearcat is undoubtedly one of the nicer comedy venues. Run by James Punnett and Grahame Limmer, it's in what to all intents and purposes appears to be a classic village hall or scout hut, behind the Turk's Head pub. Removable seating is lined up in rows, there's a bar at the back, a stage at the front, and an aisle down one side. Behind the stage are two tiny rooms, inside one of which the artist stands and waits nervously before making an entrance and beginning their act. I was a little bit anxious, but deep down felt sure that my collection of impressions would go down a storm, just as they had on the tape. I was introduced by James and walked out, smiling at the crowd as I ambled towards downstage centre, took the microphone out of its stand and began.

It only took twenty seconds to realize that the audience hadn't made up their minds about me yet. It took another ten to realize that they had, after all, made up their minds, and the newly made-up minds had decided

I wasn't up to much. They didn't laugh. At all. Worse than that, they didn't heckle either. With a heckle, at least you have something to work with, something to bounce off. They just sat there in silence, staring at me with blank faces. If I detected anything from them, it was a hint of sympathy. Nothing I said was getting a response.

Nothing.

I hadn't expected this; at worst, I thought I'd get weak laughter, just a few titters. But here I was, completely dying in hushed funereal silence. While continuing to trot out the memorized act, in my mind I was panicking. *What the hell am I going to do?* I had been so confident that this evening was to be the beginning of a new chapter in my career. It had seemed like the natural next step; everyone kept telling me how funny I was, and how I really ought to do stand-up. I couldn't take in how badly it was going.

Things then became worse as my mental anguish took on some physical properties in the form of a dry mouth. When I say a dry mouth, I don't mean a slightly dry mouth, I mean a completely arid, cracked riverbed, drought-ridden dry mouth. Along with this my tongue seemed to be getting bigger and began to stick to my dried-out mouth, which made performing the impressions almost impossible. I couldn't form the sounds for the words needed to speak as myself, let alone as Hugh Grant, the master of bumbling charm. I desperately tried to moisten my mouth. One way to do this is to bite your tongue; I bit mine so hard I let out a little yelp of pain, which the audience assumed was yet another unfunny moment in a consistently unfunny act.

Nothing worked.

The dry mouth as a result of nerves problem is one that has stayed with me to this day, although thankfully it happens far less now. But it still occurs. Sometimes it'll be when I know I'm unprepared for something and not getting the laughs I want. But also, more worryingly, it can happen when things are going OK. It'll sometimes just begin, and I'll have to try to trick my body into relaxing and my mouth into releasing moisture. If you ever come to see me onstage and I begin to make strange shapes with my mouth – like a horse eating a mint – then you'll know I'm not happy and I'm trying to get some moisture into my mouth.

If I had wanted to do an impression of the Elephant Man then things would have been fine, but I didn't, and they weren't. It got to the point where I literally couldn't get any coherent words out and so, having made the rookie's mistake of taking to the stage without a glass of water, I had to ask a girl in the front row if I could have some of her pint. She of course obliged, and so I had to bend down in silence to get the drink, take a few sips from it, and then regain my composure and carry on performing to the big wall of silence that was wrapping itself around me and squeezing out my last drop of self-belief. It probably took no more than five to ten seconds to take a sip of her drink, but it felt like longer than for-ever, played out to the backdrop of the deafening quiet. I pushed on through to the end of my act, then quickly left the stage to scattered showers of politely sympa-thetic applause.

When a gig has gone badly, I like to leave the venue as

quickly as possible, avoiding the embarrassment of looking anyone directly in the eye. A bad gig does two things to you. In the long term, it makes you better; you really do learn from your mistakes, and it does thicken your skin to know that you've survived a bad show and carried on to fight another day. It enables you to look at a difficult audience and think, *No problem, I've had far worse than you*. But in the short term, it can be very damaging.

After this first disastrous attempt, I didn't return to the stage for a whole year, I was that traumatized by it. It upset me hugely to think that I could have been so wrong in my opinion of my abilities, that I could have misjudged the picture so wildly. I limped back, bruised and battered, to the lucrative and comfortable world of voice-overs. Here, amongst the bowls of sweets, I was a success and could continue to perpetuate and luxuriate in the received wisdom that if I did at some point decide that I had the time to do stand-up, I'd be very bloody funny indeed.

Nine or ten months into my self-imposed sabbatical, I began to get the itch once more. This time, though, I told myself it would be different. This time, I wouldn't just stand there doing impressions. I would instead dazzle them with my wry observations on life – like a smaller, Welsh Jerry Seinfeld. I'd have them eating out of my hand with my pithy one-liners and my well-constructed tales of my semi-truthful misadventures.

I arranged some more open spots at clubs around West London, and there was a competition, held at a venue above a pub in Hanwell, that I entered and did well in. There was a red-haired girl on the bill that night who went down quite well too. She talked about being an actress, but not getting anywhere with it, she did a bit about *The Bill* and showed off an array of voices. The audience liked her but they certainly weren't going crazy over her. I remember standing at the back of the room watching her and thinking, *Is it just me or is she actually very good indeed?* She was Catherine Tate. What a fucking liberty.

My material had developed into a mixture of voices, characters, observations and impressions. It wasn't great. I did a bit about those sales you see on Oxford Street where some hucksters have illegally taken over an empty shopfront and begun an auction of sorts. They have a black bin bag full, if they are to be believed, of expensive big-name electrical products. They then tell you it's not fifty quid, it's not forty quid, it's not even thirty quid . . .

'Who'll give me twenty quid? Hold your money up now!'

And then, unbelievably, a concentrated throng of the capital's most gullible hoist their hard-earned banknotes aloft and head off into the distance with their bags. My take on it was to have the 'auctioneer' listing incredible things, such as a speedboat, a BMW, or a seven-bed-room detached home, all waiting inside the bag. As the price comes down, a Scottish couple are standing at the back watching the action. The price reaches twenty pounds and the husband cannily says, 'Wait, Sheila . . . he'll come down.'

Hmm, it got a laugh sometimes.

I did some very basic stuff about the difference between posh British Airways pilots and downmarket Virgin pilots (I was still flogging a version of that one ten years later) and ended with the thing that always guaranteed a strong finish, my Tom Jones impression. He had been in the charts again with the charity recording of 'Perfect Day'. My take on it revolved around the sophisticated observation of how much louder he was than everyone else on the record. It climaxed with an as-loud-as-I-could-make-it 'Aw, you're gonna reap just what you sow . . .', all held-out notes and big eyes. Generally, people were surprised that such a little chap could have such a big voice; as cheap and gimmicky tricks go, it was pretty cheap and gimmicky. But it usually got applause, and it gave me a big ending, so its place in the first team was secure.

I seem to recall making it through to the semi-final of this competition above the pub, before coming a cropper. At the same time I was picking up more gigs here and there and, slower than very slowly, gaining in experience and confidence.

Confidence is a fragile fellow, and mine took its biggest beating yet at a notorious club in Greenwich, Up the Creek, run by the late and also notorious Malcolm Hardee. First off, and this may strike you as an odd thing to factor into the equation, the drive from East Sheen to Greenwich is a long and horrible one, made more so by the knowledge that you're making this effort for a five-minute spot in front of a crowd that will in all likelihood be leaning towards the hostile. I had heard so many horror stories from other battle-scarred open spots about how tough it could be, and I struggled to put them out of my mind as I crawled along in the traffic heading slowly east. *Maybe I'll be different; maybe they'll like me. Some-one has to do well there, surely?* I kept up the internal pep talk all the way, parked nearby and tried to affect a confident gait as I walked into the club. I don't remember anything else of the evening, other than the time spent on the stage and the drive home.

I began the act with a remark about being Welsh. Immediately a man near the front of the audience made a sheep noise.

'*Baa!*'

People laughed.

I chuckled slightly and carried on, pleased with myself for having taken this almost-heckle in my stride. Five seconds passed, and from a far corner of the room another sheep piped up, as though responding to the first.

'*Baa!*'

Hmm, OK. Just carry on.

'*Baa!*'

Don't worry, they'll get bored with it.

'*Baa! . . . Baa! . . . Baa!*'

There were more now, but I carried on regardless, as though it wasn't happening.

This isn't a good tack. You can pretend not to have heard the odd isolated heckle – in truth, due to the acoustics in certain venues you often *don't* hear the things that are shouted out from the audience – but when it's something as concentrated as this, it's madness to ignore it. It makes a mockery of your relationship with the audience; in fact, it only highlights the fact that you *don't* have a relationship with them. When you do, you bounce off the spontaneous things that happen and the evening is enriched by the knowledge that we're all experiencing something uniquely in and of the moment. The sheep were now getting their act together beautifully; the more of them that baaed, the more the rest would follow. Like sheep – the very same dumb defenceless creatures they were so cruelly satirizing.

Soon it was a deafening flock. The sheep were angry now, yet still I carried on with my carefully memorized act, behaving as though it wasn't happening. In my head I was frantic, desperately running up and down corridors in my mind, opening doors and searching for something funny, something that would turn it around, something that would save me. A border collie of a line that would round them up and lock them safely back in their pen.

I didn't find one. I was dying. I was probably already dead.

I remember Malcolm Hardee laughing as I came off, looking at me as if to say, *I've seen some bad ones in my time, but this took the biscuit.* Actually, that wasn't what his look said. That's how he seems in the version I've built up in my mind, the version of the story I've told to friends and fellow comedians over the years. I suspect the truth is more mundane. I think his look said no more than, *There goes another one.*

Far worse.

As quickly as possible, and making eye contact with no one, I made my way towards the exit, consoled by the thought that at least there was no one in the audience who knew me.

'Hiya, Rob!'

Shit. It was Bleddyn, from Cardiff. What the hell was he doing here?

He had worked on *Except for Viewers in England* with Ruth and me; he'd been a runner and had, in my opinion, a complete disregard for the unwritten rules of status on such an enterprise. I had been a runner myself, in 1989, on a BBC Wales television show, *The BBC Guide to Alcohol*. The job had involved coming up to London and loitering backstage at *Top of the Pops*, grabbing the acts and persuading them to do brief interviews with our presenter, Gaz Top. At that time it was an exciting gig for me, as it meant a visit to the very famous set at TV Centre where I noted, like many before me and with clunking predictability, how much bigger it appeared on television. In my increasingly infrequent diary I went on to observe:

I saw Dave Lee Travis, who by the way was carrying a portable phone, as was anyone who was anyone.

These fantastical glimpses of the future – or 'portable phones', as I felt they were destined to be called – obviously hadn't reached Cardiff at this point.

I digress . . . The runner, with the best will in the world, inhabits the very bottom of the bottom of the food chain. He or she runs, fetches, carries, makes tea, takes tea, fetches tea and then carries tea. They do, up to a point, whatever is asked of them. Many of them go on to occupy positions of power further down the road, but when they run they just run. The good ones are always helpful, polite and above all enthusiastic. The *very* good ones will always do a little more than is asked of them, cleverly making themselves indispensable in the process.

Bleddyn – that's not his real name (after all, I don't know what he's doing now, he might have befriended a very good lawyer and consider my version of events to differ significantly from his own) – was not that sort of runner. He was the sort that quietly chipped away at the fragile veneer of my confidence during rehearsal, with the odd sigh here, a raised eyebrow there. At one point during the production, I made the mistake of asking him what he thought of the show we were making. It was my own fault; I was fishing for compliments.

He didn't bite. Or, rather, he did. He said it wasn't really his kind of thing, he preferred stuff like *Blackadder*. Well, so did I! That's what we were trying to do, stuff that might be as good as *Blackadder*; we weren't deliberately setting out to make something bad. There was sympathy in his voice too – he was speaking from a position of comedic superiority. One could be forgiven for thinking he'd actually *made* Rowan Atkinson and Co.'s masterpiece, not merely joined the rest of us in watching it.

Anyway, here he was in bloody Greenwich, on the one night that I happened to get up on the stage and suffer a ritual disembowelment. As I approached him, his face twisted into a sympathetic smile that took Schadenfreude to new heights

'Hiya, Rob! A baptism of fire, eh?'

Bastard.

Five minutes later, I was in the car driving home.

Oh my God, I was low. I was devastated. I was traumatized, and I was depressed. By now I was making a very comfortable living with the voice-overs, but on that long drive home I convinced myself that I would never earn another penny through performing, through art, through any branch of show business. I told myself that it would be best to spend none of the money I had saved up; there would be no more coming in. I had been a fool to think that I could be a comedian, an actor, a writer, a voice-over artist, indeed any of the above. I was humiliated and defeated. I really cannot convey to you how desperately low I felt on the drive home.

It was all over. I was bereft.

The morning after has a wonderful way of making what happened the night before seem not so bad; except for when you've done something absolutely appalling the night before, in which case the cold light of day just makes things worse. In this instance, it was the former. I resolved to one day return to Up the Creek, be hoisted shoulder-high at the end of my act and then carried through the streets of Greenwich on a triumphant parade of celebration and affirmation, banners twirling and party poppers popping, as those small unfurling paper trumpets are blown hither and yon with gay abandon. And I did. Nearly.

I went back, some months later, more scared than before (if such a state were possible) and proceeded to perform five minutes of material to general disinterest and perhaps the odd lone chuckle. You'd be hard pushed to describe me as a success. But, in my mind, the absence of sheep noises was akin to being presented with an Academy Award.

My ill-concealed glee on leaving the stage must have perplexed anyone watching, leaving them with the impression that I'd somehow set myself spectacularly low standards and then shocked myself at being able to rise to them.

17

My period on the London comedy circuit was mercifully brief. After the first competition gig in Hanwell, I'd come off the stage and been taken aback to be handed a business card by an agent, Paul Duddridge. I wrongly assumed that this happened at every gig and therefore waited a while before calling him, to see who else had been dazzled by my obvious potential. No one had.

A fellow Welshman, Paul saw something in me that others had missed, and he began to arrange a few gigs for me. I played mostly at Ha Bloody Ha in West London, a few times at the Chuckle Club in the West End, and at various Jongleurs outlets. I never made it to the Comedy Store, although I often meet people now who swear they saw me there. At most of these gigs I would go out feeling underprepared. I was lacking in material, and relying on tricks – the impressions and the big finish with the Tom Jones song, which by now was getting longer and longer. Occasionally I would go off script and chat with the audience; these moments would always harvest the biggest laughs, and a feeling began to grow in the back of my mind that this was where I was at my best. Paul would come to the gigs and we would analyse how they'd gone, both agreeing that if I could tap into the kind of humour I produced around friends, when I was just messing about, then we might be on to something. In other words, *be myself*. It was easier said than done.

As I was notching up my modest tally of gigs, I came across a whole host of other comedians also trying to make their way up the ladder. As well as Catherine Tate, I played on bills with Al Murray, Sean Lock, Rich Hall and Mackenzie Crook in his guise of Charlie Cheese. You could never tell who would go on to break through and make it. There were many who stood out as being ones to watch, and it was certainly easy to tell who was going down best in the room that night. But that, in itself, was no indicator of future, wider success – or, to put it another way, who would end up on the telly. I saw acts absolutely own the room at Jongleurs, their audience crying with laughter, struggling to catch their breath, yet these same acts ten or twelve years down the line are still there, still storming it, still living the strangely antisocial late-night life of the circuit comedian.

It was one of the reasons I came to stand-up so late; I would peruse the listings in *Time Out* magazine and read of comedians described as 'circuit veterans, guaranteed to raise the roof' and ponder on why, if they were so hilarious, I'd never heard of them. It seemed there was an embarrassment of riches, and I had a great aversion to joining that embarrassment. A large part of it, I'm sure, was a fear of failure: if you don't join in the game then you can be pretty sure that you won't lose. So, when I did begin – ever so tentatively – to join the circuit, it was done almost as an experiment while at the same time answering a long-held desire to perform onstage as a stand-up.

One of the first things I noticed on entering the world of the stand-up comedian was the smoke. This was before the smoking ban, and clubs would exist in a positively Dickensian fug of cigarette and cigar smoke, which would catch at the back of my throat and make the impressions and singing especially difficult. It would get so bad that I would arrive at a club, let them know I was there, and then stand outside in the fresh air until it was my turn. After a while you acclimatize to the smoke, and I got to the point where I didn't notice it at all.

Mostly I would gig at the weekends, on Friday and Saturday nights. This wasn't conducive to family life and, because of what I'll politely describe as a 'nervous stomach', meant that I basically couldn't eat anything after an early lunch on the Saturday. By the time I got to the venue on a Saturday night I'd be starving, my blood sugar levels low, and desperately wanting to eat something. I'd usually give in and have a Mars Bar, or similar, and this would be swiftly followed by an anxious trip to the toilet where the recently consumed chocolate bar would continue on its journey. It would have saved me some time to just buy the thing, take it to the loo, and flush it away unopened. As I did more gigs, I'd begin to feel an ever-so-slight lessening of the nerves and this would trick me into believing that I could maybe eat something before the show. Always a mistake.

The nervous stomach was one thing; the general feeling of impending doom was another. Again, it would start after lunch on the Saturday and slowly creep up, the fear that I might die onstage. *What if they hate me? What if I don't get any laughs?* The act in those days was so flimsy, so reliant on a good crowd, a good ad-libbed line, so many variables beyond my control, that it was like starting afresh each time. As the afternoon progressed, I'd become more and more quiet and increasingly irritable. Lovely.

Then to the gig itself: you're announced; you walk on to the stage. No one knows who you are, so there's a period at the beginning of your spot where you can feel the crowd sizing you up. *Hmm, what's this one like? Is he any good?* I'd always make a superhuman effort to appear calm and confident (it's amazing how people are willing to accept the appearance of relaxation as genuine relaxation). It buys you some time. I would just act the part and wait until laughs came. Hopefully, the wait wouldn't be too long, and then I'd be away.

I still fall back on this now when things don't fly from the start; just try and look relaxed. Audiences can smell fear in a comic, if you let them, and the minute they do you're in big danger of losing them. All audiences want to feel that the comedian is in charge and knows what he or she is doing; they want to feel that all they have to do is just sit back and enjoy the show. I've had numerous times onstage where a few lines haven't gone as I'd hoped and I'm beginning to worry; I'll try to slow things right down, smile a bit and look like I couldn't be happier while inside my mind is turning over at a hundred miles an hour.

It changes once you build up your own audience; they've made the effort to buy the ticket months in advance and have been looking forward to coming to see you. It buys you time at the top of the show when

you're greeted with enthusiastic applause, a mini celebration. You're the one thing that the whole audience
has in common – their liking for you, the comedian. I
say the whole audience, but it's often painfully easy to
spot the partners who've come because their wife/girl-
friend is a fan, or there was a spare ticket going at work.
I'll scan the front rows: smiley face, smiley face, smiley
face . . . scowl. You learn after a while to block those
faces out, to pretend they're not there; they get filed
under the heading 'You Can't Please Everyone'. It takes
a while to learn the discipline required to phase those
faces out. I've known so many comedians who will fixate on the one bloke who's not enjoying the show; I've
done it myself.

During my West End run a couple of years ago, I was
five minutes into the act when I noticed a man in the
front row looking at his watch. He then turned to his
wife and made a gesture as if to say, 'At the first chance
we get, we'll go.' The thing was, we just happened to
catch each other's eye – and he knew that I knew exactly
what had just happened. I was furious. I felt embar-
rassed, insulted, angry. He looked mortified.

I decided to direct everything at him and, for the next
twenty minutes, after every laugh I would look at him,
stare him down as if to say, 'See? They think I'm funny!'
He was looking more and more uncomfortable until
suddenly (and imperceptibly, at first) he turned the tables
on me. He began, rather cleverly, to laugh a little too
much at the jokes. This unnerved me enormously; it
really put me on the back foot. You won't be surprised
to hear that the couple did not return after the interval.

I now wish I'd simply ignored him. What I did was futile; it's just self-flagellation, and ultimately pointless. It's also unfair on the rest of the audience, who are enjoying the show, as it gives the comedian a warped view of the crowd as a whole, which in turn impacts on how he relates to them.

If I'm giving the impression that I feel I can predict how an audience will behave, then I'm giving the *wrong* impression; an audience can so often surprise you. When you're on tour and a rhythm is built up of good show after good show, it can be easy to become complacent. This is when the shock usually comes along. I remember walking out to an audience somewhere in the north of England with great confidence after a run of excellent shows in similar towns.

Within ten seconds, I knew tonight would be different.

It was as though they'd all had a little meeting before I came on, the conclusion of which was that they'd give me a chance but that each and every one of them should be on their guard and treat me with the greatest suspicion. Very weird. After a while, things settled and the show was fine. But that initial shock was disconcerting and only overcome through experience and being able to keep faith that they (the audience) would eventually come around if I just carried on and did what had worked every other night.

While slowly building up my experience as a stand-up, I was also picking up the odd television gig here and there, always in tiny roles that never seemed to make a difference to the overall picture as far my career was concerned.

I was in a couple of one-off films for Hat Trick Productions. The first, *Eleven Men Against Eleven*, starred James Bolam and was set in the world of football. I played a commentator, and we filmed on a hot summer's day at The Den, home of Millwall FC. The only thing I remember from this job was my delight at watching James Bolam during the read-through; it was another of those moments when you get to work with someone you've grown up watching.

The next film was *Lord of Misrule*, starring Richard Wilson, in which I played a policeman. We filmed in the beautiful seaside town of Fowey, in Cornwall. My part involved no more than standing on a ferry boat as it crossed the river and asking Stephen Moyer, playing the lead in his pre-*True Blood* days, if the car belongs to him.

He then dives overboard and Prunella Scales steps out of the car and says, 'Well, go after him then.'

It would be nice to report that Prunella and I sparked with the kind of brilliant onscreen chemistry she'd enjoyed with John Cleese in *Fawlty Towers*.

But, alas, all that happened was I replied, 'You go after him, ma'am . . .' and the scene ended.

As with James Bolam, it was great to work alongside Prunella and Richard Wilson but, beyond that, I knew it was unlikely to have any real impact on things. A couple of weeks after I'd returned from Cornwall, I received a call asking me to head back and reshoot the scene. Driving from the unit base to the location, I was sitting in the car with Jimmy Mulville, former comedian, star of *Who Dares Wins* and now head of Hat Trick Productions. Fishing for compliments, I cast my line and asked, in an admittedly light-hearted way, whether the scene was being reshot due to any shortcomings on my part.

'Is it my fault?'

Without missing a beat, and slightly too chillingly for my liking, Jimmy replied, 'If it was, you wouldn't be here.'

I quickly put away my rod.

Perhaps I had expected a bit of unsolicited praise after my recent experience on *Married for Life*, the short-lived British remake of the hugely popular and long-running American series *Married with Children*. Our version starred Russ Abbot and was filmed up in Nottingham. I had a small part in one of the episodes as a co-worker at the shoe shop where Russ's character is employed. I got on so well with the team that they wrote me into another episode, this time as a newsreader. The series also featured a little-known Hugh Bonneville and we would often all eat together at the hotel at the end of the day's filming. At one of the meals we were joined by some of the executives from the television company. After dessert, with everyone chatting away ten to the dozen, Russ began to sing my praises to the executives, saying how funny he thought I was and that there was quite a buzz going around on the show about me. When they weren't looking, he gave me a sly wink and a smile.

Later, when the executives had gone, he came over and, in conspiratorial tones, whispered, 'That's what you've got to do, get them talking about you.'

What a nice man.

As 1997 progressed, the television roles began to dry up again – as a result of my poor performances, I feared (with perhaps a little paranoia). I was getting by handsomely on the money coming in from voice-overs, and in the evenings I'd slip out and try my stand-up routines at tiny clubs.

Martina was pregnant again, although this time not in the presence of Sir John Gielgud, and as the summer came to an end she gave birth in September to a baby boy – my first son, Harry. Having had a girl when we'd suspected it would be a boy, we now had a boy when we were expecting a girl. We were both surprised and over-joyed at our beautiful new addition.

Hurrah!

A new member of the family meant more responsi-bility for me and, while money was no longer the problem it had once been, I still felt unfulfilled creatively and dreamed of wider success, the chance to create and act in something of substance. At night I would lie in bed wondering what more I could be doing. Why wasn't I breaking through to where I wanted to be? The more I wondered, the more I'd stay awake, and so I developed a routine that would help me get off to sleep.

I'd imagine myself on television, being interviewed on *Parkinson*, coming out at the top of the steps, strol-ling down with confidence as the crowd cheered and Michael stood waiting, arms outstretched and smiling.

'It's been a remarkable journey, hasn't it? Tell me about your roots . . .'

He would quiz me about my incredible rise from voice-over artist to beloved actor and comedian, express-ing amazed admiration that I'd been able to make the leap from the one world to the other. Sometimes it would be a one-on-one interview, sometimes I would be the final guest in a line-up that would include perhaps Steve Martin, Paul Simon and James Taylor, who would all at some point interrupt Michael's flow to offer up their own praise. After twenty minutes or so I would drift off to sleep perfectly content. It was, I suppose, a form of positive visualization – and, given that some years later I went on to descend the steps for real, it could be considered to have been very effective and successful (although the reality, as is often the case, was not quite as sweet as the fantasy).

It was 2002; I was a couple of years into my eventual success and had finally been asked to appear on *Parkinson*. I'd already appeared on a few other chat shows and been interviewed by a generous handful of journalists and presenters, yet none of them came close to the excitement of appearing on the show that I'd watched for as long as I could remember. While waiting in my dressing room before the recording, there was a knock on the door and in walked Michael Parkinson himself, to welcome me to the show and to generally wish me well. He mentioned what he might cover in the interview: how the Celts could be prone to depression, and that he'd heard I did an impression of Anthony Hopkins which he might ask me to do. With that, he was gone. To say that I was nervous about appearing on the show was an understatement. I had a real fear that I would bomb – that I would *die* on the show – although whenever I'd have these thoughts, I'd reassure myself that I was being silly and that while I might not storm it, there was no real chance that I'd die. The worst that could happen, I reasoned, was that I'd be OK, nothing special.

Waiting in the wings, I was sitting with fellow guest Timothy Spall while Chris Tarrant was already out in front of the audience being interviewed. Soon I was standing at the top of a rickety stairway waiting for my introduction, heart pounding in time with Bryan Ferry who was singing his latest song, unseen, just feet away. Peter Sellers, Morecambe and Wise, Kenneth Williams and Richard Burton had all made this same entrance; had they felt as nervous as this? Suddenly it was time to make my move, I stepped forward into the lights as the band played loudly to my left, and I descended the stairs (trying desperately hard to look relaxed while battling the thought that I might well slip and slide my way to the bottom). I remember walking across to Michael Parkinson with my arm outstretched, we shook hands and I sat down, still trying to affect the air of a very relaxed man.

He spoke.

I stared.

Rabbits and headlights sprang to mind.

The thing about appearing on *Parkinson* is that it's not like watching it at home. While this is of course true of every interview programme, it is especially true here due to the frankly iconic nature of the show. Firstly there was the proximity to Mr Parkinson; I remember very quickly noticing how close we were to each other, our knees practically touching. Then there was the fact that, when looking at Michael, he didn't appear to be sitting on the set; the chairs were angled in such a way that it looked as if he was sitting in front of an inky blackness that stretched off into the distance. On top of this, there was the sound of the audience – or, rather, the lack of any sound from the audience. They were so quiet, so reverential; it was quite unnerving.

Michael began by saying something or other – I don't remember what, and I certainly can't bring myself to watch the video recording I have of the show. I answered. It was evident that most of the audience had no idea who I was and weren't overburdened with curiosity. After a couple of minutes, Michael said something about the gloomy nature of the Welsh. *Ah!* I thought. *This is my cue to do the Hopkins impression.* And so I answered that, in my opinion, we could indeed be a little gloomy but I bet there was one Welshman who wasn't that gloomy right now, what with his success and all – Anthony Hopkins! I then began to do my impression.

Now the thing to remember is that, although I can be insecure and nervous about a myriad subjects, areas or aspects of myself, there is one topic on which I am quietly confident, and that's my ability with voices. I'm not the best there is, but I'm pretty good and can hold my own in most circumstances That was the mindset with which I began to do Anthony Hopkins: *I'm on safe ground here.* My impression involved having him say words I'd heard him trot out many times in interviews regarding the fact that as a recovering alcoholic he no longer drank and didn't take life seriously; he considered it to be 'a game'. Added to this, I squinted into the distance and tugged at my right earlobe, both little physical quirks that I'd witnessed him exhibit on many occasions.

'Well, I don't drink any more, I don't like to talk about it, very dull, very boring. It's all a game really, isn't it?'

Within the first few words I noticed that there was not

the slightest, smallest, most imperceptible response from the audience. There was nothing at all, and it threw me slightly. What then unfolded can have taken no more than five or six seconds, yet it seemed at the time to last an appalling eternity. My thought processes went something along the lines of: *They're not laughing! They're not even making a sound! This is awful, I'm dying, I'm dying on* Parkinson, *my worst fears are coming true!* I scrambled around, searching for something to say that would redeem me and prompt the audience to laugh. Or, if not to laugh, then to cough or at least mutter, anything but the desert of silence I was currently stranded in.

It was at this point that I unexpectedly and inexplicably went into a very fleeting impersonation of Tom Jones, in particular his cough. This is the aspect of his voice that I'd seized on to some comic effect many times before – the loud throat clearing that accompanies almost every interview with The World's Greatest Welshman. In and of itself it's amusing enough, but it has no place midway through Anthony Hopkins. Unplanned, unexpected and unwanted.

'Well, I don't drink any more, I don't like to talk about it, very dull, very boring. *HARRUMPH!!!*'

I don't think I've ever been more shocked than I was at the arrival of an involuntary Tom Jones cough. I couldn't believe I was getting it so wrong; I never messed up with voices; they were one hundred per cent safe ground for me. *What are you doing?! You're doing Tom Jones! Why? Why? Why?* I stopped short of saying 'Delilah'. *Right, come on, keep it together, do something crowd-pleasing, finish with the sucking in of breath between the teeth that Hopkins does in* The Silence of The Lambs, *that little thing he does after mentioning how much he'd enjoy a fine Chianti. That's bound to get a response.* It seemed a good plan and so I began to suck the air between my teeth – or rather, I didn't. For reasons I still don't understand, I began to hiss. I hissed like a snake. More panic. *What are you doing? You're hissing like a snake! He doesn't hiss like a snake! Why are you hissing like a snake?*

Immediately post-hiss, my little impression was over – along, I feared, with my career. I spent the rest of the programme in a daze, smiling at Michael, laughing at Timothy Spall's anecdotes, but all the time contemplating what had just happened.

If my imaginary bedtime *Parkinson* had been at all like the real thing, I'd have never got to sleep.

Meanwhile, in 1997, I had become a father again and was managing to provide for my expanding family quite comfortably, thanks to the voice work, but decent acting jobs were as elusive as ever. Then one day I was pottering about in my kitchen, making lunch, when the phone rang. It was a casting director I'd been bothering for some time, and my little heart leapt when she clearly used the word 'film' in association with the part she was about to describe. It then sank when she went on to preface the part with the word 'nerdy'. I had developed an aversion to the word; it had begun to seem as if the only way I'd ever be considered for a role was if it contained an element of nerdiness. I had played a variation on the nerd theme in *Cold Lazarus*, *Married for Life* and *Lord of Misrule*, and had more or less had my fill. I was making enough money by now for a comfortable life and was of the opinion that another nerdy role would not be a great help in furthering my artistic cause and getting me closer to a part with some substance. When she went on to say that it wasn't just a nerd per se, but a nerdy traffic warden, I was ready to say 'thanks but no thanks'. What was the point of another tiny inconsequential part? I had begun to say, when people asked me about my latest small role, that it was so tiny a part, 'a Labrador could play it'.

It must have been the fact that it was a film rather than something for TV that stopped me from making an excuse and hanging up. Instead, I thanked her for thinking of me and took down the details. The film was called *Lock, Stock and Two Smoking Barrels*; I was to go to Ealing Studios and meet the director, a man named Guy Ritchie. I already knew the famous Ealing Studios from watching numerous documentaries on Peter Sellers and seeing footage of him filming *I'm All Right Jack* there. I pictured the place in my mind; it was a very distinctive building on the North Circular. Whenever I passed it in the car, I would point out to whoever cared to listen that this was where the great Ealing Comedies had been shot, and that we were driving past a site of great cultural importance.

On the day of the meeting I set off in good time, full of the ridiculous hope that I might be edging my way into films. I turned the car off the North Circular and into the studio compound, looking for a reception area. I was surprised that there appeared to be no security to speak of, or indeed any of the paraphernalia usually associated with film studios. Where were the sound stages, the golf buggies, the people carrying huge pieces of scenery past old rotting props? As I drove around a little more, it became apparent that I had in fact come to a block of flats whose only connection with the celebrated Ealing Studios was that they vaguely resembled the location I'd seen on the Peter Sellers documentary.

I arrived for my meeting with Guy Ritchie half an hour late, and more than a little flustered. But he was very relaxed and, after the usual pleasantries, almost apologetically asked me to read some lines for the part. It was chillingly reminiscent of my casting for *First Knight*, once again reading a tiny bit of script, once again playing a man being assaulted – although this time I was only knocked out, not shot with a crossbow. It's also worth saying in First Villager's defence that he wasn't at all nerdy; he was, after all, just trying to protect his family from evil Ben Cross (worried, perhaps, that he might be forced to sit with his wife and children watching *Chariots of Fire* again and again, while Ben loomed at their shoulder monitoring their reactions).

I read the part – it basically consisted of, 'You can't park here . . . *Argh!*'

Guy said, in effect, 'Sorry about that, of course you can do it,' and then told me when the filming would be.

Directors often do this during an audition. Sometimes it means you've got the part, and this was how I interpreted it. He looked at my CV, saw that I had appeared in *First Knight* and asked me how I'd found the experience. For reasons best known to someone smarter than me, I began to tell him (with no small amount of detail) the story of my little chat with Hunt Lowry, how

I'd refused to do the extra filming that had been asked of me, and how it had all ended a little unpleasantly. I had almost reached the conclusion of my tale before realizing that it probably didn't show me in the best light for potential employers. I could feel my grip being prised open by my own idiocy and the part slipping out of my hands – but short of saying that I'd entirely made up the last five minutes of our chat, there was nothing I could do. We shook hands and I left. What an idiot.

A couple of weeks went by . . . and I heard nothing. Then a month or so . . .

I became convinced that it was my retelling of my 'Bad Employee of the Month' tale that had cost me the part. Then one day, some months later, the same casting director called once more and said the part was mine; it had been mine all along, but the film had lost its funding not long after my casting, hence the delay.

We were back on. Cock-a-doodle-do!

The night before the filming of my first scene, I received a call from the production team. My first instinct was to expect the news that my line had been cut, and did I still want to play a nerdy *mute* traffic warden? I was wrong, they were actually calling to tell me there was a chance I might be stood down tomorrow as one of the stars of the film, Vinnie Jones, had been arrested for allegedly threatening a neighbour with a shotgun ('We've all done it . . .') and so the schedule might have to be rearranged to accommodate his enforced absence. Ten minutes later, there was another call – this time to say that all was well and we were going ahead as planned.

I arrived at the unit base late the next morning; it was

almost midday, they weren't ready for me, and so I was told to wait on the lunch bus. I grabbed some food and sat down. There was a *Daily Mirror* on the seat next to me and I flicked through it, arriving after a few pages at their report on Vinnie's altercation the previous day. As I read, I felt someone sitting down opposite me at the other side of the table. I looked up from a picture of Vinnie Jones, over the top of the paper, and there he was, in the flesh, sitting opposite me. I looked straight back down at the paper. It was not unlike the moment in so many films when the fugitive is making his escape across country and manages to get on to the safety of a train, only for a fellow passenger to spot his picture in a paper and raise the alarm. (I didn't raise any alarms.)

The filming was a lot of fun – if lying in the back of a transit van as it is towed around the East End and pretending to be beaten up is your idea of a lot of fun. Of the actors in the van, Dexter Fletcher and Jason Flemyng were especially friendly, always apologizing at the end of a take and checking that they hadn't hit me for real.

I did two, maybe three, days on the film and then went back to my normal working life of voice-overs.

I had forgotten all about the film when, some months later, I began to notice it being talked about here and there. I had just come out of a voice-over, and was walking along Wardour Street one day, when I bumped into Stephen Moyer (who had played the lead in *Lord of Misrule*). He'd been in LA, where he had heard great things about *Lock, Stock and Two Smoking Barrels*. There was a buzz going around, people were talking about it, and apparently a special screening had been arranged for no less a Hollywood luminary than Tom Cruise. Even though my role in the film was tiny, I was excited to be part of something that was causing a stir in America.

I was invited to a cast and crew screening of the film, ahead of its official release. The screening was in the West End, just a stone's throw from the Odeon Leicester Square where, a few years ago, I'd sunk down in my seat in horror at my *First Knight* performance. My nerdy traffic warden doesn't appear for some time, but even through the long wait and the ever-present fear that I was about to be revealed as an actor out of his depth, I couldn't help noticing that the film really was rather good. It was funny, stylish, slick and, perhaps most of all, it felt remarkably *now*.

As for myself, when I finally appeared, I thought I was OK, certainly not bad, and while Dustin Hoffman wouldn't be losing any sleep I felt that I hadn't let myself down – I'd improved, if only ever so slightly. Overall I just came away hugely impressed with the film and sure that it was going to be a hit. The distributor obviously thought so too. The subsequent advertising campaign was huge; the posters were everywhere.

When the film finally came out, it was to great acclaim. In those days I was a big film fan, that is to say, a fan of films and film-making – the excitement and glamour of the whole world – and I would read *Empire* magazine each month. They gave the film a glowing review; I bought a copy in a newsagent's on the Upper Richmond Road in East Sheen and stood on the pavement to read it. I was pleased enough with the review but absolutely flabbergasted to see that I'd been given a mention, something along the lines of 'an extremely unlucky traffic warden, Robert Brydon'. I was amazed, and straight away began to wonder if I could use this to my advantage. I was in a hit film, a trendy, fashionable, 'of the moment', zeitgeist film; I must be able to hitch a ride on its back somehow.

I'd been toying for a while with the idea of putting together a showreel of characters I'd created myself, not just the tiny parts I'd been getting up to that point, and decided this would be the perfect time to do it. I'd write a script, then shoot the thing and, using the money that was flowing in from voice-overs, I'd pay to have it edited, dubbed and packaged.

In a shameless display of bandwagon-jumping, I called it *Rob Brydon: An Extremely Unlucky Traffic Warden*.

18

Earlier that year, we had been on holiday with friends to a beautiful old farmhouse in Tuscany. There was a pool, you could eat outside, and it was all on its own, surrounded by the most stunning countryside. It had been exceptionally hot and I'd taken to wearing a rather fetching bandana around my neck, to protect my skin from burning. As hard as it might be to believe, this bandana, worn at a jaunty, rakish angle, had given me a slightly camp appearance and so I began to mess about and build a character to go with the look.

I named him Colin; he'd come to the farmhouse to get himself together after a difficult time in his romantic life. He spoke in a posh, clipped Welsh accent, the kind that pronounces the word 'university' as '*ewe*niversity'. I'd loved this kind of voice for a long time but had never managed to do anything with it. The character would get lots of laughs around the dinner table and by the pool, so I decided to make the most of the incredible location and film a little video of Colin, just for fun. When it came to costume, I stripped down to my boxers, tucked them in so they resembled a posing pouch, and oiled my body until it glistened. The final touch was the bandanna. With the magnificent Tuscan hills rolling away behind me, I stood by the pool, glistening in the sun, and began to speak to the camera as though recording a video message for a dating agency website. The comedy was helped by the unplanned additions of an intermittently barking dog and a curious wasp, both of which caused Colin to lose his composure.

I'd liked the results of this messing-about-on-holiday tape, and had thought for a while that there was more I could do with the character. So, once I was home, I sat down to write another few minutes around Colin, which involved him going on his first date – to an amusement arcade, with Steve Speirs. In the finished video Ruth Jones pops up in the final scene as she waves Steve and me off on holiday.

I wrote two other characters. One was a Londoner, named Terry, who we see enjoying a night out in Cardiff and interacting with the drinkers and clubbers he meets on the streets. I also revived a character from my earliest days at Radio Wales, Chuck Webb. Chuck was an American reporter, again interacting with real people as he filed his reports for an imaginary US network. The joke was an old one – his misunderstandings of British culture – but there were some nice moments. I went to the Museum of Welsh Life at St Fagans, on the outskirts of Cardiff, and interviewed visitors, asking them what they thought of the place. The museum has many buildings from all over Wales that have been transported from their original location and then rebuilt, brick by brick, at the museum. I pronounced St Fagans as 'St Fagin's' and questioned whether Fagin, famously brought to life in *Oliver Twist*, should ever have been made a saint, and whether it was fair that he'd forced street children to steal the houses brick by individual brick and bring them to Cardiff.

Remarkably, no one questioned my logic, one chap saying that at least these kids weren't on the streets and we should be thankful to St Fagin for that.

The final character on the tape was Keith Barret, who I hadn't visited since *Who Died Earlier Today*, two years previously. I wrote a brief episode for Keith; it involved him visiting a fellow taxi driver in hospital who had been attacked by a passenger. Talking to a camera set up on the dashboard, Keith tells us that he himself has never been attacked, as he simply doesn't look for trouble. He then of course inadvertently does just that, and gets set upon after searching for his pick-up, a Mr Anka, in the course of which he leans out of his window and loudly asks a passer-by if he is Mr Anka.

'Excuse me, Anka? Are you Anka?'

It wasn't the most sophisticated gag I'd ever written. We see the passer-by approach the car and grab Keith as the camera slides to the floor, and we hear the savage beating that ensues.

I recorded all the sketches over a couple of days with Rhys as cameraman and director, and then set about compiling and editing them. I designed a cover for the VHS cassette in the style of the posters for *Lock, Stock and Two Smoking Barrels*, packaged about thirty of them in padded envelopes and sent them off to a variety of casting agents, directors and producers. Almost all of them were never heard of again, or plopped sadly back on to my doormat unwatched; the only positive response was from Carlton Television, whose casting department put me in *Barbara*, a sitcom starring Gwen Taylor and Sam Kelly. The show also featured the brilliant Mark

Benton, who would go on to appear with me in *Human Remains* and *A Small Summer Party*. Other than that, there was nothing.

Undeterred, I would carry a copy of the tape around with me wherever I went in case I should run into anyone whom I thought might be able to help. One day, I was walking down Sherwood Street in Soho and saw Sir Peter Hall walking towards me. We were both strolling along the middle of the road; this was a hell of an opportunity. I reached down to my bag, my fingers itching like a gunfighter's. Did I dare to accost the great man of theatre and press a copy into his hands? Did I have the nerve to step forward and take control of my destiny? Did I have what it took to seize the moment. To *carpe diem*?

No, I didn't.

This was a shame – at the very least, I could have told him how much I had enjoyed his production of *The Merchant of Venice* at the Phoenix Theatre in the West End a few years previously. Dustin Hoffman played Shylock; I'd watched a *South Bank Show* on the making of the production and was beyond excited at the prospect of seeing Hoffman onstage. As we milled about outside the theatre, I did a double take at the unexpected sight of Benjamin Braddock/Ratso Rizzo/Dorothy Michaels himself strolling past. It was Hoffman, complete with appropriately Venetian merchant facial hair, walking unimpeded through the crowds and into the theatre, giving a little wink to the stage-door attendant as he entered the building, as if to say, 'Fooled them, again.' I was so flabbergasted I had to sit down. That's not just a figure of speech; being ten feet away from an undetected Dustin Hoffman really did cause me to have to sit down.

Meanwhile, here I was, stalking the West End with my new showreel, showcasing all my own characters, hoping to catch someone's eye. Amongst the many people I had considered sending the tape to was Hugo Blick, a name from the distant past of my college days in Cardiff. I hadn't seen him for some time but was very aware of his progress. He had worked as an actor, appearing in films like *Batman* and *The Wind in the Willows*. I had seen him pop up on shows like *Jeeves and Wooster* and *Blackadder*. He was now at the BBC as a writer and producer, and was credited as such, as well as for his acting, in the comedy series *Operation Good Guys*.

It would have made sense to send the tape to Hugo; given our history, I could at least be sure that he'd watch it. But I didn't. The thought of a polite 'no' from someone I'd been at college with was too much to contemplate – although I had thought to myself that if I ever bumped into him by chance I might casually bring up the fact that I'd made a tape and possibly pass it on for his opinion. This was one of the reasons for carrying the cassette around with me everywhere I went.

A couple of weeks after I'd failed to make a connection with Peter Hall, I was at the BBC TV Centre. I had just recorded a voice-over ('. . . and with *Match of the Day* at ten, that's Saturday night on BBC1!') and was walking through the corridors on my way out. Knowing that Hugo worked in that same enormous building, I imagined how fortuitous it would be to bump into him and be given the opportunity to hand over the tape in person. At that very moment, he walked round the corner and almost bumped into me. Television Centre is a huge building containing an enormous number of people; the chances of bumping into one specific individual must be very slight indeed. I burst out laughing. This was a bizarre piece of synchronicity.

We went and had a drink together and caught up with what we'd been doing over the years. He explained that part of his job at the BBC was to read new scripts and find new talent; he also had a modest development budget for any projects he felt showed promise. Hmm . . . a very small light bulb illuminated a far corner of my mind. All through our chat the tape was sitting in a bag at my feet, but still I hesitated to bring it into the conversation, worried by the possibility of rejection from one of my contemporaries.

Eventually, and after much internal debate, I quietly mentioned that I'd done this thing, this video, this collection of characters: 'I have a tape and, if you like, you could watch it . . .'

He was probably just being polite but, to my surprise, he said he'd love to see it.

I handed over the box, and left.

An hour and a half later, I was back in my second home, Soho, sitting in a café on Broadwick Street, just along from the public toilet where Peter Cook and John Lennon had filmed a sketch in the year of my birth, when my phone rang. It was Hugo. He'd watched the tape and, while the first three weren't to his taste, he liked the last character of the four, Keith Barret, and suggested I come back to the BBC and talk about it.

I didn't know it at the time of course, but this phone call was a fantastically important, game-changing, pivotal moment in my life. It was the beginning of a whole new chapter.

The next day, we met in his tiny office and straight away seemed to be in tune with each other as to how we saw the character and where it might develop. There was a great deal of very fortunate timing involved in this coming together, for both of us. For my part, I was absolutely desperate to play a character with some depth, some substance, a character with a story arc – something I had yet to do on television with my gallery of five-line nerds. I think that Hugo was looking to develop something less slapstick and perhaps more subtle than the knockabout humour of *Operation Good Guys*. The idea we had – that Keith would continue, as he'd done on the demo tape, to simply drive around while telling us, albeit unreliably, about his life – was a relatively simple and, more importantly, inexpensive one to attempt.

We began to construct a rich backstory for Keith. All that existed at this point was Keith, his taxi and his wife, Marion. Together we decided that Marion had left Keith for a man named Geoff, taking with her the two boys, Rhys and Alun, so named in honour of Rhys John and Alan Thompson. Alan was changed to Alun, the Welsh spelling, pronounced 'Alin', for no other reason than that it used to annoy Al when I called him that. Childish, I know. We placed our hero in London and sent Marion back to Cardiff, Keith's natural home, so that he was left struggling to survive on his own, far from his native land, living in a single room in a house shared with loud and noisy students. This was surely inspired by my horrible room in Grangetown, sleeping on a mattress on the floor, just feet above the noisy architect. Keith drove around in his taxi for hours on end, telling the camera about his life and inadvertently revealing his true self by degrees.

The story of what became the first episode began to emerge: how Keith was going to drive to Cardiff and surprise Marion at the anniversary party of Edith and Neville, his former in-laws; how he had bought presents for Rhys and Alun, his 'little smashers', worrying that one of the gifts, a gruesome action figure, might be too violent for his son, 'But, like his mother said, he's a very violent child.'

When we were happy with our story, we arranged the shoot. A camera was borrowed from *Noel's House Party*, handed over rather bizarrely by Noel Edmonds himself. Hugo, with the pioneering use of a large wad of Blu-tack, then stuck the camera to the dashboard of the rented car and we were away. We shot the pilot and the subsequent first series primarily on the streets around my home in East Sheen; local residents familiar with the geography of the place would have been well placed to point out the absurd routes that Keith often appeared to take as he doubled back on himself and drove along the same stretch of road several times in succession.

We would shoot the script we had written but I was also able to improvise and create material on the spot, which could be instantly edited and added to by Hugo as he sat crouching out of sight in the back of the car. When I was trying to deliver a gag or tell a story with a sudden humorous twist at the end, I'd know if I was on to something if I could feel the car vibrating ever so slightly as Hugo struggled to contain his laughter. It was a wonderful way of working, a little two-man underdog team pulling together to create our own very special, very different story.

Looking back at this period of my life now, I can see that all the strands and fragments of work that I had experienced, if not endured, over the years since leaving college were finally beginning to come together in a coherent way. While I had been trying, with a straight face, to sell Paula Yates Hand Cream (no, really) on the Shopping Channel ten years earlier, I had yearned for a move into the unattainable world of acting; in film, in a TV show, in a fringe theatre, anywhere but that brightly lit, smelling-of-make-up studio in Osterley. But I'm sure that the television shopping, the roving reporting, the radio-show hosting, even the playing of a thrush-cream salesman in a hotel in Glasgow, all contributed to the person who finally managed to produce some work he could be proud of.

It was during those few days spent driving around and filming the beginnings of *Marion and Geoff* that I finally gave an acting performance that represented what I'd hoped I was capable of, a performance that wasn't forced or overplayed but that just *was*. I realized what I had been doing all these years whenever I'd had a chance to prove myself on something, such as *First Knight*, was simply overacting. I'd had a terror of trying to give a subtle, naturalistic performance and then looking up to see the director recoil in horror, saying, 'Woah, woah, what are you doing?' So, to deny anyone the chance, I would always crank it up just so they could see that I was doing something, I was 'giving a performance'. It was always hard coming into a big production to play a small part, and having to judge the tone of the whole piece; my default mode was simply to go big, in the vain hope of being noticed. Sitting in the car was the first time I'd felt secure enough to try to give the sort of performance I admired in others. It was a wholly conscious decision, an effort to go for it and try to be the sort of actor I'd always wanted to be.

Alongside the excitement of finally being part of something good, something of quality, in July Martina gave birth to a beautiful baby girl, Amy. We now had gone girl/boy/girl, and I rather admired our completely random symmetry; it was as though we were planning a Eurovision act. I was present at the birth, as I had been for Katie and Harry – a nervous wreck, even more so than before, convinced that we had been lucky so far and surely something must go wrong this time?

Thankfully, it didn't.

To describe this time of my life as an exciting period of creative rebirth might smack of hubris, but that's really how it felt; as well as the good fortune of bumping into Hugo, I was once again in contact with another old friend, Julia Davis. After our More Fool Us days in her native Bath, Julia had seemed to vanish off the face of the earth, only to pop up again some years later after relocating to London. Rather than being intimidated by her surroundings and following my own deathly slow progress, from shopping channel to thrush convention, she had immediately begun to work with the very best people around. We would talk on the phone and I'd listen wide-eyed as she told me how she'd already been involved in projects with *Father Ted* creators Graham Linehan and Arthur Mathews, as well as the man on the cutting edge of the cutting edge, Chris Morris. One day, she called and said that she'd just got a job alongside the still-unknown Simon Pegg as one of two supporting actors on Steve Coogan's forthcoming tour of the UK.

Wow. Gulp. Oh my. This was the one that I especially envied.

I had followed Steve's career for a long time and had watched his television appearances with huge admiration, in particular the peerless *I'm Alan Partridge*. Martina and I used to watch the first series on the sofa, and at the end of each episode I'd look across at her with an expression that said, 'Perfection.' It was as though the programme had been made just for me. Knowing that Steve had started his professional life as a voice-over artist had seemed to me to be the much-needed proof that I might still, one day, be able to clamber across into the world of comedy.

On the day of her first rehearsal, I called Julia in the evening to ask how it had gone and to offer up that classic fan question: 'What's he like?' I told her how I already had tickets to see the show when it came to the nearest venue to my home, the Reading Hexagon. Indeed, that was the next time I saw her – and the first time I met

Steve. It was a brief meeting after the show, at a local hotel, where he was surrounded by well-wishers and some of the large travelling circus that made up the show's cast and crew.

I drove home from the encounter elated and deflated all at once. I clearly wasn't doing what I wanted to be doing with my career and, having spent just a little while with Steve and his acolytes, the world of which I had just enjoyed the most fleeting taste and wanted so much to inhabit seemed further away than ever. I had planned to mention to Steve that I'd made a videotape of a few characters I'd written, and maybe even suggest that I try to get it to him for his perusal. But when it came to the crunch I wimped out, once again afraid of rejection. Other than saying how much I'd enjoyed the show, I think all I did was mention that we had a mutual friend in Peter Serafinowicz – so, essentially, I came away from our meeting no closer to success than when I'd arrived. I returned to my life of voice-overs, ever so slightly depressed.

Eventually, the tour came into London and took up a residency at the Lyceum Theatre, where it was packed with fans for a record-breaking five-week run. Rather conveniently for me, the theatre was just up the road from where I was to be found every Friday afternoon, whipping out my funny voices, recording *The Treatment* for Radio Five. One such Friday, on my way through the West End to the recording at Bush House, I knocked on the stage door at the Lyceum and dropped off a copy of *An Extremely Unlucky Traffic Warden* for Julia, who had promised to pass it on. My hope was that it might at some point be opened and watched, while my expectation was that it would probably meet the fate of most of its siblings and return home, tail between its legs, landing with a defeated thud on the doormat.

The Treatment was a weekly radio show looking back at the news of the last seven days. In front of a very small studio audience, and I mean *very* small – they made Derek Jameson's lot look like the O2 – a panel of assorted wits and political writers would each read a prepared piece on a given subject before it was thrown open for discussion. The contributors were an eclectic mix. Comedy writers like David Quantick and Jane Bussmann, political journalists Peter Oborne, Patrick Hennessy and Kevin Maguire, and comedians Lucy Porter, Jo Caulfield and a pre-ascendant Graham Norton all appeared on the show. Their talks were punctuated by a series of sketches performed by the very talented Laura Shavin and myself, as a variety of characters real and imagined.

It was a very good show, although I soon tired of the lightweight nature of the sketches and began to resent being given a cassette with the voices of the politicians of the day lined up for me to learn to mimic. Doing voices was always just a laugh; as a rule of thumb, I only really do people I'm fond of, or admire, so being given a list tended to irk me. The production team was a great bunch of people, though, and I'd always look forward to spending time with them – especially the host, Stuart Maconie, a splendid northern chap, a gentleman broadcaster with a wonderfully dry and understated wit. Stuart is one of the few people to share with Rhys John and myself a love of the line, 'What could possibly go wrong?'

He and I soon had a list of sayings that would make each other laugh. When talking about my brief warm-ups in front of our threadbare studio audience, he would refer to me as, 'Little Bobby Brydon . . . He fills the stage with flags.' He would always have me in stitches as he'd drop into conversation, apropos of nothing, 'What was it the doctor said, Rob? A complete mental and physical breakdown . . .'

I liked Stuart so much that, if you watch the first episode of *Marion and Geoff*, as Keith is driving through the night to Cardiff to gatecrash the anniversary party, Stuart's is the voice of the contestant on the radio quiz. I'm the DJ. Such versatility.

There was a researcher on the show named Mark Mason, with whom I was friendly. Mark has gone on to become a published author with several titles to his name, but in those days his great love was blues guitar. He played at a club on Kingly Street, round the corner from the home of the floral-print shirt, Liberty. This was such a time of change for me (I was grabbing any and all chances to perform in front of an audience, whether it was brief spots at comedy clubs or warming up the regulars in *The Treatment* audience) so when Mark suggested I join him at one of his blues nights I jumped at the chance. I think we sang 'Reconsider Baby' (the Lowell Fulson song that I knew via Elvis's version), along with James Taylor's 'Steamroller Blues'.

The bar was an intimate venue with a tiny stage at one end, and the performers would just step up and do their thing without much fuss. I went along three or four times and learned an important lesson from Mark, the very first time, when he noticed how I would sit back and wait for instruction from the band as to when to come in on a verse and when to sit out for a solo. He explained to me that I was in charge; I was the one who led the little band and decided who would do what. This seemingly obvious piece of advice was very significant for me – coming, as it did, at a time when I was beginning to take a bit more control of my working life and was becoming increasingly proactive. It was the realization that if you're out front singing, in essence leading the band, then that's what you have to do, you have to *lead*; you're in charge, and you have to make the decisions. I was always too polite, waiting to be told when to come in. Since then, whenever I'm singing with a band I'll always be sure to let them know where we're going, with a hand gesture or a look. And whenever I do, I remember being in the little bar on Kingly Street with Mark.

One of the clearest memories from my time on *The Treatment* has nothing to do with comedy or music; it was the feeling I'd get after the recording, when everyone would reconvene at the bar of the BBC Club at Bush House for a few drinks. I was still teetotal and utterly bewildered at how content my colleagues would be to stay in the club for a couple of hours – talking, it seemed to me, about nothing in particular. I would have a Diet Coke and, after forty minutes or so, I'd make my excuses and leave – just as I'd done at teenage parties back in Porthcawl. This puritanical approach to pleasure became especially evident when the show escaped to Edinburgh for the Fringe Festival one August and we all found ourselves sharing a flat together. It was very much a 'crash where you find a space' arrangement – not one that I have ever endorsed (liking, as I do, excessive, perhaps even opulent comfort).

On the first night, the small flat soon filled up with friends and acquaintances, and before long everyone was under the influence of something or other. I'm sure it was just drink; I can't imagine anyone in the media being interested in anything illegal. I of course was drinking only soft drinks, but this didn't stop me from entering into the spirit of things. The writer David Quantick recalls watching in amazement as I stood up and sang 'Delilah' to a room full of drunken revellers, while completely sober. I wasn't going to let the opportunity of an audience go to waste.

I went to bed around one or two in the morning, bagging a mattress that someone else had already claimed with the placing of their holdall on the pillow. If they were going to stay up this late at night, making a noise, then they didn't deserve a bed. I tried to go to sleep while the party carried on along the corridor, eventually nodding off around four o'clock, and waking again after a rejuvenating three hours' sleep at seven. It was quiet now, a little too quiet, and I wandered out of the bedroom, past an unidentified body in the other bed, and along to the living room. Here I found, to my horror, assorted corpses asleep on sofas, chairs, a table and the floor. It looked as though a friendly genocide had occurred while I slept. Around the window some curtains had managed to come free of their mooring and now lay defeated on the carpet.

I think it was the sight of the curtains that did it.

I like fun as much as the next man, but when that fun involves a blatant disregard for the welfare of curtains or soft furnishings in general, it's time to stop. I immediately got dressed, grabbed my bag and left. I walked briskly through the fresh August morning into the centre of Edinburgh and checked in at the Balmoral, a lovely five-star hotel with splendid views of the castle. Within half an hour I was reclining by the pool in my fluffy white robe, enjoying a breakfast of smoked salmon and scrambled eggs. This was my home for the remainder of the trip.

A few weeks had passed since Julia had handed the tape over to Steve. I was impatient to know what he thought of it, so I set about contriving a spontaneous random encounter with the King of Comedy. After another recording of *The Treatment* and an alcohol-free spell in the BBC Club, I wandered over with a friend one Friday night to the pub that I knew the cast of 'The Man Who Thinks He's It' frequented after their curtain had come down. I planned to chat to Julia for a while until Steve joined us, at which point I'd casually mention the tape and wonder out loud if he'd had a chance to see it? I hoped that this would be enough to prompt a positive response and subsequent career enhancement.

When we arrived at the pub it was crammed with post-theatre drinkers but in amongst the crowd I spotted Julia. We went over and joined her, asking how the show had gone that night. She replied that it had been good, but she was tired now and so she was going to head straight home. With that, she left.

So, now I was in the bar but without anyone to reintroduce me to Steve, whom I doubted would remember our fleeting encounter at the Reading Holiday Inn some months previously. I was just about to leave, when suddenly there he was, the reigning monarch of Comedy Land, and he was heading in my direction.

Unless I was the poorest judge of body language, he seemed to be smiling in recognition.

'You're Rob, aren't you? I saw your tape. I thought it was really good. I think you've got something, not many people have. Julia has, and Simon has, and I think you have too. I'd like to work with you one day . . .'

I don't remember anything else that was said between us.

I couldn't believe what I'd heard. This was huge.

If it had been ten years later, I might have been tempted to say, '*OMG!*'

When I think back to that night, I seem to have floated back home several feet off the ground, my mind buzzing. I arrived at the house; it was dark, the children were all in bed asleep. I went straight upstairs and woke Martina.

I couldn't wait to tell her: 'I've just met Steve Coogan; he's seen the tape. *He likes it!*'

19

It wasn't long after this thumbs up from Steve that Julia mentioned something Henry Normal had said to her. Henry was a former performance poet and writer responsible for, amongst others, *Paul Calf's Video Diary* and *The Royle Family*, as well as now being Steve's business partner. The two were in the process of setting up the production company that would go on to become Baby Cow Productions. Henry had one day mentioned to Julia that, if she ever wrote anything, would she bring it to him and Steve rather than, say, Talkback? This was the hugely successful production company set up by Griff Rhys Jones, Mel Smith and Peter Fincham, which was responsible for many of the most highly regarded comedies of the day. Julia told me of her chat with Henry, and suggested that we try to write something together.

This sounded like a good idea; we'd always had a chemistry when we'd been part of the More Fool Us group in Bath, and we shared a sense of humour and love of making each other laugh. After some thought as to what it was specifically that we should do, we settled on the idea of writing about couples, about relationships. We both loved Woody Allen and felt that we'd like to explore similar territory – the ins and outs of relationships, the odd shorthand that develops through intimacy and familiarity. We realized also that, in writing about a couple, we could keep the whole thing self-contained and wouldn't be reliant on others.

We decided to meet in town at a private members' club I'd just joined, Blacks on Dean Street, and spend the day writing in one of their many elegantly faded Georgian rooms. We sat opposite each other, one of us holding a pen and pad, and waited for the muse to descend.

We waited.

And we waited.

Nothing happened. I should, perhaps, say *incredibly* nothing happened, as we'd arrived full of enthusiasm with the expectation that by the end of the day we'd have taken the first steps towards a substantial piece of work. We were both such fans of each other's talent that the thought of a day spent staring at a blank piece of paper was one that we had never considered. By the end of the afternoon, it was clear that nothing was going to come and so we decided, in a mood of great disappointment, to call it a day. Perhaps this writing partnership lark wasn't for us.

As an afterthought, I suggested that maybe it would be better if we just did what we'd done back in Bath – improvise and see what happened.

The next day, with nothing to lose, I set off across London with my video camera, a microphone and a tripod and made my way to Finsbury Park, where Julia had a room in a shared house. We set up the camera, sat down on the sofa and began to talk. We had no preconceived idea of where we were going, the type of characters we were trying to create, or the situations we were trying to engineer; we just talked. To begin with we spoke with Birmingham accents. Immediately, characters came tumbling out.

> *Gordon:* How long has your sister been with us now?
> *Sheila:* Seven years . . .
> *Gordon:* That's it, seven years. But she doesn't judge us, she doesn't judge.
> *Sheila:* Well, that's the beauty of a coma.

That was the beginning. Two characters, Gordon and Sheila Budge, running a guest house, Budge Lodge, complete with playroom for similarly broad-minded couples, and all the time caring for Sheila's bedridden and coma-stricken sister, Val.

We were able to talk and talk, in character, for hours at a time, often making each other howl with laughter, weaving intricate storylines that arose entirely naturally and unforced. At the end of each session, I'd transfer the audio from the videotape on to a cassette and send it off to a freelance secretary I'd found who lived close to my home in East Sheen. She would then transcribe the sessions and send us back what she thought she'd heard. There would be a lot of mistakes where the sound hadn't been clear enough, or Julia or I had gabbled a line. We didn't always correct the mistakes, as they were often quite funny, so we'd just go with the flow. In *Slither In*, the episode featuring Gordon and Sheila, Gordon says, 'Some people think that swinging is all about jerking off over other men's wives . . .' When the transcription came back, 'jerking' had become 'junking'. We both liked the sound of junking – it seemed like the sort of thing a long-established couple might say – and so it stayed in.

We would each receive separate copies of the sessions and then go through the material independently, highlighting what we thought was usable in terms of storylines and dialogue, after which we would compare notes. The plots and stories were worked and reworked as the rewriting progressed, but much of the dialogue remained unchanged from the original improvisations. There's something about the spontaneity of good improvisation that offers up material far superior to anything I could ever conjure up while sitting in front of a computer. One of the keys to the success was trust. We had complete trust in each other, and were unafraid to go off down dark avenues that could turn out to be dead ends; nor were we afraid to fail in front of each other.

From Gordon and Sheila we next came up with Peter and Flick Moorcross, the upper-class couple trapped in a quietly hostile marriage lived in the shadow of Flick's former love, Geoffrey. On top of this was Flick's debilitating illness, extreme vaginismus.

> *Flick:* During intercourse the vaginal walls contract to the point where penile accommodation is absolutely impossible.
> *Peter:* Even a small penis feels like an aubergine.

From Peter and Flick we went to the other end of the social scale. Stephen and Michelle were a young couple preparing for their wedding day, living on next to nothing in the Rhondda Valley in South Wales. Stephen was a character I'd wanted to try for a long time – a basic, seemingly monosyllabic boy yet with incongruous flourishes of language, which he struggled to articulate. I thought of him as a computer with a large hard drive but small processor, who chose to be with the slightly mentally challenged Michelle as she was someone he could dominate and feel intellectually superior to. I had heard his voice so many times when I was growing up in South Wales, but had never seen it used in drama or comedy on the television.

Stephen and Michelle socialized with Michelle's brother Leighton and his girlfriend Elaine who joined them at the bridalwear shop as Michelle tried on an assortment of wedding dresses. Michelle wanted something that surely all girls dream of, a dress that simultaneously captured the spirit of both Princess Diana *and* Mariah Carey, while amongst Stephen's concerns was the following instruction: 'Top of the tit . . . visible.' He was also keen that she should have a veil or, as he put it, 'a long hat'. When Stephen was satisfied that the outfit in which Michelle eventually emerged from the changing cubicle was provocative enough, he asked, 'Who's got wood?' Holding up his own hand as proof of his aroused state, he waited until Leighton, Michelle's brother, reluctantly did the same.

This was the only episode on which Julia and I found ourselves in disagreement with Henry and Steve. There is a scene in which Stephen and Michelle sit at their dinner table discussing the seating plan for the wedding. They are using household objects to denote the guests; Stephen is a very phallic black torch while Michelle is a peach with glasses drawn on in marker pen. Michelle is shocked to discover that Stephen plans to sit next to Leighton during the reception

Michelle: But you'll be sitting next to me . . .

Stephen: I'll be sitting next to Leighton, this is my day, 'Chelle.

Michelle: I'll be your wife . . .

Stephen: Exactly! I'll have you on my back all bloody day like a big pencil, won't I?

Stephen then leaves the table in disgust and walks into the kitchen. While he is gone, Michelle moves the peach and places it next to the torch. On his return, Stephen sits down, notices this change and, without saying a word, calmly picks up the peach and eats it, places the remains back where they came from and puts Leighton, in the form of a pepper grinder, back at his side. Originally we had written that when he sees that Michelle has moved the peach, Stephen picks up the torch and smashes the soft fruit into oblivion. Steve Coogan was unhappy about this; he felt that it was condoning violence towards women and said that he wouldn't allow us to include it in the final cut. We shot the scene both ways; in the take with the torch hitting the peach, some of the fragments of splattered fruit ended up on Julia's face. It was perfect, but we had to go along with Steve – it was, after all, his company. This was the only disagreement in the whole of the series. I still prefer the version that condones violence towards women, and it's on the DVD extras if you want to see it.

Our next couple, Tony and Beverley, again came from improvisation, just evolving from seemingly random conversations. With these two we knew that we wanted to do something concerned with extreme religion and I was interested in playing someone who was determined not to let guilt get the better of him, regardless of how badly he had behaved. This was an attitude I'd witnessed in characters on early-morning shows like *Tricia* and *Vanessa*. We also liked the idea of a couple at war with their neighbours, so the episode kept coming back to the bedroom window where Beverley and Tony spied on the couple next door as they sat in their garden, innocently minding their own business.

Tony: Very strange pair. Started out perfectly well, and then it all blew up.
Beverley: It all blew up at the barbecue, didn't it?
Tony: They took exception to us barbecuing dove.
Beverley: Can't see a problem with that.
Tony: It represents peace. Dove burgers to represent peace, and red wine for the Boss's blood. Now, they took exception to it and there's been a lot of bad feeling, a lot of resentment, and it's culminated in some very abusive daubing.
Beverley: Had to do something, didn't you?

Tony and Beverley kept an assortment of dogs in a large fenced-off area at the bottom of their garden, were keen fans of Scottish dance and held regular prayer meetings at their home. They frequently visited the home of their pastor, Vicar David, and his close friend Dennis, clutching a curly sausage casserole, but usually left it on the doorstep after their repeated knocking had gone unanswered.

I can't imagine how we would have created such a fully realized world without just sitting there and talking in character to each other over many hours, then painstakingly reducing it to the best bits and shaping what was left into a script.

We had completed two episodes before showing them to Henry and Steve. By now, Julia was living in a flat in Marlborough House on Osnaburgh Street, one floor up from the flat in which Kenneth Williams had lived and died. I knew the number of his flat from reading his diaries; as I'd ride the old-fashioned grille-fronted lift up to Julia's, I would pass his door, always offering up a nod of acknowledgement and respect to the great comedian. There was no printer at Julia's, so when we were happy with a script (written on Final Draft software) and had allowed ourselves the reward of filling in the title page – always the last part of our process – we wandered down Great Portland Street to Kall Kwik, or some such store, where we would have copies made. These would be paid for, a couple would be placed in envelopes addressed to Mr Normal and Mr Coogan, and then we would ceremoniously drop them into the postbox.

I can't overstate how confident I felt with what we were producing. I *knew* it was good; and I knew that, if Henry and Steve liked it, then it would get made. I remember sitting on a plane, about to head up to Edinburgh for the festival with my *Treatment* colleague Laura Shavin, and her asking me what I was doing at the moment. I told her how Julia and I had by now written three scripts and were going to make a show called

Coupledom (its original title, rejected by the BBC, as was its follow-up suggestion *Beautiful Love*) as soon as we were finished with six. She asked if it had been commissioned. When I said no, but that I was sure it would be, she looked at me with a mixture of pity and bewilderment.

On another occasion, I was at the BBC doing more Saturday-night BBC1 promos ('There's trouble in *Holby* at eight!) and I remember the producer asking me what I was up to. When I replied that I was writing a comedy series with Julia her face screwed up with inquisitiveness and she shot back, 'Has it been commissioned?'

I think it may well have been commissioned by then, but I'm sure she couldn't imagine someone who was voicing promos managing to get something off the ground. There can be a terrible competitiveness at that level of show business, almost an anxiety brought on by the sudden and unexpected progress of others. I think Hugh Laurie once described how he eventually came to realize that there was not a finite amount of success in the world, and that someone else gaining great success did not necessarily mean that there was now less to go around for everyone else. It's a good thing to remember.

Henry and Steve loved the scripts and were keen to present them to the BBC, where they would go on to become Baby Cow's first proper commission, along with *Marion and Geoff* (which was a co-production, but more of that later). In the meantime, Julia and I carried on writing, trying to progress towards the magic number of six couples, which would be enough for a series.

*

We had always loved the idea of creating something that featured American characters, as so many of our reference points and influences were American. We began to improvise an antagonistic couple, constantly needling each other. We walked around Julia's flat, often creating scenes on the hoof as, in the absence of a camera operator, I held the camera in one hand, as far away from us as I could get. It felt as though we were in *Husbands and Wives* or *Crimes and Misdemeanors* territory, and this was one of the most enjoyable episodes to write, certainly in the early stages of pure creativity and improvisation. This Woody Allen feeling was as much a curse as a blessing for me, in that I was wary of simply doing an impression. I was determined to find a voice that didn't sound like Woody Allen – but, I have to say, I think I failed on that score. I ended up with a hybrid Woody and Shaggy from *Scooby-Doo!* type of voice and, with hindsight, should have worked harder to come up with something original.

Putting my voice to one side, we ended up with two very individual characters, Barne Willers and Fonte Bund, who together made up the Fonte Bund Band. I'm sure that a big part of the reason for giving the band that name was simply that it sounded funny to our ears. There was something about the American accents that gave us a delight in saying certain words and phrases. We talked of how Barne had worked in a health-food store entitled The Bean, The Pulse, The Berry and this would have us rolling with laughter as we tried to say it ever more quickly. I find the thought of someone refusing to abbreviate a name like that, especially when they are saying it several times in the space of one conversation, to be hilarious.

> 'Well, to really understand The Bean, The Pulse, The Berry, you have to understand what The Bean, The Pulse, The Berry represents to anyone who comes into The Bean, The Pulse, The Berry. Uh, The Bean, The Pulse, The Berry is more than a store, it's a . . . [etc.]'

Whenever we were improvising around the idea of the health-food store, I of course always pictured in my mind the one from my schooldays in Porthcawl, with Katie Davies Williams standing beguilingly at the till.

We eventually settled on calling the episode *Hairless*, a reference to Barne's obsessive paranoia regarding his hair loss – although what could possibly have put that idea into our heads, I still don't know. *Hairless* would be the first time that I would play the guitar in public; just about managing to negotiate my way around a simple three-chord song that Julia and I had written entitled 'The Cat and the Mouse'. We came up with this and many other songs during breaks in writing, when she or I would pick up a clunky old Spanish guitar that lived in Julia's flat and start messing around and recording the efforts on to minidisc. 'The Cat and the Mouse' was just one of a larger collection made entirely for our own amusement, until we realized that it would work perfectly for these characters.

I have a couple of CDs full of our rambling, made-up-on-the-spot songs. We've sometimes talked about releasing them – perhaps on a website, or as extras on a

The More Fool Us team, including Julia Davis and Ruth Jones.

Photographed at the opening of an envelope.
Reading the *First Knight* script, July 1994.

With Hugo writing *Marion and Geoff*.

From the look of this we're either writing *Human Remains* or forming an electro pop band in Berlin.

With Julia as Sheila and Gordon.

Watching a rough cut of *Human Remains* with Julia and Henry Normal.

With the make-up team during the filming of *Human Remains*.

Winner of the Best TV Comedy Newcomer 2000 at the
British Comedy Awards. 'The student becomes the master.' *

* Unless you're reading this, Steve, in which case, 'The Best Day of My Life.'

With Mum and Dad, celebrating my success
at the British Comedy Awards.

Islands in the Desert.

On location for *Cruise of the Gods* with James.

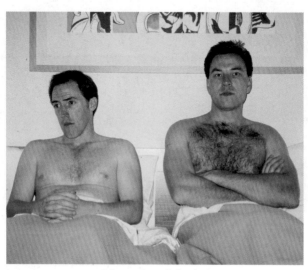

It's not how it looks.

In Venice with David.
James is tagging along.

'I confidently predict that
one day you *will* remake
Dudley Moore's *Arthur*.'

'Bruce! It's really, really, really . . . really good to meet you.'
'All right!'

DVD. Some of them are rather good, some of them are not, and many of them are filthy.

One of the songs, a bizarre dirge about potatoes, ended up on the bonus episode found on the *Human Remains* DVD, in which Barne and Fonte got to perform with the genius that was John Martyn. We went on as his support act in Guildford and were met with bemusement bordering on light anger, even after a heartfelt introduction from John himself. At one point, Barne tells the crowd how he once saw Rod Stewart at the LA Forum and how Rod had kicked footballs into the crowd. Barne wanted to emulate that with the Guildford audience but had been told that it was a health and safety risk. So, instead, he took out a table-tennis bat and hit ping-pong balls into the gathering of impatient John Martyn fans.

I am sometimes asked which of the six episodes is my favourite. Although it's an ever-fluctuating chart, the final instalment is often at the top. *More than Happy* began through a series of improvisations in which a chipper British Gas engineer, named Les, talked with a clinically depressed florist, named Ray, about how they'd met all those years ago. These discussions went on to include the many and varied items sold in their seaside shop, Ray's love of arts and crafts, and the couple's coded references to the absence of the twins.

> *Les:* You know, me and Ray, I think you've got to say we've been very happy, very happy indeed. I mean, apart from losing the twins, obviously.

Ray: Yeah, that was . . .

Les: Ooh, that wasn't very nice, that ruffled a few feathers. I'll be very honest with you, when they was taken from us, when the twins was taken from us, early . . .

Ray: Ruffled a lot of feathers.

Les: Ruffled feathers we didn't know we had. Let's be, you know, but uh . . . Smashing kids, you see, but when you got to go, you got to go, and go they did, didn't they?

Ray: Totally unexpected.

Les: They went, they went.

Ray: Brought us together.

Les: All we've got is each other, you see.

Ray: Brought us together.

Les: All we've got is each other.

Ray: Brought us together.

Les: All we have is each other.

One thing that characterized the conversations was Les's refusal to listen to the heavily medicated Ray or to acknowledge that she was at all depressed. He would refer to her as 'the teacup' or 'the trumpet'; and when she answered his enquiry as to whether she was happy with a firm *no*, he would reply, 'That's it, more than happy.' We both delighted in this lack of communication and wrote as much as we could along these lines.

The two of them ran a doomed shop, selling bras, flowers, coffee, snacks and grotesque models made from the driftwood that Les would cheerfully collect and hand over to Ray, who would decorate the models with all the skill of a visually impaired four-year-old. Much of the episode takes place at the picnic table that the couple would erect on the beach. For this, our location manager found a fantastically bleak concrete promenade at the foot of a cliff, separated from the sea by a man-made concrete sea-defence wall. It wasn't what we had imagined at all, but it worked perfectly. We also hadn't expected the glorious weather that we enjoyed for the week's filming; we had always pictured Les and Ray on the beach with a gloomy overcast sky, perhaps even rain. When the day arrived, we were greeted with clear blue skies and bright sunshine, but this again worked in our favour, highlighting the gloom of the couple against the vivid colours of nature.

20

The series was green-lit by the time we'd finished first-drafting the third or fourth episode. It was a difficult commission; the scripts were dark and dense, and Julia and I were completely unknown. It was only the power and persuasion of Steve and Henry that convinced the BBC we were the right horse to back. They were in a very good position to do so. It was an especially good time for Steve – he was riding high on the back of the much-lauded *I'm Alan Partridge* as well as the live show, and he had just signed a production deal between Baby Cow and the BBC. This was another of the increasingly regular occurrences where I was simply in the right place at the right time and, just as importantly, with the right people.

We set about gathering the team that would help bring our ideas to the screen, and met several directors before settling on Matt Lipsey. Matt seemed to share our view of the world we had created, as well as welcoming our continued input and accepting our desire to be able to create stuff on the spot once the cameras were rolling. It was vitally important to us that we were able to retain as much creative control of the project as we could – from the writing all the way through to the editing – and Matt was happy to go along with that.

When it came to casting, there were a few people we already had in mind. In particular, in the episode *All Over*

My Glasses, we asked Mark Benton and Ruth Jones to play Leighton and Elaine, which they did brilliantly. I think we made a horrifically convincing foursome. When Ruth, Julia and I had been members of More Fool Us in Bath, we had worked alongside Jane Roth. Jane and Julia had performed as a double act for a while, the Sisters of Percy, and she came in to play the owner of the bridal shop who goes along admirably with Stephen and Michelle's enquiries, even tolerating being put in a headlock by Stephen ('I'm only pissin' around. Look at her! Fuckin' cackin' herself, she's cackin' herself . . .'). Jane gives a beautifully understated performance; at the time the show came out, I remember being asked repeatedly if it was a real shop owner featured in the episode. This was one of my favourite scenes – Leighton laughing along for fear of being out of step with Stephen, Elaine telling Stephen to stop, and Michelle cowering in the cubicle as Jane keeps a smile on her face despite being afraid of the idiot who's invaded her shop.

We used another of our More Fool Us colleagues in *Hairless*, when Toby Longworth played Dr Boxer, the therapist with the unusual, if not unethical, methods. Toby had always been the star of the improv group; he had been part of a double act with Bill Bailey, the Rubber Bishops, and had always seemed a few years ahead of the rest of us. He came in to audition for Dr Boxer and blew us away with an improvisation in which he asked Barne to imagine a number between one and ten.

Then, on hearing which number Barne had chosen, he replied: 'OK, that number is you. Now I want you to imagine another number between one and ten . . . it could be a number of greater numerical value, or it could be a number of lesser numerical value. The important thing is that it is your number.'

Barne offered up another number.

Toby paused, before replying: 'OK, that number is you *now*.'

We loved this and lifted it in its entirety into the episode (with Toby rightly receiving an additional material credit).

In *An English Squeak* we struggled to find an actor to play the clown with whom Flick has a brief encounter in the bedroom until a then unknown Stephen Mangan walked in and played it perfectly. It was one of his first jobs, something I now like to remind him of at every opportunity. For the part of Nana, the domestic help, we were very lucky to get the also then unknown Joanna Scanlon (long before she became celebrated for shows such as *The Thick of It* and *Getting On*).

We worked and worked on the scripts, right up to and during the filming, which took place around Brighton in the summer of 2000. We began with *An English Squeak*, finishing each day with a trip to Henry's house, where we would go over the script again and again, looking for areas that could be improved upon. It was an intense and exciting way to work; in addition to any changes we'd made the night before, we would also record looser takes once we felt we had the scripted version in the bag. We would also just keep going, once we'd reached the end of what was written, and see what happened.

We shot an episode a week; once the first episode was

finished, it went off to be edited into a rough assembly. I remember us watching the first pass at *An English Squeak* and being hugely disappointed. This, I was to learn, is a common response to seeing a rough cut, but at the time I was unaware and just knew that what we'd done wasn't anywhere near as funny as I'd thought it would be. We set about writing new stuff for the episode; the bits by Geoffrey's grave, the croquet, the tennis and the scenes with Peter pushing Flick around the grounds in her wheelchair were all shot in one day at the end of the six weeks. If you look closely, you'll notice that I'm wearing a wig in these shots (my hair having been shaved off to play Gordon and Barne).

The extra day of filming came about as a result of an insurance claim after Julia injured her hand in the door of one of Steve's cars – probably a Ferrari. She had been due to play the guitar as Fonte in *Hairless* but was unable to use her hand properly after the accident. That is why I was playing the guitar in the episode. But, again, this happy accident worked perfectly with the characters. It made complete sense that someone like Fonte, who claimed to be a great artiste while merely covering the songs of another (in this case, Alanis Morissette), would happily get someone else to play the guitar for her. It made further sense that that someone should be poor Barne, who did all the donkey work in the relationship while sitting at the back of the stage, out of the spotlight.

Our make-up artist for the series was Vanessa White, who had just done excellent work with *The League of Gentlemen*. It was Vanessa who persuaded me to bleach and cut my hair and then ultimately completely shave my head for the shoot. I wanted Stephen in *All Over My Glasses* to have bleached blond hair, and had assumed we would achieve this through a wig or temporary dye, but Vanessa was having none of it. She convinced me that bleaching my hair was the only way forward for a serious actor, so off I went and had it bleached. The following week, I had the top shaved off to play Gordon and then Barne, so the sides were still blond but the top was bare. When we had to do some pick-ups as Stephen, Richard Mawbey (the renowned wigmaker) made me a little blond toupee that sat on my head. I'm wearing it in the scenes set on the train, as I talk to the camera while Mark Benton moves stock around – although, thanks to Richard's skills, you'd never know.

Vanessa also introduced me to the world of prosthetic make-up, something I'd never experienced before and a great help in bringing a character to life. Teeth were made for a couple of the roles and eye bags fitted for a few. The great thing about eye bags and ageing make-up in general, beyond what they bring to the characters, is the moment at the end of the day when you're sitting in the make-up chair getting it all taken off. As the eye bags are peeled away, you suddenly look ten years younger and fresher.

This feeling of rejuvenation can last a good fifteen or twenty minutes. If you're lucky.

We began filming at the end of July and went through a mostly hot, blue-sky summer to early September. I remember being in the make-up truck with Julia one day, the door fixed wide open to allow a slight breeze as my eye bags were being forcefully evicted, and seeing my first piece of press in relation to *Marion and Geoff*. The series was scheduled to begin going out on BBC 2 at the end of September, and this was a little piece in *Red* magazine featuring the photo that most of the papers ran in association with the show – Keith staring out of the window of the car, his reflection caught in the wing mirror.

Marion and Geoff came about, again, through the support of Henry and Steve. Hugo and I had made our pilot episode (it would go on to be episode one in the eventual series) and had submitted it to the BBC, where it sat for nine months without a response. In the meantime, two things happened: I began to write *Human Remains* with Julia; and I started to receive a great deal of very positive feedback on the pilot from everyone who saw it. But from the BBC there was only silence. Looking back, nine months without a response was perhaps another way of saying 'no thanks', but I still held on to the hope that we might get good news any day soon.

As the time passed, I kept hearing of other shows which I knew had been submitted at the same time as ours and had already heard that they'd been commissioned. Eventually, and in some desperation, I called Henry Normal at his home in Brighton; by now, we were well into the writing process for *Human Remains* and I told him that we'd still heard nothing from the BBC about *Marion and Geoff*. I knew that he and Steve had seen the pilot; he'd told me that they'd watched it together in his living room one evening and it had so moved them that, at the end, they couldn't look each other in the eye for fear of betraying their emotions.

I asked Henry if he and Steve would be interested in

adopting it as a production for their new company, Baby Cow. He said yes straight away and the BBC, with the weight of this endorsement behind it, commissioned the show. Better than that, they commissioned ten episodes. Our show was ten minutes long and the BBC had also commissioned ten episodes of a fifty-minute show called *Attachments*, so they needed something to round up the hour.

It had been the best part of a year since we'd filmed our pilot episode, and in the intervening time Hugo and I had come up with lots of ideas and directions in which we might take the story. It was wonderful to finally get the chance to create more stories for Keith, knowing that they would make it to the screen and be seen by the viewing public.

While keeping everything focused inside the car, we expanded the world outside to include tales from Keith's past. How his 'one proper job was for a Japanese company, at the very cutting edge of technology, and I'm very proud to have worked for a company that was so advanced that it was able to do away with manpower'. How his honeymoon with Marion hadn't been an entirely happy affair, 'But then, what honeymoon is?' We sent him up and down the M4 motorway, desperate to see his beloved boys. When Marion and Geoff took Keith's little smashers to Disneyland Paris, Keith simply got on the Eurostar car transporter and followed them, delightedly telling us of his plan to surprise them in a restaurant with the greeting, 'Avez-vous your real dad?'

His job as a minicab driver was one for which he was

clearly not cut out. In the first episode, he fails to make radio contact with the taxi company and later in the series, while delayed on his first airport job ('quite glamorous, really'), he fills his time by going to a safari park, on his own. Before leaving the airport, he speculates about how much of the five-hour delay he could fill within the terminal building.

I could look around the shops. Not for five hours. I could do that for about forty minutes. I could have something to eat, half an hour, another forty minutes, that's one hour twenty minutes, then I've got another three hours and forty to fill. Uh, three hours and forty, I could play on some of the games in the arcade. Say I could do that for half an hour, if I played slowly at low levels. Got another three hours to fill, have another drink, coffee or something for . . . ten minutes, that's . . . I'm pushing it, really pushing it. I could browse in Smiths for . . . if they don't move me on, I could do that for an hour . . . It's not going to happen, is it? Whichever way you look at it, it doesn't add up. Hmm, right . . . Bloody hell. What to do? What to do?

I would imagine that the line about browsing in Smiths came from the endless hours I'd spent in the Hounslow branch. Once at the safari park, Keith begins to wonder why the plane is delayed.

They never tell you why a plane is delayed, have you noticed that? They never . . . give a reason. Keep you in the dark. Technical fault, could be, um, maybe it's a hijack situation . . . [PAUSE] Imagine how stressful that is, eh? Terrible. A hijack situation. Very stressful. I mean, in the old days with the propeller planes, the smaller planes, it was much easier. You would stand at the end of one aisle, wave your gun about, show who was boss. Nowadays with the bigger planes you can have three or four aisles, different sections, how do you police it? Um, you know, do you, do you treat people differently because they're in different sections, are you a little less cruel to the people in First Class? I mean, you're no fool, you know they've paid more. [PAUSE] You imagine, delivering a bomb somewhere, I mean you've got the bomb with you, could go off at any time, you've got to remember the secret code to alert the media, and I dare say you're not allowed to . . . I wouldn't imagine they encourage you to write it down. Like a PIN number, you've probably got to memorize it. [PAUSE] At any moment 'ba-boom'. [PAUSE] It's the modern curse, you see, stress. Doesn't matter what you do really, if you're a terrorist or a doctor. Or a zebra.

A little later, Keith is parked near some passing camels and is prompted into a memory of his parents.

See these camels now, I'm told they mate for life. Smashing. Like my mum and dad, really, they mated for life . . . literally. I mean Mum . . . Mum died on . . . the Thursday, in hospital [PAUSE] and then the following Monday, Dad shot himself.

The idea of the gun had been planted in episode two, when Keith drives to Cardiff with the weapon that had belonged to his father and uses the telescopic sight to spy on Marion and Geoff. The safari-park episode is a good example of how we would often create material on the hoof. On arriving at the park, we discovered that there were no monkeys (they had all been shot after contracting a virus). We came up with a lovely little moment for Keith as he sits eating biscuits in the car park and reflects on the news.

> Well, quite a shock [PAUSE], they've all been shot. They had a virus, Herpes ... Simian Herpes B. Uh, don't know what they've been getting up to. I've had a virus, umm, not one like that, and I'm all right, I'm still standing. [PAUSE] Imagine that, 'What is it, doc?' 'It's a virus, Keith' 'What are my chances?' 'Well, if you start running now, pretty good.' [HE MAKES THE GES- TURE OF SHOOTING A RIFLE WITH HIS BISCUITS] Dear me ...

Music plays a big part in the series. Hugo and I would raid our respective record collections, searching for the perfect choices, settling eventually on Slade, Bruce Springsteen, Tom Jones, Catatonia, the Bee Gees and Radiohead. With his brilliant editor, Graham Hodson, Hugo did a superb job in the edit. Creating an entirely distinctive look and feel for the show, he paced the stories wonderfully. He also did great things in the dub, very subtly manipulating the sound to enhance the narrative.

It was a great advantage that *Marion and Geoff* was spread out over ten episodes; it gave a chance for the word-of-mouth factor to build on the show, and build it did. Slowly at first, then slowly but surely, until it seemed as though everyone was talking about it. The critical response was exceptionally good from the start.

The Times said it was 'a beautifully judged tightrope act both in the writing and in the delivery . . . like an Escher drawing'.

The Sun considered it 'unmissable', the *Mirror* felt it was 'bleakly funny and achingly poignant', and the *Telegraph* 'brilliant'.

In London's *Evening Standard*, Pete Clark declared it was 'the funniest British comedy effort for years, and it is also the most heartbreaking . . . a *Madame Bovary* for our times . . .'

Andrew Billen in the *New Statesman* called it 'a work of art'.

Wow.

This response was more than I could have hoped for, and I was quite taken aback by the sudden attention and praise. I began to have a sneaking suspicion that I might have *arrived*, finally. While this was going on, Julia and I were often holed up in a windowless room on the South Bank in the edits for *Human Remains* with Matt Lipsey and his editor Charlie Phillips, agonizing over what should stay and what should go. In the episode *All Over My Glasses*, the original ending (a whole subplot involving the principal characters going off on a coach to see Texas at the NEC in Birmingham) was dropped. A bold and, frankly, unsettling decision.

We were told that *Human Remains* would begin transmission two weeks before *Marion and Geoff* had finished, and this bothered me. I was worried that all the work I'd been involved in for the last couple of years would be splurged onscreen and gone in the course of three months. As it turned out, it was the perfect way of showcasing my work. If anyone had thought that Keith was my one-trick pony then *Human Remains*, with its six very different couples, showed a range and versatility to put those suspicions to rest. The critical response was again fantastic, with *The Times* saying, 'Rob Brydon and Julia Davis, who demonstrate a level of invention, observation and sheer versatility that defies comprehension . . . This is extraordinary television, so effortless and inexplicable that it is touched with comic genius.'

Affirmation, vindication, validation – these are all good words to describe how I felt. But along with my sudden notoriety came an unsettling new experience. Most people go through life hearing about themselves only what is said to their face; it's very rare that anyone will come up to you and offer a disparaging comment with regards to your appearance. Once I began to be written about, this all changed, especially in the broadsheets – where a profile piece inevitably contains a degree of psychoanalysis for good measure. I was genuinely surprised, albeit perhaps a little naively, when so many of the writers who interviewed me would then include in their piece a comment or two on my appearance. As more and more articles were published, a theme began to emerge.

The *Observer* told its readers of my 'sorrowful brown eyes and lugubrious features'.

Jasper Rees in the *Evening Standard* saw me as 'a wiry Welshman with a long thin knife of a face'.

The *Daily Express* opined that I was 'deadpan and tombstone featured'.

Jasper Gerrard, in the *Sunday Times* had given the subject considerable thought.

> So does he have five-star potential? His appearance is utterly ordinary. Women would probably consider him boy-next-door crumpet, were it not that he is saved from any hint of matinee idol looks by his bad complexion.

Ouch!

The first year of the new millennium was coming to an end. And so too, it seemed, was my era of terrible job after terrible job. Everything had changed; I felt now as though I was on a wave, and all I had to do was ride it. After becoming used to a life of rejection letters, returned VHS cassettes thudding on to the doormat and a phone unable to make a call that could stretch beyond a secretary, I was suddenly receiving invitations to events here, there and everywhere.

One such invitation was to a party being thrown by the BBC to celebrate something or other relating to Light Entertainment. It was held in one of the large studios at Television Centre and was full of the great and good of the day. It was the first of many occasions when person after person seemed to want to come along and congratulate me on *Human Remains* and *Marion and Geoff* – I of course was only too happy to receive their praise. Early in the evening, through the throng of besuited bodies, I spotted Ronni Ancona coming towards me. I had met her some years earlier, while making the pilot *The Strip Show* for Channel Four, since when she had gone on to the BBC and great success with

Alistair McGowan on *The Big Impression*. I had noticed her earlier across the room, talking to Ronnie Corbett and Ronnie Barker, in the process effortlessly forming a new comedy team, the Three Ronnies. Knowing how big a fan I was of the two, she offered to introduce me.

Ronnie C., all tartan-trousered warmth and charm, told me how much he'd enjoyed *Marion and Geoff*. I returned the compliment and gushed over him (probably a little too much), telling him how not just I, but my whole family, had loved his work over the years and how I had performed some *Two Ronnies* gags at school just before the world premiere of *Star Wars* onstage.

I wondered whether Ronnie Barker was aware of my work, and what he might have thought of it?

Ronnie C. introduced us: 'Ron, this is Rob Brydon.'

Mr Barker looked over at me quizzically, his eyes narrowing. 'Ah, you're the chap who does that *Human Remains*.'

'Yes . . .'

There was a pause.

'I saw four of them.'

'Right . . .'

There was another pause.

I stood waiting. Was he going to give me a compliment to add to my list? Surely he was; why else would he have brought it up?

He thought for a moment, before offering: 'You should tell the girl that does it with you, she shouldn't always play dowdy.'

And that was it.

*

329

But there was one more treat in store, a cherry on the cake of my success, when I discovered that I had been nominated for the Best Newcomer category at the British Comedy Awards. I was thirty-five years old; I had watched the awards every year since their inception, sitting on my sofa, sure that I would never be a part of it. How could I be? It was another world. I particularly remembered seeing Steve sweep the board with three awards just two years ago. It had seemed to me then like something from another universe.

The nomination was for *Marion and Geoff* and I wanted very much to win. The awards at that time took place at the ITV London Television Centre on the South Bank, just up the road from the National Theatre where, all those years ago, I had seen Anthony Hopkins in *Pravda* while on the college trip. It was also not far from the editing suite where, just weeks earlier, we had been arguing over *Human Remains*.

It was a good year, in which Alan Bennett won the Lifetime Achievement Award. When I was at college, there was a video library and each week *The South Bank Show* would be recorded and added to the shelf. I would often sneak in, between classes, and take out the show devoted to Bennett's *A Private Function* and watch it again and again. Now here I was at the same ceremony as him, potentially winning an award on the same night. Victoria Wood was given the Writer of the Year prize. I had watched her stuff for as long as I could remember – Julia and I were both influenced by her when writing *Human Remains*, and Duncan Preston banging his head on the boom microphone in *Acorn Antiques* is one of the funniest things I've ever seen – and now here she was in the same room.

When the moment for the Best Newcomer category arrived, Jonathan Ross turned to introduce the presenter and I remembered how I'd interviewed him down the telephone line on Radio Wales aeons ago as he burst on to the scene with *The Last Resort*. Was I about to share the stage with him? Mum and Dad were watching the broadcast live, back home in Baglan, as the guest presenter took to the stage. It was Steve Coogan – a good sign, surely? He read the nominations, some clips were played, and then he opened the envelope.

Time stood still.

I prepared my magnanimous loser's face.

And the winner is . . . Rob Brydon.

That was the first award; the next year I returned and won the Best Actor Award for *Human Remains*. In the meantime, Julia and I both won Royal Television Society awards, *Marion and Geoff* won the *South Bank* Award for Best Drama and a Broadcasting Press Guild of Great Britain award. *Human Remains* was awarded Best Comedy at the Banff International Festival in Canada, beating *Frasier* and *Friends* in the process.

It felt good.

It also felt a little unreal. Had I really crossed the divide? And, if I had, would I be able to stay on this new side – where, I have to say, the view was much nicer. As I did the round of interviews and photographs that always follow the receipt of an award, I remembered the words Jimmy Savile had spoken to James Lovell and me all those years ago, at St David's Hall in Cardiff, after we'd just performed our first paid gig.

'It's very hard to get to the top in this game, but it's a damn sight harder staying there.'

Was he right?

I was about to find out.

Epilogue

Six years later, I was sitting on a bench looking out onto the water at Manly, one of the many glorious beaches that Sydney has to offer. I was in Australia for the second time, filming the second and, as it would turn out, last series of *Supernova*, a lovely, silly show that I made for the legendary Beryl Vertue and her Hartswood production company. I was eating fish and chips, and sitting next to me was James Corden; we'd stayed in touch after *Cruise of the Gods* and had hooked up in Sydney, where he'd found himself as part of the world tour of Alan Bennett's *The History Boys*. They'd already been to Hong Kong and New Zealand, and after Australia would go on to win a record number of Tony awards on Broadway.

We were talking about a new project, *Gavin and Stacey*, that James was writing with my old school chum Ruth Jones. The two had met while filming the ITV series *Fat Friends* and had come up with the idea of a one-off film set at the wedding of an Essex boy and a girl from Barry, the seaside resort in South Wales.

There was a part in it for me – the part of Bryn West, Stacey's uncle – and Ruth and James had sent me a couple of scripts. Although I liked them very much, I was unsure of accepting. The problem, as I saw it, was that Bryn was a little too close to Keith Barret – both big-hearted men, both rather naive and, more importantly, both Welsh. I was concerned at becoming pigeonholed as someone who only plays Welsh characters. It's an odd fear; after all, no one says of Robert De Niro, 'Oh, here he comes, playing yet another New Yorker.'

James was keen for me to take the role, and we talked around it for a while. He explained that Bryn's love of technology came from the uncle of his then girlfriend, who had once sat him down and told him all about digital cameras, unaware that James was already in possession of his second. I liked the sound of this and began to improvise around this idea so that James could see if we were both thinking along the same lines.

I took the camera that James had brought with him to the beach that day, and began to invent stuff.

'Now, this is a digital camera and that means there's no film in there, none at all, so you never take a bad picture.'

I took a shot of my hand.

'There we are, now no one wants that, why would they? Not a problem, just press this and it's deleted, gone, you won't see that again. And it's full of features . . . not sure about this one . . . sepia, seepia? I'm not sure what it does but I think it's faulty, it just makes the pictures brown.'

We had a laugh, messing around like this under the glorious Sydney sunshine, finished our remarkably tasty fish and chips and then, with full stomachs, went for a swim.

James later told me that, when he was back in his apartment, he got straight on the phone to Ruth and told her about my riffing around the camera and how they just had to persuade me to do the show.

I'm pleased to say they did.

Acknowledgements

For their help in remembering the things I thought I remembered already but didn't . . . Mum and Dad, Pete, David Charles, James Lovell, Jacqueline Gilbrook, Rhys John, David Broughton-Davies, Dougray Scott, Alan Thompson, David Williams, Roger Burnell, James Corden, Steve Coogan, Julia Davis, and David Walliams. For his help in keeping me keeping on and offering invaluable advice along the way, my editor at Penguin, Daniel Bunyard and his team.

In conversation with . . .

The following are transcripts of conversations with friends and family for inclusion in the enhanced ebook edition, available at the iBook store, and are reprinted with their kind permission.

Steve Coogan

RB: When did we meet?

SC: In a bar.

RB: We met prior to that. We met at the Holiday Inn, Reading . . .

SC: That's what I meant . . .

RB: . . . after your show . . .

SC: . . . it was a bar at the hotel.

RB: Oh, in a bar at the Holiday Inn in Reading . . .

SC: That's what I mean; it was in a hotel, a very unremarkable hotel bar when Julia [Davis] introduced you to me, in '98.

RB: What do you remember of that?

SC: Very little.

RB: That's true, isn't it? It was a bigger deal to me than it was to you, it has to be said.

SC: It was, at the time.

RB: You were at the height of your powers.

SC: It was a good year for me. One of the peaks. Before a few troughs. In quick succession.

RB: You don't have to go there – don't beat yourself up! Yes, you failed, massively at times, but don't feel you have to . . . So, I'd been to see the show. I knew Julia, she got into your live show, and I was so excited when she told me, so excited. I phoned her up at the end of the first day of rehearsal and said 'What's he like?' and she told me about a trick you played on Peter Baynham, when you asked him to go and get sandwiches or something, do you remember this? And then berated him in front of everybody when he came back?

SC: For what?

RB: For comic effect, but nonetheless there was a degree of beratement.

SC: For what?

RB: Getting the wrong sandwich or something.

SC: Are you sure?

RB: Yes, but in a very jokey way.

SC: Really?

RB: You don't remember that?

SC: Wasn't it about croissants?

RB: Ah, it might have been.

SC: Pete used to say 'croissant' [pronouncing with a 'KR' rather than 'KW' sound] and I said, 'Pete, can you come in here and sit down for a second? I need to have a word with you.' And he was like, 'Yeah, fine, sure' and sat down. I said, 'Pete, we've been working together for a few months now, and I didn't want to bring this up, but I feel it's the right time: it's *croissant*, not "croissant".' And that was it.

RB: Pete's Welsh.

SC: Yeah. So, Peter Baynham, who went on to write for Sacha Baron Cohen. Very difficult for me to book him as a writer these days.

RB: He's done very well.

SC: Very well, he's done very well for himself.

RB: Very well . . . He wrote that Partridge line about the chip and pin, didn't he? Lovely line.

SC: Er, yes he did. What was that again?

RB: Alan said, 'My father always dreamt you'd be able to pay for something with just a card. They did it, Dad, and they called it "Switch"!'

SC: Ah, that's it, 'My Dad had a dream of a plastic card, that one day, unlike a credit card, would debit directly from your bank account. People said he was mad. He was *crazy*. These were the dreams of some fool. Well, Dad, they did it. They did it, Dad, and they called it '*Switch*' . . .'

RB: So . . . we met there but then we met again at the pub you used to go to at the end of your live show. And by then Julia had given you a tape of me, do you remember?

SC: Yes, I do remember that tape – 'a very unlucky traffic warden' it was called, from your memorable performance as a traffic warden in the film *Lock, Stock and Two Smoking Barrels*, and it was, er, a, um, er, a mixed bag . . . I have to say. But I definitely remember thinking . . .

RB: It showed promise . . .

SC: . . . I did, I thought 'this guy's got something'. What was good about it was that it wasn't derivative. I thought, 'he's doing his own thing – he's not just watched lots of things he liked and sought to imitate them.' It was quite small, quite nuanced, and I thought, 'he's good . . .'

RB: It's kind of odd, isn't it, because I remember you saying to me in the bar, 'I like it, I think you've got something, I'd like to work with you one day,' and it must be quite rare that two people end up working together quite as much as we have.

SC: Well, weirdly it happened similarly with Julia Davis. She sent me a tape and I remember sitting down and watching it and thinking 'Oh my god, this woman's weird, and funny', but I was worried – I had to meet her before I asked her to join the tour, because I was worried that she might be genuinely . . .

RB: Well, that tape she used to have was very dark, I remember that.

SC: It was, and weird and twisted, but incredibly compelling. I remember thinking I wanted to meet her before she toured with me to support with the sketches and things, but when I saw it I was genuinely worried – I thought 'she's either a genius or she's mentally disturbed,' and in the end she was a bit of both.

RB: She was a bit of both.

SC: So then you did a longer version of . . .

RB: What became *Marion and Geoff* . . .

SC: But what did you call it at the time?

RB: For a while it was called *Head Shots*. I think *Marion and Geoff*, the title, came quite late. But I did that with Hugo and then I got involved with him, and the two of us made what became episode one, and it was bouncing around the BBC . . .

SC: Well, Henry and I – Henry who runs Baby Cow – I think that was one of the very first things that as a company we pitched and we said, 'look, this is really, really great' and then you and Hugo took off and made it and it was, er, genuinely laugh-out-loud funny and genuinely moving, I remember I wept at, I think, the last two episodes; they made me cry. And I was very admiring and a little bit professionally envious of the way you sort of tapped into the pathos.

RB: It's similar, because you know I'm very influenced by you, I was a huge fan so I was so excited to watch what you were doing, so you can probably see, you know, I think a lot of people like me, like Pegg, you know Simon, I think you can see things that he does that are influenced by your stuff.

SC: It's interesting because there are things that Pegg does and you do that – it's weird because it goes both ways – because I find myself doing something and thinking, 'ah, I probably nicked that off Rob, or I might have nicked that off Simon Pegg,' but . . . they nicked it off me first.

RB: [*laughs*]

SC: Well, you know, you find yourself doing these things . . .

RB: No, you're right, you admire it, it soaks in . . .

SC: And it comes out in your performance and you think, well I'm probably doing that there . . .

RB: Well, hopefully what happens is it goes in and goes through the mixer and then comes out as something that is then yours . . .

SC: Yeah . . .

SC: You used to write at my house, didn't you? With Julia, in the early years. And I suppose I got to know you bit by bit. And I knew Julia a bit more because she was living with me, not in the biblical sense, and when you did *Human Remains* I still think that your performances in that were fantastic. All of them were really good and really varied – lovely – and 'Slither In' is my favourite, I've told you before. I play that to people if they haven't seen it, if they stay at my house there are a few things that I play them and I say, 'you have to watch this', and I know it so well that when I say something now I find myself hearing bits of that . . . the bit where you turn round and bend down and go, 'I have entered into men on some occasions . . . if that makes me homosexual, so be it' . . . [*Rising from his chair with apparent difficulty and discomfort.*]

RB: I talk in the book about that bit that we disagreed on in *Human Remains* which was in 'All Over My Glasses'; Stephen and Michelle, the peach, and you didn't like the smashing of the peach with the torch, when they're doing the wedding plan, and you insisted we shoot it again with me eating the peach, because you felt it was condoning violence towards women, do you remember?

SC: I do remember that. And I sometimes feel, and do feel with Julia's stuff, that it's diminishing returns . . . if you do a disturbing joke you have to tickle the audience, or massage them, before you slap them round the chops with a slightly disturbing joke. And I felt it happened then. If you do too many disturbing jokes it's like an assault on the senses – you need to do some nice gentle stuff then whack them over the head, then seduce them again. It's like saying, 'Come here, I won't hit you . . .' – *WHACK!* – and then going, 'Oh, sorry, I won't do that again,' and them coming back . . . Otherwise it's just hitting someone over the head again and again, and it's not pleasant.

*

SC: It's weird; there is, especially in comedy, a sort of comfortableness amongst heterosexual males, of broaching effeminacy, in relationships. With that idea of the femininity that men have within them, even if they're not gay, and not being uncomfortable with that.
RB: Yeah, I think that's very true.
SC: Not being worried about it.
RB: I mean, I have entered into other men . . . If that makes me homosexual, so be it.

*

RB: That's the nightmare scenario, a bit like when we went to the Baftas the other week.
SC: It was very funny – we did go to the Baftas the other week. You were nominated for your show, *The Trip* was nominated as a show, and I was nominated for my performance in *The Trip* . . .
RB: And I wasn't.
SC: And you weren't, but to be fair you were nominated for a Comedy Award in *The Trip* and I wasn't.
RB: Yeah, but who cares about those . . .?
SC: I didn't like to say that, but obviously . . .
RB: Everybody knows that! The Baftas are *Baftas*!
SC: So, you said to me, the worst scenario for you would be if you didn't win, if *The Trip* didn't win either, and just I win . . . You said, 'If *The Trip* wins we're both happy, but if it doesn't win and *you* win then that's the nightmare scenario,' – and that's exactly what happened. And I did feel, well, as you've been nominated several times . . .
RB: Never won . . .
SC: But you did leave early that night.

RB: Yeah I did! Because the fact of it is, what are you going to stay for?! You're cheesed off!

SC: Well, you know, you're with your mate . . .

RB: Yeah, well you buggered off with all the other winners! You were like Charlie Sheen that night.

SC: Yeah, like a low-rent, poorer . . .

RB: . . . but with most of his sanity.

SC: . . . yeah, I had the lucidity of Charlie Sheen that night.

RB: You did.

SC: Can I go now? [*Gets up and leaves*]

Howard Jones

HJ: I can remember when spaghetti bolognese came along, and lasagne – your mother thought it was the end of the world! 'Where the hell are we going?!' She said something like that, didn't she?

RB: Well, do you remember when I went to Australia first to do *Supernova*, in about 2003 or 2004, and do you remember I phoned you and Mum because I was down by the docks, by the Sydney Harbour Bridge, and I was eating oysters for the first time and squid and all these different things, and I phoned up and went, 'We're in Sydney Harbour! And I've just eaten squid!' and Mum said, 'Ooooh . . . you'll pay for that. Your father had crab in 1973. He was sick!' [*Both laugh*]

RB: And what about the time when I fell out the tree?

HJ: That was very memorable. We had a pub, didn't we?

RB: Well *we* didn't have a pub; we didn't own the pub; I know you behaved as though . . .

HJ: Yeah, yeah, I'd have liked to have owned it. And I should have done with all the money I spent in it. I went out, as I did on a Sunday lunchtime, for a couple of pints before lunch and, walking back to the house, someone I knew was leaning over in this tall grass. He looks up and says, 'Howard, do you know whose boy this is?' And I walked up and there, lying in the grass unconscious was you, and I was really shocked and upset and worried, so we ran around and we got a neighbour to come and look at you, your mother came out, and we were all panicking like mad. We get you into the car and we take you to the hospital . . . and you're still unconscious. So you're on this stretcher in the hospital and I'm looking over at you, your mother's looking over at you, and then this nurse is looking over at you and the first thing she said is, 'Does your son drink?' and your mother said, 'He certainly does not!' But she'd smelt the beer that was on my breath and she thought you must have passed out after having a few drinks. But, thank god, you were okay. And you'd fallen out of a tree where you'd been cutting a –

RB: I was cutting a branch to make a den and I was pulling the branch and cutting it at the same time, so as soon as it came away I fell.

HJ: And you had the misfortune of landing on your head . . .

RB: Yes . . .

HJ: . . . so we don't know what effect that's had . . .

RB: . . . what were the long-term effects . . .

HJ: . . . correct.

RB: I mean, were there any, do you think?

HJ: Um, yes, I think so . . .

RB: I haven't put in the story about the orange. Was it in Greece?

HJ: No, that was in Spain and you were about six or seven at the time – and I clearly remember the three of us were walking along and this Spanish guy comes over with a donkey and all these earthenware pots and jugs hanging off it, all very colourful, and we stop and we look at these things and the first thing this Spanish guy does is, he's got this plastic rubber orange in his hand, and he squeezes the orange and a huge penis shoots up and the first thing you say is, 'I'll have one of those!' whereupon your mother says, 'You certainly will not!' [Both laugh] But because we were so taken with this guy's presentation we then decided we'd buy a couple of his pots and things and we still have them out now at home at the top of our landing. And every so often when I'm feeling rather low I look at those and it lifts my spirits because I think of that delightful organ that was exhibited on that occasion . . .

RB: You think of his inflatable penis.

HJ: Yes, yes.

RB: And everything seems nice . . .

HJ: . . . perfectly formed . . .

RB: . . . well in proportion . . .

HJ: Absolutely. So, er, yeah, that was on holiday, Rob . . .

Alan Thompson

AT: I remember going to a Christmas party at your house; you had an annual Christmas party, do you remember that?

RB: Well, Christmas only comes once a year, Al.

AT: It was like our equivalent of the Hootenanny.

RB: It was a bit – we used to have a crowd of people and would always end up singing in a circle on the floor.

AT: You had a small house, at the time . . .

RB: Tiny . . .

AT: . . . and if you were invited to that, then you were in. It was like David Frost's summer garden party.

RB: Except in a small end-of-terrace house in Llandaff, Cardiff.

AT: It was just up that road, wasn't it, and you said, 'Al, would you like to come to my Christmas party?' And I thought, 'I've arrived! I'm in! I've only known him three months and I'm there . . .' And do you remember that we – Ruth was there as well, Ruth Jones, she sang a song – and we did, we were at the party, all sat around, and you did a speech, didn't you? You used to do a little sort of speech, you'd go around the room, you'd talk about people who were at the party and then you did a few songs. And, the night before, you and I rehearsed, with me playing the guitar and you singing, because Michael Jackson's 'Black or White' had just come out – 'Black *or* White' or 'Black *and* White'?

RB: 'Black *or* White' – it didn't matter whether you were black or white; you could be my baby. If it had been black *and* white it would have been about his enthusiasm for old films.

AT: . . . and you did a speech and you said, 'Al, I've taken to him.' Wow. So I picked up the guitar and we did an acoustic version, which we rehearsed the night before – you insisted on a rehearsal – and we played 'Black or White' and you moonwalked across your carpet. In your slippers. That was the moment I thought, 'There is a man . . .'

Roger Burnell

RB: Do you remember when we met?

RBnl: I do, actually, the very first lesson, it was a Friday afternoon, you might have forgotten that.

RB: You don't seriously remember that?!

RBnl: Yeah, yeah, I do – and the room, it was one of those pre-fab rooms that we were assigned to on the day, and I was introduced to you: 'This is Rob, he likes doing a bit of acting.' There was no room so we just did some play-reading and I immediately thought, 'Of course, well, what a talent this is . . .' [*Rob laughs*] No, I did!

RB: What, that first thing?

RBnl: Yeah, quiet, quite introspective actually, at that time . . .

RB: . . . at that time . . .

RBnl: . . . and then the monster was unearthed and that was it!

RB: Were you aware that I had a particular interest in comic acting?

RBnl: Yeah, for me the two things were almost separated and diverse, in that you'd do the acting thing and then on the other hand, for example, we'd ask you to go on the mic for sports day and then you'd be different characters with different voices, and not everybody understood that you were actually quietly taking the mick out of all the teachers, pupils, students! So that was that, but I suppose the two things sort of converged then – some of the roles you took were comic, so that necessitated looking at how you saw things in comic terms.

RB: But the role of Billy in *Carousel* was quite heroic – that's far more like me as I actually am. Quite a heroic figure. So that was more me . . . People always say, 'Are you like Keith Barret? Is that what you're really like?'

RBnl: Of course, people when they're talking about you, will refer to Uncle Bryn.

RB: It wouldn't be so bad if you were Daniel Craig: 'Are you Daniel Craig? Are you like James Bond?' – 'Yeah, yes, I am.' – 'Oh, you're just like your character!' – 'Oh, well thanks very much!' It's not quite the same with the roles I've played . . .

RBnl: No, no, but there's the darker side of characterization and acting; with *Human Remains*, it was obvious that you were looking at other parts of you and performance that were darker and which had lots of layers.

RB: Did that surprise you?

RBnl: It did, yeah, and I think because you were so engrossed in those characters and the situations that's what made it such a stunning series to be honest, and . . . maybe you should do more things like that?

RB: You're not the only person who's said that. But it took so long to write. We keep talking about it and almost starting. But it took over a year, on and off, to write that series. I would like to, but I like doing everything – I like hosting shows and I like acting and stuff.

RBnl: But I suppose with those characters, with that series, you do spend a lot of time improvizing.

RB: Yes, and it's much harder to find that kind of time now, where the two of you can devote that much time to doing it . . .

David Walliams

RB: So, as people are reading my autobiography . . .

DW: I can't wait to read it.

RB: Oh, it's very exciting . . .

DW: Is there an index?

RB: I've been promised an index.

DW: Ah, well then I can just look for my name and just go to those pages.

RB: Yeah . . .

DW: It's weird when you start featuring in other people's autobiographies, because I think I'm in Russell Brand's and Simon Pegg's, who I was at university with.

RB: You'll be in James Corden's. You might be in mine, depending on how this goes. [*David sighs.*] Well, all I'm saying is let's just see how this goes . . . Who wrote a book – was it Gore Vidal? – and there was a contemporary of his who he doesn't mention in the book but he put his name in the index because he knew he'd look for it, and next to his name he put 'Hi!' [*Both laugh.*]

DW: Well, you know I'm going to be writing a book.

RB: Yeah. Will you be mentioning me?

DW: Of course I will. But again, I think I'll go up to a certain point.

RB: Just before you meet me.

DW: Well, no, because people actually said it can be a bit boring when you're talking about the period of your life when you're successful, that it just becomes a list.

RB: I think it's much more interesting, all the . . . I mean, this book, when you read it, it's basically a catalogue of heroic failures, because I keep trying and I keep trying . . . You'll probably find, as you write yours, how much you've forgotten and how hard it was trying to get ahead because once you have had some success it's very easy to forget what it's like, what the struggle is like, and to not have your phone calls returned, to be sending things all the time . . .

DW: You told me a very chilling story about an agent meeting you who'd seen a picture of you. And then he met you. And he made a comment about your skin.

RW: Yeah, that's in the book – he was a guy who cast for commercials, and I sent him this photograph of me . . .

DW: Had you been airbrushed?

RB: No, no! It's just all light, isn't it? I mean, if you've got nice light . . . So, I walked in and he went, 'Oh . . . oh dear . . .'

DW: [*laughing*] . . . like you were the elephant man?

RB: He was looking at me a bit shocked; he said, 'Oh . . . Oh dear . . . Your photograph doesn't really . . . I could hardly put you up for a chocolate commercial, could I? "Eat our chocolate and you'll look like me".' Isn't that terrible?!

DW: It's chilling, because you'd think you would not be quite that direct. Anyway, where is he now?

RB: He's probably more successful than ever. But you must have had a lot of that, though, when people actually saw you in the flesh and they were just . . . repulsed? Not so much because of your skin, but more of a general disfigurement?

DW: [*Ignoring him.*] No, but it's that thing, isn't it, where you can't really get a gig but then as soon as you're successful everyone wants you to be in things, and you go, 'Well now I'm really busy! You could have asked me before!'

DW: So . . . we got cast together in *Cruise of the Gods*, which was a fantastic experience; very strange because no one has really seen this programme other than the people in it.

RB: . . . and we bang on about it all the time!

DW: . . . yes, in Russell Brand's book there's a big section about it which mentions you and me and James Corden, Steve Coogan . . . and immediately I really liked you; I put you on a pedestal.

RB: Well, you had to. I couldn't reach the basin.

DW: But you and Steve were the stars of that. I was really thrilled to get that job. I thought, I'm playing with the big boys now. Because at that time I hadn't done *Little Britain*, I'd done it on radio . . .

RB: But that was all you talked about; I remember you saying, 'Me and Matt, me and Matt . . . *Little Britain*, me and Matt, me and Matt . . .' and you kept talking about it – were you about to make the pilot?

DW: Yeah, we'd made the pilot, but between the pilot and the series was quite a long space of time, and then the next year we made the series. And the rest is, well, history!

RB: Yes, history!

DW: Yeah, but it was a great experience. Because there's something about when you work with people and you actually go away with them that you bond a lot more than you would if you were just turning up.

RB: Because we were sailing around the Mediterranean weren't we?

DW: It was idyllic. So you work all day with people and then in the evening you socialize with them . . . It's on YouTube, isn't it? A lot of *Cruise of the Gods*? But there's some really lovely scenes between you, James and me. I was basically a massive creepy fan of yours, lurking behind you . . . And then, of course, the boat crashed.

RB: We hit a rock; everybody had to get off, wasn't that exciting?

DW: It was exciting, because you really don't expect it, do you? On a cruise ship? But it tore a great hole in the ship, much like the *Titanic* . . .

RB: And do you remember, we got off the boat and were looking back as we were being taken away and it was night-time by then, it was all lit up, it was *just* like *Titanic* . . .

DW: Was it Mykonos, where we were? It was a Greek island . . . anyway, and then we got put on another boat and had a few days in Athens . . .

RB: . . . but, hang on, we shared a cabin on that first boat, do you remember? We were in a really basic little cabin and I was on the top bunk, I think, and you were on the bottom – do you remember that?

DW: I remember being on the bottom but I don't remember there being bunks . . .

RB: And the engine was going [*makes loud engine noise*] and I remember you going [*in a camp voice*], 'Ooh, it's relentless! Will it ever stop?'

DW: And then we were in Athens for a few days, and then we got on another boat . . .

RB: But before that we visited the Acropolis together, and it was like Kenneth Williams and Joe Orton or something, so camp . . . You would walk around and say [*in a camp voice*] 'Well, it's just a pile of bricks, isn't it! Don't know what the fuss is about!'

DW: And then we were put on this other boat that was much fuller . . .

RB: And there weren't enough rooms so they said, 'Who will share with each other?'

DW: Well, I mean, I was first to put *my* hand up . . .

RB: You said, 'I'll only share with Rob!'

DW: Well! Steve had his then-wife there and was flying back and forth, I could have shared with James . . . But we were put in a room and there were two beds, and they were pushed together.

RB: When we went into the room there was probably a millimetre gap between them . . .

DW: . . . and we asked the maid to separate the beds, and she separated them by about an inch . . . So we thought 'to hell with it' and just pushed them back together. But it was nice. You were sort of, I think you'd been through quite a tough time, emotionally, and me too, so we were sort of sharing quite intimate thoughts with each other.

RB: It was the beginning of our friendship.

DW: I think it was. And you've been a very, very caring and loving friend.

RB: When you've leant over the balcony of a cruise ship and pulled a man back up, with your bare hands, as you did . . .

DW: No, but it was nice. And in the middle of the night you'd get up to have a pee, and I'm not a great sleeper, so when you were peeing I'd go [*in camp voice*] 'Ooh, my Rob!' to the sound of the water, gushing . . .

RB: . . . cascading down . . .

DW: 'Oooh! My Rob!' And we became so relaxed with each other than in the end you'd be like having a bath and I'd come in and bring you a gin and tonic! Which was great. And then . . . and then what happened? And then unfortunately we had to stop making that programme.

RB: Then we finished, then we came back, and we had to do some pick-ups at Shepperton, do you remember? They reconstructed the ship – I don't think you'd ever tell when you're watching it that some of the scenes are not on the ship.

DW: It was a lot easier doing it on a stage rather than on a boat.

RB: Yep, so then we did that, and I think that was the last time I saw you, wasn't it?

Index